THE CANADIAN ARMY
ON SALISBURY PLAIN

THE CANADIAN ARMY
ON SALISBURY PLAIN

The First Canadian Contingent
October 1914–February 1915

T. S. CRAWFORD

HALSGROVE

First published in Great Britain in 2012

Copyright © 2012 T. S. Crawford

British Library Cataloguing-in-Publication Data
A CIP record for this title is available from the British Library

ISBN 978 0 85704 155 5

HALSGROVE
Halsgrove House,
Ryelands Business Park,
Bagley Road, Wellington, Somerset TA21 9PZ
Tel: 01823 653777   Fax: 01823 216796
email: sales@halsgrove.com

Part of the Halsgrove group of companies
Information on all Halsgrove titles is available at: www.halsgrove.com

Printed in China by Everbest Printing Co Ltd

Contents

Generations of soldiers based on the Plain have visited Stonehenge.

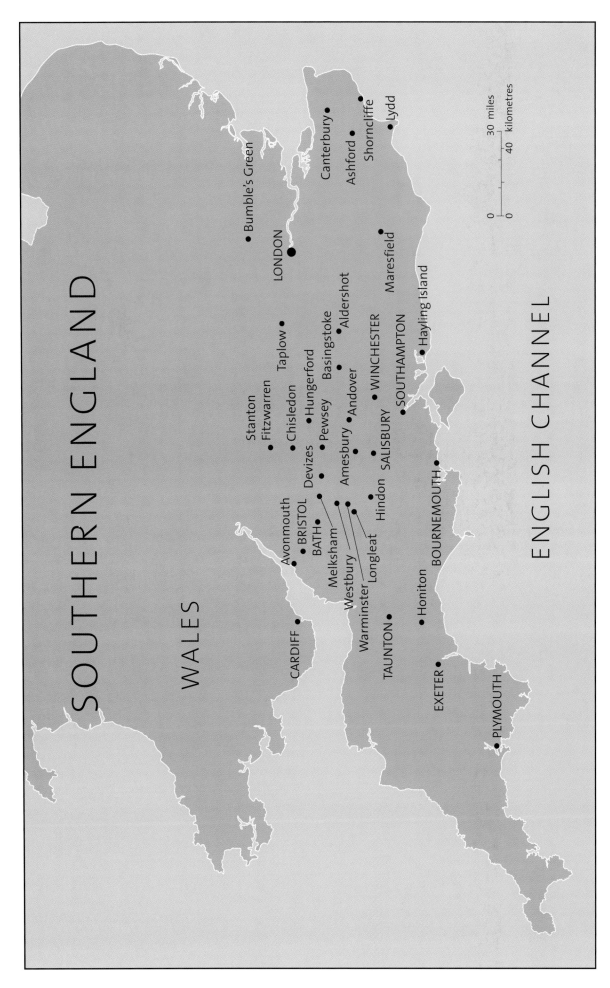

SOUTHERN ENGLAND

WALES

ENGLISH CHANNEL

Bumble's Green

LONDON

Canterbury

Ashford

Shorncliffe

Lydd

Maresfield

Taplow

Basingstoke

Aldershot

Hayling Island

Stanton
Fitzwarren

Chisledon

Hungerford

Pewsey

Andover

WINCHESTER

SOUTHAMPTON

Devizes

Amesbury

SALISBURY

Avonmouth

BRISTOL

BATH

Melksham

Westbury

Longleat

Hindon

BOURNEMOUTH

Warminster

Honiton

CARDIFF

TAUNTON

EXETER

PLYMOUTH

30 miles

40 kilometres

0

0

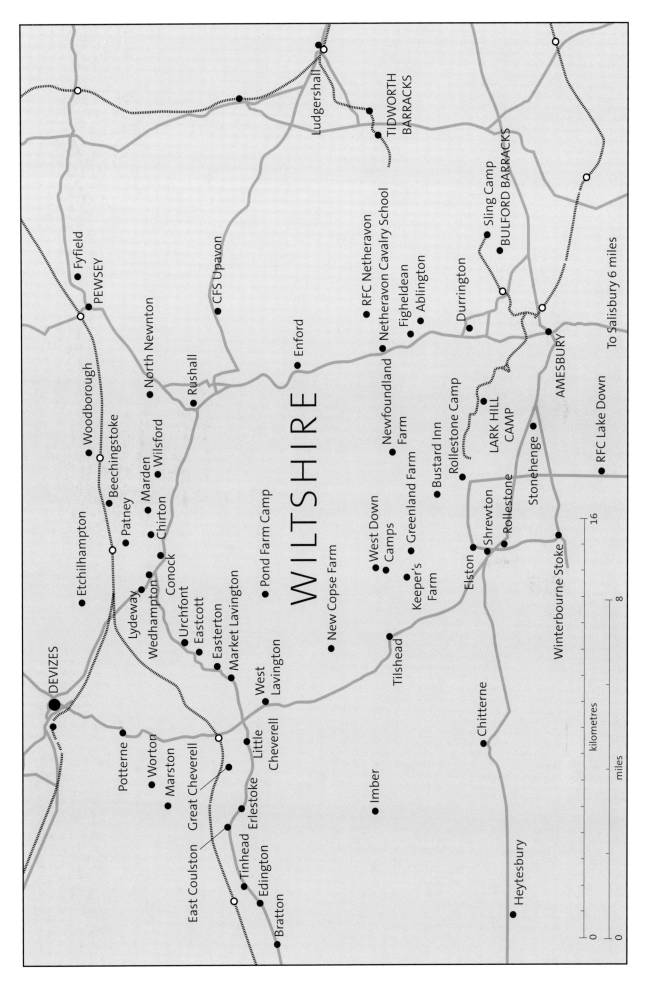

The Contingent is drawn up for parade in 1914.

Introduction

The First Canadian Contingent, later the First Canadian Division, was conceived and born in the British Empire's rush to respond to the outbreak of the Great War and was the first part of a Canadian Expeditionary Force formed to serve overseas. Together with accompanying units such as the Newfoundland Regiment, it totalled more than 31,000 men and 105 nurses, the vast majority of whom were volunteers. If the soldiers were somewhat rough and ready during their training under arduous conditions in England in 1914-15, they quickly won glory when they went into battle and set a fine example for their countrymen who followed them.

A problem in researching the Contingent was reconciling soldiers' details given in personal accounts with its official roll (compiled in early November 1914), attestation papers (usually completed at the time of recruitment but in a few cases some weeks later) and service records. In some cases the names could not be traced or, if a form of them did appear, the details were not always complementary. There are three main reasons for this:

The rush with which the Contingent was recruited and assembled did not help accurate record-keeping. Divisional orders on Salisbury Plain several times listed men and asked whether it was known if they were part of the force. Inevitably clerical errors occurred. For example, William Francis McInnis had his name mis-spelt 'Macinnis' by one local newspaper reporting on his court appearance in January 1915 and in the Contingent's own roll complied two months earlier he is given the army number of Walter MacInnes.

Though the Pay and Record Office was based in London (with a branch in Salisbury), it relied on information from units camped in atrocious conditions. On at least two occasions gales blew down tents, including those of staff officers at Bustard Camp, scattering paperwork across the surrounding countryside.

Names may have been misremembered by the narrators, who might also have deliberately changed some for the purposes of anonymity.

Other anomalies can occur with the timing of unit movements and incidents, with war diaries, unit histories and private accounts giving differing dates. Some units arrived by train on Salisbury Plain very close to one side or another of midnight, leading to discrepancies. In official diaries a sequence of events was sometimes compressed into one day's entry, as may have been the case in the death of William Hartley and the subsequent inquest (see Chapter Eight.)

Though the name 'Canadian Army' officially existed only from 1940 to 1968 and again from 2011, the term has been used colloquially and semi-officially from confederation into a dominion in 1867 to the present.

There are many references in this book to Canadian units with Scottish Highland identities, a reflection on the sizeable numbers of people of Scottish origin living in Canada (some 15 per cent before the war) and an eagerness to continue the tradition of Scottish soldiers for bravery and devotion.

Frequently soldiers over-estimated the miles they had marched, exaggerations by no means confined to Canadian troops. I have walked on many of the public rights of way on the Plain, wearing light clothing and carrying a modest rucksack in contrast to a soldier's encumbrances, and can vouch for one mile seeming like 2,000 yards or more!

The official exchange rate in 1914-15 was about $4.95 to the British pound, which then consisted of 20 shillings, each worth 12 pence or pennies. Thus a Canadian dollar was worth about four shillings. Prior to decimalization of the British currency in 1971, amounts of money were expressed as, for example, £3 6s 8d. (Confusingly the 'd' stands for 'denarius', an ancient Roman coin.)

Today the Plain has much to offer visiting military historians but there is little specifically for those seeking evidence of the Canadians, with the sad exception in local churchyards of the graves of those died. (Details are given in Appendix Two.) Of the camps well known to the Canadians, Lark Hill (now rendered as Larkhill), Bulford and Tidworth all have been much re-built, though some of Tidworth's original barracks can be seen from public roads. The camping-grounds of Bustard, West Down and Pond Farm were never built on and are now just wild grass-land.

Some public rights of way are still open on the central ranges north of Amesbury where the Canadians did much of their training, but only when there is no artillery practice. So it is possible to retrace parts of the marches the Canadians made when de-training at Amesbury, Lavington and Patney & Chirton stations, perhaps imagining their exertions when climbing the steep hills up to the Plain from the last two stations. The site of Pond Farm Camp is within an area where shells fall and is permanently out of bounds. Several rights of way cross the sites of the West Down camps and another passes close to that of Newfoundland Farm, where there are now modern military buildings. (The sites of the original West Down camping-sites are a mile north east of today's Westdown Camp.) A good impression of Salisbury Plain can be gained by driving along the old Devizes to Salisbury road from the Bustard Inn to the top of Red Horn Hill when it is open to the public. One stretch of four miles is poorly surfaced but can be driven with care in dry conditions in a saloon car.

Scenes of so many arrivals and departures, the stations at Amesbury, Lavington and Patney & Chirton have long been closed and demolished. The site of the first has been developed and the branch line to it closed, with a main railway line still running through the locations of the last two.

T. S. Crawford

"Look for Your Friends."
Canadian Contingent on Salisbury Plain, England—1914

CR Series

Made in England.
Copyright

Sitting and waiting – all part of a soldier's life.

King George's Canadian Boys on Salisbury Plain, 1914.

THE EMPIRE'S BOYS.

Many centuries ago on Salisbury Plain,
  A terrible battle was fought,
The men on both sides strove with might and main,
  But dearly was victory bought.

Their duty they did and to martial strains
  Died thousands of brave men and true;
And now are encamped on the same ancient plain
  The Empire's CANADIAN BOYS——True Blue.

Real British Sons, steadfast and brave,
  As their father's were of yore;
Each fond of a "gal" and true to a "pal,"
  Earnest in play or in war.

Though short is the time since the Empire's Call,
  You hastened at once to obey;
You are doing your "bit" for the dear homeland
  Each minute you work or play.

You're anxious to get to the Front at the Foe,
  And sure—you're fine lads and true;
Mighty proud was His Majesty when he saw the fire
  In the eyes of his troops on review.

You have come up like men to play a man's part,
  (For slackers the Empire's no use);
And when the dare-devil CANADIANS get to the front
  KAISER BILL *will* think HELL's been let loose.

——————
B. WINTON.

Copyright.   *Renton & Co., 60, North Road, Brighton, Sussex.*

The verse is poor and one wonders about the 'great battle', but the sentiments cannot be faulted.

Acknowledgements

I am grateful to the following for access to their collections and for specific information:

Bodleian Library, Oxford
British Library
British Postal Museum and Archive, London
Jim Busby, Winnipeg, for information on Nathan Agranovitch
Devizes Library, Wiltshire
Jim Fuller, Amesbury, for permission to reproduce postcards published by T L Fuller
and for supplying images from original plates.
Imperial War Museum, London
Library and Archives Canada
Brian Mosley, Plymouth, for a photograph of the First Contingent at Plymouth
National Archives, Kew
Marika Pirie, Calgary, for suggestions of source material
Plymouth Library
Rod Priddle, Chirton, for local information
Reading Library
Rhodes Library, Oxford
Barbara Saunt, Corton, for information on diphtheria cases
Wellcome Library, London
Wiltshire and Swindon History Centre, Chippenham, Wiltshire

Remarks by J. E. Sutton are included with the consent of the Trustees of the Imperial
War Museum in whom copyright is vested.

Many of the illustrations in this book come from picture postcards in the author's collection.
Some bear publishers' names, others do not. As with certain documentary material,
the author has tried to identify and contact the owners of the copyright, but this has
not always proved possible. Those who believe they may have unacknowledged copyright
are invited to contact the author so the matter can be rectified in any future edition.

Chapter One
Canada Musters an Army

The assassination in Bosnia's capital, Sarajevo, of Archduke Franz Ferdinand of Austria on 28 June 1914 sparked off a war that many had been anticipating throughout the century, with European countries grouped in two opposing parties. But few would have predicted the four years of warfare that followed, nor the ten million deaths that were suffered. Famously the belief was that it would all be over by Christmas.

Austria blamed Serbia for its Archduke's death and issued it with an impossible ultimatum before declaring war. Austria's ally, Germany, announced that it was at war first with Russia, which was mobilizing its army in support of Serbia, and then with France, demanding passage for its troops through Belgium, whose neutrality was guaranteed under an 1839 treaty signed by Britain, Russia and France (and, incidentally, Austria and Prussia). After attempts to preserve peace, Britain felt obliged to come to Belgium's aid, not only because of the treaty but because of fears of a German presence on the other side of the English Channel on the Belgian coast. It declared war on 4 August .

As part of the British Empire Canada also found itself at war. Constitutionally it had little choice though it could decide exactly how and how much to participate. On 4 August its Governor General, the Duke of Connaught, had given a firm assurance of the Canadian people's resolve to make 'every effort [and] every sacrifice necessary to ensure the integrity and maintain the honour of our Empire'. The Duke (British by birth and the youngest son of Queen Victoria) was re-affirming the statement in 1910 by Sir Wilfrid Laurier, then Canadian Prime Minister, that 'when Britain is at war, Canada is at war. There is no distinction.' The following year, Colonel Sam Hughes, the Minister of Militia and Defence, had stated that Germany needed to be taught that Canada was behind Britain.

Many Canadian people vigorously supported this stance. As with much of the British population, it is unlikely that very many grasped the political reasons for an European war (as it was to be regarded, albeit inaccurately, for some time). There were parades, flag-waving, speech-making and a rush of men to enlist. There was similar patriotic enthusiasm in Britain and other European countries, which at least had large, well-trained Regular armies and reserve forces. In the case of Britain, Lord Kitchener, newly appointed as Secretary of State for War, had deep doubts about the efficacy of its part-time Territorial Force, but at least some of it could be deployed to replace Regulars, in India for example, and all its members had some military training. The Force had been created in 1908, assimilating militia, yeomanry and volunteer units. Apart from regular weekly parades, members were supposed to attend a summer camp, though were sometimes inhibited from doing so by their employers being reluctant to release them from work.

In contrast, in 1914 Canada's Permanent Active Militia of full-time soldiers (also known as the Permanent Force) had an authorized establishment of 3,110 men of all ranks and 684 horses, formed into two cavalry regiments (the Royal Canadian Dragoons and Lord Strathcona's Horse); the Royal Canadian Horse Artillery; the Royal Canadian Garrison Artillery; and one infantry battalion, the Royal Canadian Regiment. Their primary functions were to garrison coastal fortresses and assist in training the Non-Permanent Active Militia, which by 1914 had grown to an authorized establishment of 77,320. Little more than a police force, its members were voluntary part-time soldiers organized into local regiments who trained for only 12 to 16 days each year.

Equipment for both the Permanent and Non-Permanent Milita was insufficient and of questionable quality. Canada depended on British factories for its artillery and had to compete with Britain's War Office for supplies. At least from 1905 it had produced its own .303 rifle designed by Sir Charles Ross, though this was a departure from the principle of uniformity of armament within the Empire. Much modified and well regarded as an accurate target weapon, the Ross as a battlefield rifle was heavier than and inferior to the British Lee Enfield, though patriotic pride rejected some of its continuing shortcomings, not least the propensity to jam in muddy conditions – a problem exacerbated during the war by the fact that British ammunition was inclined to worsen the problem.

At least there were plans to place the armed forces on a war footing, including service overseas. Just completed in July 1914 was a War Book (actually a number of war books compiled by individual departments), detailing what actions should be taken during a period of severely strained relations with foreign powers and on a declaration of war. In the days after 4 August these plans were smoothly implemented, with guards being posted on key installations, the Royal Canadian Garrison Artillery and Royal Canadian Regiment placed on active service and Militia called out in the two coastal military districts.

Initially Britain, perhaps pre-occupied with its own mobilization problems, deemed that there was 'no immediate necessity for any request on our part for an expeditionary force from Canada'. However, two days later it did accept Canada's offer to send a contingent, and asked that it 'be despatched as soon as possible'.

Sam Hughes, Canada's controversial Minister of Militia and Defence.

The Canadian Cabinet authorized the raising and equipment of such units as might be determined by the Governor General in Council, 'to be composed of officers and men who are willing to volunteer for Overseas service under the British Crown'. The strength of the force, soon to be known as the First Canadian Contingent, was set at 25,000. On 6 August Colonel Sam Hughes, the Minister of Militia and Defence, ignored the pre-determined procedures and authorized a letter to 226 unit commanders of the Non-Permanent Militia. This instructed them to prepare and forward direct to Militia Headquarters by the 12th rolls of volunteers between the ages of 18 and 45 who could meet prescribed physical standards. After some confusion and modifying of instructions, including one that not more than 125 men would be

accepted from rural regiments, most volunteers joined through existing Militia units in a similar manner to that prescribed before the war. In addition there were several independent bodies of volunteers.

On 28 September the Duke of Connaught was to write to Kitchener about 'the peculiar manner in which the selection of this Force has been made by the Minister of Militia who would do everything himself and who would not listen to any advice'. He went on to describe Hughes as 'an arrogant and conceited barrister who would commit any folly if there were not someone to keep him straight'.*

Then Britain accepted an offer of four additional Canadian units of a thousand men each, made after

---

*At the age of 16 Sam Hughes had enlisted in the 45th Regiment and by 1902 had become a colonel. He believed that he should have been awarded the Victoria Cross for his part in the Boer War, though he had been sent home for military indiscipline. He had many of the abilities needed by a front-line officer but boastfulness and impatience told strongly against him. 'Eccentricity' is a kindly word to use of him and 'monomanic paranoia' barely an exaggeration. For several years he had been warning of the danger of hostilities with Germany and strongly supported the principle that the colonies should support Britain in time of war.

Hughes had reported proposals from three provinces to provide battalions. In the event, New Brunswick denied having made such an offer and Manitoba and Calgary were financially unable to undertake what was suggested. More substantial was the offer of Captain A. Hamilton Gault, a Montreal veteran of the Boer War, to raise an infantry battalion of ex-soldiers and to contribute $100,000 towards the cost. The battalion, named Princess Patricia's Canadian Light Infantry (popularly referred to as the Princess Pats and occasionally Pat's Pets) after the daughter of the Duke of Connaught, was speedily recruited in Ottawa, its ranks being filled by veteran soldiers from all parts of Canada. The Government ruled that it could not recruit existing Militia members and the battalion itself strongly preferred experienced men; this was to make the 'Pats' the most efficient element of the Contingent. Of its 1,098 officers and men, 850 were ex-regulars or had seen service in South Africa; of the others 219 were picked men from auxiliary forces, the remainder being described as prize-fighters, cow-punchers and pipers. Men originally from England constituted 65 per cent of the Pats, 10 per cent were Canadian, 10 per cent Irish and 15 per cent Scottish. Any Welsh representation appears to have been overlooked. Their commanding officer was Lieutenant Colonel Francis Farquhar.

The 102nd Rocky Mountain Rangers provided more than 100 men for the First Contingent. They left Kamloops for Valcartier on 29 August.

The Pats were never officially part of the First Contingent. After their rapid formation they boarded a ship at Montreal in late August but were halted at Quebec, being told it was too dangerous to cross the Atlantic without a naval escort and that they should wait until the main force could sail. Some suspected that the delay was due to Sam Hughes wanting to split the battalion up and distribute around the Contingent its members – especially the non-commissioned officers – because they were so experienced. Whatever the reason, the Pats had a month of training at an old militia camp at Lévis. This was time usefully spent, as however impressive their individual records the men would have needed welding into a cohesive force. After testing the Ross rifle, Farquhar urged a switch to Lee Enfields (used by the British army) as 'experiences we have had with the Ross … can hardly fail to have shaken the confidence of the men in that rifle'.

Valcartier, 16 miles north-west of Quebec City, was selected as the mobilization camp for the Contingent. The site had been acquired as a central training area for the Quebec Militia in 1912, with further land being bought after war broke out. Hughes was to note that the site had been taken over on 8 August and that within 12 days 3½ miles of ranges had been completed, 1,500 targets put in position, 12 miles of water mains laid and 15 miles of drains established. Railway sidings and streets were set down and electric lights and telephones installed. There appears to have been some typical Hughes bombast here, for when the Calgary Highlanders arrived in very late August they noted their camp to be 'all brush', with no latrines. Hughes may have exaggerated the speed but certainly the camp was constructed quickly and the achievement was considerable, and doubtless the Canadians remembered it when they had to help build their own camps in England. An impartial verdict is given by Elisabeth Flagler MacKeen in *With the First Canadian Contingent*:

> Electrically lighted, with purified water and baths for every unit, with broad roads and board walks, with post-office and hospitals, a network of telephones, a bank and Y.M.C.A. tent, with canteens for soft drinks, goodies and smokes: in two short weeks it was ready for use….

> The camp was scrupulously clean; metal incinerators, like burning-ghats, lined the streets; left-over food was hourly consumed, while, nightly, carts removed all refuse. There were entertainment shows, some free, and a cinema – which got trashed and its cash box stolen after overly repeating the same programme.

Those who did not admire Hughes, including some of his ministerial colleagues, were concerned that he had awarded the camp-building and other contracts himself and without Cabinet approval. Certainly there was a steady stream of people approaching his office to offer help, to suggest bright or not so bright ideas and to seek contracts, Some of these were awarded for political reasons, Hughes being as guilty as most, if not more so, of allowing politics to influence decisions.

When he inspected the Contingent at Valcartier he ordered Lieutenant Colonel John Rattray, who had come up against Hughes politically, to leave the parade ground, then ordered Rattray's 10th Battalion off without inspecting it

The first detachment of the Permanent Militia, comprising two officers and five other ranks of the Ordnance Corps, arrived at Valcartier on 10 August, to be followed by more ordnance personnel, and cavalry, artillery, medical, veterinary and postal units and four Army Service Corps companies. The first Non-Permanent Active Militia volunteers for overseas service arrived on the 18th. They were assigned to provisional battalions which often had titles denoting their provincial origins: Toronto, Eastern Ontario, British Columbia, for example. By 8 September 32,665 men were at the camp.

Many of the localized Militia units were disappointed to be combined into new battalions, even if these were formed on geographical lines, and to be stopped from wearing their insignia. Some did retain their original unit names; the 6th Battalion was often referred to as the 'Fort Garrys' because the largest proportion of men – 234 of 814 – came from the 34th Fort Garry Horse (which was to spend its time on Salisbury Plain

as infantry). Likewise the 8th Battalion was sometimes known as the 90th Winnipeg Rifles, which supplied 776 of the 8th's 1,359 members. The composition of the units would be changed several times, not only at Valcartier but also in England.

Troops of the Permanent Militia were busy at Valcartier in administration and training and at first there were no plans to include them with the Contingent. However, on 26 August the order was given to mobilize the two Royal Canadian Horse Artillery batteries and a composite regiment from the two regular cavalry units, the Royal Canadian Dragoons and Lord Strathcona's Horse. On 14 September it was decided that both of these would go overseas complete. This meant that it was not possible to meet a request from Lieutenant Colonel George Tuxford of the 27th Light Horse that a mounted Militia unit under his command be sent overseas. But he was given permission for mounted Militia units from the West to go to Valcartier as dismounted troops of the 5th Battalion. They came to be known as 'the Disappointed Fifth', 'the Wooden Horse Marines' and 'the First Mounted Foot'.

Britain had wanted the Contingent to be drawn up on the lines of one of its own divisions, comprising 18,000

Seen here at Valcartier, the 101st Edmonton Fusiliers comprised nearly all of the 9th Battalion.

soldiers and including 12 infantry battalions, each having a thousand or so men, formed into three brigades, with support units accounting for the other 6,000 men. Its War Office became concerned that the Canadian force exceeded this greatly, even allowing for those units that were only attached to it. The number of recruits was enough to make up 16 infantry battalions, hence the creation of a 4th Brigade, to supply troops to quickly replace casualties in the other three, All four brigades would move over to Europe together, Hughes pointing out that otherwise it might take ten weeks for replacements to arrive from Canada.

There were various and varying summaries of the national breakdown of members of the First Contingent. Harold Peat suggested in his memoirs that 78 per cent were English, Irish or 'Scotch' – an over-estimate. A Canadian correspondent writing from Toronto reckoned that only 20 or 30 per cent were native Canadians, others made an estimate of about 50 per cent. Of the 10th Battalion, only one-fifth were native Canadians, three-quarters being British and the remainder from a large number of nations. Figures compiled in 1988 split the birth places of the members of the First Contingent thus: Canada 9,159; British Isles 18,495; other British possessions 662; United States 756; other foreign countries 523; country of birth not stated 1,032. (These figures total 30,627, a hundred more than the figure often given for the force, not that its personnel records were very accurate.)

Most of the men from the British Isles had settled in Canada in the 15-year wave of immigration that had preceded the Great War. The high numbers enlisting may in some part be attributed to patriotic fervour, though contemporary cynics suggest that some at least had failed to make a success of their new lives and had seized the opportunity to return home, see family members and perhaps remain in Britain after what some were predicting would be a short war. Mackenzie King, a former Canadian Minister of Labour and future prime minister, reckoned that the volunteers from Ottawa were mostly unemployed who had joined up in desperation for $1.10 a day (including a 10c field allowance). 'I should think 80 per cent [are] East Londoners or old country [British] failures,' he said.

The response from French-Canadians was muted. Canada's initial outburst of enthusiasm for the war had centred on loyalty to the British Empire. 'There are no longer French Canadians and English Canadians. Only one race now exists, united ... in a common cause,' proclaimed the Montreal newspaper, *La Patrie.* But whilst English-speaking Canada felt itself very much part of the British Empire, French-speakers believed themselves to belong to a separate nation that had been incorporated into the Empire against its will. And their sympathy with France was limited, those with long memories recalling that following the end of the Seven Years War in 1763 France had given up all of Canada in order to retain control of Martinique.

Thus only about 1,000 (some say 1,200) men with French backgrounds enlisted in the Contingent. There were just two French-speaking companies (G and H of the 14th Battalion) comprising 240 officers and men in all, with other Frenchmen scattered among other units, notably the 12th Battalion.* There were some Russians, such as Privates Michel Alek and Jack Strombek in the 48th Highlanders, both of whom had served with the Canadian 31st Grey Regiment, and the 9th Battalion's Ajanaza Orischenko who had three years' service in Russia's army. The roll of the 9th's K Company includes a number of other Russians and there may have been an attempt to keep them together within the Contingent.

'Coloured' volunteers were refused, though on 27 November 1914, the *New Liskeard Speaker* was to report the death of

> Oscar Douglas, the young colored man who joined the New Liskeard company on its departure for the front. We are told ... that Oscar became connected with the cavalry division of the Canadian Contingent quartered at Salisbury Plains, and it was while training with the squad at that camp that he met with his death. It is stated that Douglas was thrown from his horse and that his foot became caught in the stirrup, the unfortunate young man being dragged and trampled to death... He it was who applied to the Captain here when volunteers were called for, wishing to know if his color would debar him from joining the regiment. He said that Great Britain had done so much for his people and he wished to do what he could for her.

---

*The Second Contingent of more than 20,000 men had a single French-speaking Quebec battalion. Of 258 infantry battalions formed during the war, just 13 were raised in French Canada and all had difficulties attracting and retaining recruits.

Later this story was declared to be incorrect and no Oscar Douglas is to be found in attestation papers for 1914 or on the First Contingent's roll, though the circumstances of his death are similar to those of the fatal accident that befell Gunner Percy Sawyer on 28 October (see Chapter Eight). However, Oscar Douglass from New Liskeard and of 'dark' complexion was to attest on 3 April 1916, claiming service in the local 97th Regiment, or Algonquin Rifles.

Nor at first were aboriginal Canadians officially accepted.* Nevertheless a few did manage to enrol, though perhaps not in the numbers fancied by some of the more imaginative journalists. There were three members of the family of Joseph Brant (also known as Chief Thayendanegea, who sided with the British in the American War of Independence), including Cameron Brant, who had been born on the New Credit Indian Reserve, Ontario. He had attended military school and served for six years with the 37th Haldimand Rifles before resigning in 1912. He enlisted on 7 August 1914, the first member from the Six Nations Reserve to do so. He received a lieutenant's commission at Valcartier and was to die at the second Battle of Ypres on 23 April 1915.

Officers of the 48th Highlanders.

According to the 15th Battalion's commanding officer, Lieutenant Colonel John Currie, there was only one full-blooded Indian in its ranks, William Lickers. One night on Salisbury Plain Lickers overstayed his leave by a few hours and was put in the guard tent. At daybreak he was found to have broken out and was discovered in the horse lines. Currie accepted his explanation that he had woken up while it was still dark and, knowing it was time for him to attend to his horses, had gone about his duties as usual. He proved a very good soldier, and when his horses were killed at the Battle of Ypres he took a rifle and ammunition and found his way four miles down into the trenches where he was wounded, gassed, and taken prisoner.

Dr Barnado's Homes reckoned that 400 of the Contingent had been Barnado Boys. Quite how the orphanage arrived at this figure is not clear, though between 1882 and 1901 it had sent 8,046 children from Britain to Canada, some being boarded with families and others staying in homes opened in Toronto and Peterborough.

Two-thirds of the 1,500 officers at Valcartier were Canadian and mainly had attended military schools of instruction. Most of the remainder were British, many lately arrived in Canada to concentrate on civilian occupations but often with some experience of the army. Many non-commissioned officers were selected simply by asking for volunteers with military experience, no checks being made on the claims of those who came forward.

Hughes appears to have acted independently to place large orders for clothing and almost every other item of equipment. Understandably, stocks of uniforms were inadequate to meet the sudden demand, especially as the non-permanent Militia had never been supplied with underwear, shirts and boots, some units not even having uniforms. On 10 August it was decided to order 65,000 pairs of boots, 35,000 caps, 15,000 greatcoats, 50,000 suits of service clothing, 100,000 suits of under-garments and 100,000 shirts, among other items. In many cases the wool had to be

---

*At first the Canadian Government had adopted a policy of not allowing 'Indians' to serve overseas, believing that the Germans considered them savages and fearing that this would result in their inhumane treatment if taken prisoner. However the policy was not strictly enforced and was cancelled in late 1915. At least 3,500 Canadian Indians enlisted. Race and ethnicity were not recorded in the attestation papers, so an accurate total is impossible to assess.

obtained and woven before clothing could be made. Again, political considerations have been suggested, with Hughes said to have favored companies who supported his party.

Purchasing agents were given honorary commissions and tasked to buy more than 850 wagons, 133 motor vehicles and 8,150 horses. They obtained eight makes of wagon and eight makes of motor truck, little regard being made to the need for interchangeability and spare parts and how these would be supplied when the Contingent was the other side of the Atlantic.

On 20 August Canadian businessmen offered to finance a motorized machine-gun unit, with the guns mounted in armoured vehicles. This offer was gratefully accepted, and on 9 September the Automobile Machine Gun Brigade No. 1 was formed under the command of a French immigrant, Raymond Brutinel, who was given the rank of major. He went to the United States and bought 20 Colt machine guns and ordered eight armoured cars made to his own design. The cars were quickly built and arrived in Ottawa with support vehicles. They had a range of up to 225 miles, cruised at 15mph and could reach 30mph. They were not intended to go into action but for use as troop carriers. About half the personnel had been chauffeurs and mechanics in civilian life.

Also from the States came 25,000 MacAdam shovels, named after Colonel Hughes' female secretary (and,

some suggest, mistress), Ena, who is said to have seen the Swiss army using the design. A combined spade and shield, the shovel was claimed to be able to stop a bullet at 300 yards and had two loopholes, one to shoot through and a smaller one for sighting; it was soon found to be awkward and ineffective and, weighing more than five pounds, was too heavy to carry. Nor could it be suspended from the Oliver harness worn by men to carry equipment.

Hughes can be credited with authorizing the birth of Canadian military aviation when in early September he was visited by William Sharpe (one of only four Canadians certified as a pilot by the Aero Club of America) and Ernest Janney, who suggested that the Contingent should have an aviation arm. By 16 September Janney had been made a captain and authorized to look for an aircraft in the United States, despite his probably never having flown, even as a passenger. Heeding Hughes' emphasis on the need for 'quick delivery', Janney, with $5,000 to spend, visited the Burgess Company of Marblehead, Massachusetts on the 17th and purchased a second-hand two-seater, tail-less Burgess-Dunne float-plane, designed by the British Lieutenant J. W. Dunne and built by the American Stirling Burgess. It is difficult to imagine what use Janney thought the float-plane would be to an army involved in an European war. With clumsy two-hand controls and no rudder, it was useless both for training and fighting.

These armoured cars attracted much interest but their open design meant that their crews were vulnerable to attack from above.

A Burgess-Dunne floatplane of the type purchased, somewhat incredibly, for the First Contingent.

junior officers were completely inexperienced, many commissions being given to youngsters from the country's public schools who had served only in the Officers' Training Corps, which provided two or three hours of training once a week, an occasional field-day and a summer camp lasting a week or so.

To command the Contingent, three retired senior British officers were considered but the choice finally fell on Major General Edwin Alderson, who was promoted to lieutenant general on 14 October. Born in 1859, he had joined the Regular Army in December 1878. He had served with the Natal Field Force, in Egypt and then in South Africa, where the Royal Canadian Dragoons and 2nd Canadian Mounted Rifles had operated under him, an experience that counted in his favour when a leader for the Contingent was being sought. He had become a major general in 1906 and in 1908 had commanded the 6th Division of the Southern Army in India.

After a rushed overhaul of the plane, Janney and Clifford Webster, the Burgess Company pilot, took off for Valcartier, only to make one emergency landing an hour after take-off, which resulted in them being held temporarily as suspected enemy agents, and another one just outside Champlain, where they had to be towed in to a mooring. When they finally arrived in Quebec, Janney was arrested by Canada Customs and the aircraft impounded. After Customs contacted the Department of Militia and Defence, Janney and the aircraft were released. Its misadventures on the flight from the States had damaged the aircraft, and Burgess had to send employees to repair it and replace its engine, this latter costing $2,500. When the Contingent sailed, the float-plane was tied to the deck of the SS *Athenia* and transported across the Atlantic.*

All in all, the Canadians fared well in their first weeks compared with recruits in Britain. They were quickly equipped, if with material of questionable suitability and quality, and their mobilization camp at Valcartier was developed rapidly. On 6 August Kitchener's first act as Secretary of State for War had been to appeal for 100,000 men to form his New Army, and he got them in a fortnight. By mid-September half a million had come forward. A massive hut-building programme was launched, but in the meantime the recruits were taken to camping-sites often to find that only tents had been delivered and that they sometimes had to cook their own food. Many were to lack uniforms and rifles for months. Often their trainers were a very few officers and non-commissioned officers of the Regular Army and others who had come out of retirement. Their

Major General Edwin Alderson, the British officer chosen to command the Contingent.

---

* The information in this paragraph comes from several different sources and one suspects that the two forced landings may have been only one, with different reasons being ascribed for the crew being held.

The band of the Legion of Frontiersmen at Salisbury in 1910. Many of the Legion's North American members enlisted in the First Contingent

Colours are presented to the Newfoundland Regiment on 1 October 1914.

Meanwhile in Newfoundland, then a dominion independent of Canada, there was also enthusiasm to raise an army. On the outbreak of war Dr A. W. Wakefield wrote to Newfoundland's Prime Minister, Sir Edward Morris, offering the Legion of Frontiersmen for active service. The Legion had been launched in Britain in 1905 by Roger Pocock, a former member of the North-West Mounted Police, as a paramilitary organization composed of men with experience of active service who might serve their country in time of need. Branches in several Empire countries were established, including one set up in Newfoundland by Dr Wakefield, who had been a member in Britain. His offer to Morris was declined, but on 21 August Sir Walter Davidson, the Governor of Newfoundland, called on all men between 19 and 35 to enlist in the First Newfoundland Regiment for service abroad, the target being 500 recruits. There was an excellent response from the Legion (whose members in Canada were also joining units being mustered there) and a number of other groups that undertook military training, notably the Church Lads Brigade, the Methodist Guards, the Newfoundland Highlanders and Catholic Cadet Corps. Such organizations taught their members the value of service to the British Empire and instilled in them in a sense of self-discipline that some Newfoundlanders came to think was lacking in their Canadian counterparts.

By 2 September 723 men had volunteered, though not all met the enlistment requirements. On the 3rd Davidson announced that 500 men would be ready to leave on 1 October. Pleasantville was chosen as the training site and bell tents were hastily erected to house the volunteers. Local manufacturers were commissioned to produce khaki tunics, trousers and greatcoats. With a lack of sufficient khaki woollen material to make puttees, the troops were issued those of navy blue, giving them the name 'Blue Puttees', soon to become an exclusive mark of honour for the celebrated 'First Five Hundred' of the almost 6,200 Newfoundlanders who eventually enlisted. Lee Enfield rifles were used in training. A delivery of 500 Canadian Ross Rifles arrived the day after the Newfoundlanders (actually 537 in number) had departed and had to be forwarded to Liverpool by a freighter. Time would show that the men would have been better off with the Lee Enfields.

Chapter Two
Arriving at Plymouth

After very little useful training consisting mostly of drill and marches and a few field exercises at Valcartier, the Contingent began to embark at Quebec on 23 September. The aim was to send to Britain for further training all of its effective personnel – 1,547 officers and 29,070 men, an increase of more than 6,000 on the figure allowed for in a plan produced on the 17th and overturned by Hughes. Included were 75 supernumerary officers. Of the original recruits, 5,081 had been released from service, 2,164 being medically unfit and others for reasons such as 'protest by wife or parent' or because they were 'undesirable' or 'inefficient'. (Inevitably, different figures are given for the size of the force and, pedantically, some units were not part of the Contingent but attached to it, notably Princess Patricia's Canadian Light Infantry.)

An advance party sailed to England from New York on 23 September, headed by Colonel John Carson who commanded the 1st Regiment (Canadian Grenadier Guards). With him were five officers, two of whom were to act as *aides de camp* to General Alderson. Already in England were two officers of the Canadian Permanent Force. Also ahead of the main body was part of a machine-gun detachment raised by Eugene Houghton from the 34th Fort Garry Horse and 96th Algoma Rifles. Some of these had joined the Contingent at Valcartier but, possibly because all space on the main convoy had already been allocated, one officer and 40 men were authorized to make their own way to England in civilian clothes. They landed in Glasgow on 11 October and travelled the near-400 miles to Salisbury Plain on the 16th, only being formally enrolled after they had arrived. There the 'Houghton Detachment' found that it had been impossible to procure their machine-guns in time for the Contingent's departure and eventually they were posted to the Automobile Machine Gun Brigade on 1 November.

On board the main convoy were 7,679 horses, 70 guns, 110 motor vehicles, 705 horse-drawn vehicles and 82 bicycles. The embarkation was chaotic, with several units failing to observe rendezvous instructions Only three ships were loaded according to the plan drawn up by the Director of Supplies and Transport before Hughes interfered and the plan collapsed, leading to much 'trial and error' in the docks. Some ships arrived at Quebec already filled with freight, including at least 92,000 sacks of flour that were not military supplies but a gift to Britain. It appears that there may have been as many as 133,275 sacks but some were off-loaded to make space. Hatchways were too small for the larger vehicles and space was wasted when guns and limbers were shipped without their wheels being first removed. The 15th Battalion claimed to have its horses, harness, wagons and wheels in four different ships. One unit was forced to disembark due to lack of accommodation and in the end an extra ship had to be found for it.

By 1 October, 30 loaded transports had assembled in the Gaspé Basin, moving out on the 3rd, with one more, the SS *Manhattan*, sailing independently on the 5th, and another, SS *Florizel*, later joining the convoy with the Newfoundland Contingent aboard. It was greeted by a British escort vessel playing 'O Canada', much to the disgust of the independently minded men

Royal Canadian Dragoons board the SS *Laconia* at Quebec.

of Newfoundland, which in 1904 had adopted its own national anthem, 'Ode to Newfoundland', Nevertheless, a band on board the *Florizel* responded with 'Rule Britannia'.

Anxious to retain as much control of the Canadian force as possible, Hughes himself crossed the Atlantic by a ship travelling faster than the convoy, ostensibly in an unofficial capacity for a holiday and under orders from his Prime Minister, Sir Robert Borden, not to assume any military command or to interfere in military matters. He was promoted to major general in late October but on arrival in London had a stormy meeting with Kitchener, who stated that he wanted the Contingent broken up and dispersed among British units. A furious Hughes cabled Sir Robert, leading to the order being rescinded.

Physical training, muster parades and lectures occupied the men on the voyage, and they indulged in much speculation as to where they were headed. Liverpool was thought to be the port of dis-embarkation, with the men than proceeding to Aldershot, Britain's best-known garrison; some held that the ships were going to Bordeaux. Towards the end of the voyage, reports of German submarines caused the convoy to alter its intended destination (which actually at one time had been Liverpool) from Southampton to Devonport, the dockyard area of Plymouth, which had inferior facilities and was further from the final destination of Salisbury Plain. The first ships entered on 14 October to a rapturous reception from a city that had long associations with North America, it having been the final departure point for the *Mayflower* and the Pilgrim Fathers in 1620.

Curiously, the *Toronto Star* of 8 October had stated that press censorship in London permitted it to announce that 'the first contingent of Canadian troops …have arrived in home [British] waters and will be landed today', with accounts of hundreds of soldiers slinging out gangways and unloading in a manner that caused admiring remarks from Regulars. One can only conjecture at what prompted this premature announcement. It was not a case of confusing the main body's arrival with that of the advance party, which the *Star* said had arrived 'the week before last'. There are suggestions that various announcements were deliberately made to mislead the enemy and the article may have been part of such a plan. Copies of Canadian newspapers dating back to 9 September had been withheld from delivery in Britain, a wise move as some included announcements of the convoy's departure. Whatever the reason, Rowland Hill of the

Star showed much imagination with his details of the Canadians' fictitious arrival. *The Times* of London made no such announcement, merely observing on the 8th that Canada now intended to contribute a force of 60,000 men. When the Contingent finally did arrive, Canadian newspapers were cautious about reporting the event until definite confirmation had been received.

At Plymouth little notice had been taken of the first ship to appear until people on the shore heard the sound of bagpipes and cheering, suggesting something unusual was happening. The news quickly spread and crowds assembled at every vantage point. There was much singing of 'O Canada', 'God Save the King' and 'It's a Long, Long Way to Tipperary'.

The Times of 19 October enthused:

> Nothing like the Canadian Contingent has been landed in this country since the time of William the Conqueror. Friendly forces and hostile forces have reached our shores from time to time; the hostile ones so badly found that they were quickly extinguished, the friendly ones coming unequipped by reason of their friendliness. But the Canadians come armed *cap-a-pie*, horse, foot, and artillery. The force has its own engineers, signallers, transport corps, ammunition parks, and field hospitals, and there are 34 chaplains and 105 nursing sisters. It would be a military offence to state the number of million rounds of ammunition brought by the Contingent, so great is it.

At first only officers were given shore leave but after three days tied up in Plymouth, the SS *Grampian*, carrying the 3rd Field Artillery Brigade and Ammunition Column, sent a signal ashore asking permission for 12 hours of shore leave for half of its men. The reply should have been 'Yes, half officers only tomorrow, the other half next day'. But at some stage the word 'officers' was omitted, so that half the men went ashore and made the most of their liberty. The next day the other half lined up expectantly but were told that no one was allowed to leave ship. The men broke ranks, booed the 3rd Brigade's commanding officer, lowered the ship's tenders and evaded the boats of Royal Marines sent to restore order. John Sutton of the 9th Battery, 3rd Brigade reported that eight boats with 200 men made it ashore, though 'W.D.D.', writing in the *Toronto Star*, mentions only one boat holding 30 men. The Canadians sent after them pickets (small groups of soldiers), who dealt with the problem sensibly by splitting into pairs, taking

Canadian troops parade on the Hoe at Plymouth. The monument commemorates the sighting of the Spanish Armada in 1588 and is topped by a statue of Britannia.

no names and telling the absconders that they had to report to the dockside by 8pm. In the event, only 20 failed to get back to ship and were gradually picked up by military policemen and sent to rejoin their units on Salisbury Plain, where their pay was deducted for the periods of absence.

The last to be held to account was, according to Sutton, Paddy Carroll, a former private in the 'Royal Irish Rifles'. This would have been Patrick Carroll of Toronto and before that Dublin, whose attestation papers state that he had served seven years with the 2nd Royal Dublin Fusiliers. He was in the same battery as Sutton, who recounted how Paddy made his own way to Salisbury Plain, where he picked up pieces of ammunition and shells from the training areas and sold them in local public houses as souvenirs from the French battlefields. After he was finally caught he was sentenced to six months in Devizes Military Prison.

Some men were allowed ashore but were confined to the dockyard area, where they formed themselves into 'military parties' under NCOs and marched smartly through the gates as if on army business. The Princess Pats, and no doubt other units, were taken ashore in tugs for route marches. Perhaps as the days wore on and with many units yet to disembark, the authorities had decided that it was wiser to allow the men ashore

rather than keep them cooped up on their ships. Two hundred gunners of the 2nd Field Artillery Brigade were granted shore leave and after weeks of abstinence in Valcartier and afloat, drank 'liberally'.

D. G. Dancocks in *Gallant Canadians* has suggested that it was the British-born members who over-indulged in the public houses, treating the occasion as a home-coming. He claims that the 10th Battalion was exemplary, putting this down to its commanding officer, Lieutenant Colonel Russell Boyle who, on the first parade in England, took off his coat (thus discarding his emblems of rank) and offered to take on four men who on the voyage had said they would like to punch the hell out of him. No one came forward.

The war diary of No. 1 General Hospital recorded:

> Streets crowded with people who accorded us a most cordial reception wishing the troops 'Good Luck' and shaking hands at every opportunity. Our route literally though a lane of populace.

Bruce Brommell of the 8th Battalion recalled how:

> we got a grand reception from the populace; especially the girls. They handed us apples and

chocolates and took all our buttons and badges as mementos; which got the Sergeant-major's goat, as he had to supply new ones.

Alderson, the Canadians' new commander, was in Plymouth to meet his men and is said to have been immediately perturbed by their lack of discipline. A local newspaper, the *Western Evening Herald*, said little of any unruliness, merely referring to sightseeing officers being pestered by crowds of youngsters for badges or other mementos. It did mention the appearance in a police court on 19 October of Private Alexander Davidson of the Divisional Supply Column who had become involved in a fracas in which a police constable was kicked in the head. Davidson claimed that he had seen a sailor being kicked about and had gone to his aid, not realizing that the other man was a policeman. He was fined 50s and costs, together with the fee of the doctor who had treated his victim, £3 19s 6d in all. The following day, two Canadians, John R. Gallway and Lionel Gallway, were in court following the breaking of a lamp, perhaps a street light. Presumably they were brothers; no one with a comparable name has been found in Canadian attestation papers and in the roll of the First Contingent. A Canadian sergeant and officer both told the court that the hospitality of the local people had prompted the misbehaviour, the officer adding that the men 'were just like a lot of schoolboys let loose and did not know what they were doing'. Both the accused offered to pay the cost of the damage and were discharged. Another man, unnamed in the press reports, was charged with using obscene language when drunk; he too was discharged.

The confusion of embarkation in Quebec meant an even more confused unloading, not only of men but especially of stores and materials (some of which, such as reserve saddles for the cavalry, never turned up in camp), and it was not until the 25th that the last unit, the 2nd Battalion, bade goodbye to its ship. It is said that the Canadians were reluctant to unload their ships themselves. Possibly this was due to their revelling in their new role of acclaimed heroes or because of sensitivities among the strongly unionized dock-workers about others doing their job. Instead a thousand 'Kitchener' recruits to Britain's New Army helped, some being unused to handling horses, with the result that a number ran loose in Plymouth.

The *Western Evening Herald* of 16 September noted:

a large number of nurses. Neat and trim, [they] looked in uniforms somewhat akin to those of

our Voluntary Aid Detachment, nurses – broad-rimmed felt navy blue hats and coats of a similar colour. Happy? They were as happy as a band of schoolgirls off for a picnic, and readily did they submit to the request of the ubiquitous camera men to pose for a photograph.

The nurses were presented with several pans of Devonshire cream, the gift of Mrs Waldorf Astor, wife of the Member of Parliament for Plymouth. A British flag covering the pans was inscribed 'To the Canadian Nurses, From Plymouth'. The nurses were to spend a week at St Thomas's Hospital in London before joining the Contingent on the Plain.

Also remarked on was the camaraderie, not to say familiarity, between officers and men, who off duty walked about arm in arm and calling each other by their first names, something of which the more rank-conscious British Army strongly disapproved.

Some soldiers had strong links with the locality, having been born in the city and still with families living there. Two such were Sergeant Charles Phillips of the 11th Battalion, son of a Devonport town councillor, and Geoffrey Clark of the Fort Garry Horse, only son of a former Plymouth coroner.

A British officer, Captain John Fuller, was sent to Plymouth to oversee the disembarkation and the dispatching of the Canadians by train to Salisbury Plain. He was:

in military control of the Great Western and London & South Western Railways [both of which served Plymouth]. I could cancel any train I liked and order whatever train I wanted, so long as I got the Canadians to their destination.

Fuller's recollections, *Memoirs of an Unconventional Soldier,* include much irony, as when he observed that the Canadian soldiers would be good enough after six months' training provided that their officers could all be shot. (Fuller went on to a very distinguished career as a pioneer of tank warfare and a military strategist, rising to the rank of major general.)

Trains carrying the soldiers started to leave Plymouth late in the evening of 15 October for Salisbury Plain in Wiltshire, the camping and training area allocated to the Canadians. Detachments of about 500 men marched to several of the city's stations through streets lined with crowds, who offered gifts of cigarettes, apples, cakes and, in the case of some girls, gloves and silk handkerchiefs. They had a wide range of mascots, including bears, goats, fowl and dogs, as well as a Montreal newspaper boy who had smuggled aboard a ship. The soldiers were not meant to bring pets ashore and there were reports of dogs being dropped from the transports into the sea and swimming to the mainland. Fuller noted how on their way to the trains:

> they were met by rejoicing crowds and assaulted by every young and old harlot in the ... city. Men fell out or were pulled out of the ranks to vanish down side streets. A few reached the railway station, but the remainder painted Devonport and Plymouth pink, red and purple.

The next day the public houses were closed early and Fuller requisitioned a disused racket-court and turned it into a prison for drunken Canadians. Each day he claimed to have dispatched to Salisbury Plain a troop train that he called the 'Drunkard's Special'. This should not be taken too literally: trains were leaving daily (and mostly at night) for Salisbury Plain, and it is unlikely that any one was specifically for drunkards. No doubt a proportion of passengers on many of them had over-indulged. There were some complaints about his insisting that men joined trains that were conveying other units' soldiers, but no doubt he was anxious to keep as closely as possible to the hastily arranged special timetable and perhaps they were the drunkards who had missed their specified departure. Some 92 special trains are said to have conveyed the Canadians and much of their equipment to the Plain. It is worth noting the versatility of Britain's railways in being able to arrange so many special trains at very short notice and at a time when there were so many other demands on the rail network.

Major David Bentley, the officer commanding No. 2 Field Ambulance lamented in his unit's war diary for 17 October: 'no trace or word what transport [ship] has my Horse, wagons & equipment & stores'. On 20 October he sent Captain Percy Brown back from Salisbury Plain to enquire about them. Thirty horses did arrive at Amesbury Station on the 23rd and that same day another captain was sent to Southampton to collect stores that had arrived there; some were missing and some wagons broken. The SS *Manhattan* had disembarked 850 horses at Plymouth and then had then gone on to Southampton, to where officers and men travelled to collect equipment. An officer from No. 1 Field Ambulance went there for its stores on the 24th and men of the Divisional Ammunition Park assembled their ninety vehicles at the docks and drove to Salisbury Plain on 30 October. The 1st Divisional

Artillery did not receive the last of its guns from Plymouth until the 29th, 14 days after it had arrived there.

Southampton would have been a far more convenient port than Plymouth, it being only 30 miles from Salisbury Plain and its facilities enabling a more rapid disembarkation. True, the rail journey would have been a little circuitous on track that was already busy with trains transporting supplies for the British Expeditionary Force, but instead the Contingent faced a train journey of more than 100 miles. For any men who made the journey in daylight it afforded a pleasant view of some of the finest country in southern England, with glimpses of the ruggedness of Dartmoor, best known to many Englishmen for its isolated prison and being the setting of Sir Arthur Conan Doyle's *The Hound of the Baskervilles.* Thereafter the trains would pass through green fields, attractive villages, pleasant towns and the old city of Exeter.

There were two direct lines from Plymouth to Salisbury Plain. One, run by the London & South Western Railway, skirted the north of Dartmoor before entering Exeter where, due to a quirk of railway rivalry and routing, trains on it from Plymouth might meet coming the other way a Great Western Railway service that had also left Plymouth and had taken a route below the southern edge of Dartmoor. The LSWR line then ran through Honiton and Salisbury. Seven miles north east of the latter, a branch line, the Amesbury & Military Camp Light Railway, led to the part of Salisbury Plain then most used by the army. From Exeter the GWR line ran to the north of its rival through Taunton and Westbury and then into the Vale of Pewsey, below the escarpment that forms the northern boundary of the Plain. Both LSWR and GWR lines continued to London.

Roy Palmer of the 7th Battalion wrote to his father, the deputy chief of police in Victoria, British Columbia:

> The funny little villages we passed through on the way to Salisbury are awfully funny. I wouldn't live in one for anybody. The thatched roofs and narrow streets looked comical, but I think England as much as I've seen is the prettiest country I'm ever likely to see.

On 18 October the SS *Royal Edward* berthed at its home port of Avonmouth, close to Bristol, with 1,000 men of the 11th Battalion, whose arrival was as

Officers of the 7th Battalion, also known as the 1st British Columbia Regiment.

unexpected as their comrades' had been at Plymouth. A Canadian drum-and-fife band played through the crowd-lined streets of Bristol but the main body of men was confined to the docks, where they entrained for the Plain. Theirs was a rail journey of 40 miles.

In its coverage of national news (in those days a feature of many British local papers), the *Wiltshire Advertiser* of 23 October described the arrival in Plymouth and the subsequent boarding of trains, but without mentioning that the destination was its own circulation area, though the *Toronto Star* had said it would be Salisbury Plain in its issue of the 8th. Whether this was out of ignorance or discretion is not clear, but for the next three months the *Advertiser* and other local papers would be full of the activities of the Canadians.

The Automobile Machine Gun Brigade No. 1 and Divisional Supply Column drove to Salisbury Plain, passing through Plymouth with cheering crowds everywhere, its cars streaming pennants bearing the words 'Canada With the Empire' and the people

showering gifts such as cakes, chocolates, newspapers and apples. The convoy stopped overnight at Exeter and Taunton, the people of the latter city arranging a dance that none of the Canadians was allowed to attend, Major Brutinel believing that a man could not drive cars well after a party and that it would not be fair to stop only the drivers from attending. Such was the demand for badges and buttons that some men in the unit had none left. There was a further overnight stop at Heytesbury, on the south-western corner of the Plain, before the Brigade reached its destination.

A small number of Canadians remained at Plymouth, a few in hospital there, others to manage a medical store. When four wagon-loads of stores for No. 2 General Hospital arrived at Amesbury on October 30 (from where is not known), they were moved down to Plymouth to be kept with the unit's other equipment. One wonders why this store was so remote from the Canadian camps. By February it appears to have been moved to Southampton, a more convenient disembarkation port for conveying stores to France.

Chapter Three

Salisbury Plain

In 1897 the training area around Aldershot, the British Army's traditional home then and now, had become too small for military requirements, so the Government started to buy up large parts of Salisbury Plain in Wiltshire, a broad upland area at one time given over to sheep and populated only by small villages in its valleys. Sometimes known as the 'Great Plain', it stretches some 24 miles west to east and 12 miles north to south. British-Canadian pathologist George Adami (author of *The War Story of the Canadian Army Medical Corps 1914-1918*) compared it to 'the rolling grass-covered country stretching around Calgary'. The *Toronto Star* correspondent with the Contingent agreed, writing that 'probably no spot in England more like Western Canada could have been chosen as the Canadians' training ground'.

One officer in the small advance party commented:

> I must say that the camp sites are beautifully situated and the turf is excellent, and will be quite an agreeable change from the sand plains which our boys have been accustomed to.

On 19 October the *Toronto Star* noted with an optimism very soon to be dashed:

> so far there has been no rain, thanks to its [the Plain's] situation, though even a week's downpour would not render the camp permanently uncomfortable.

Two main north-to-south roads (today the A345 and A360) divided the Plain into three distinct areas, the central and eastern ones being much used by the army in the 1900s. The central area had had a third major road crossing it from Devizes to Salisbury, but civilian traffic on it had been increasingly restricted in the early twentieth century because the surrounding land was used for artillery practice. This road would be much travelled by the Canadians as it ran close to several of their camps. The western area, east of Warminster, had been little used by the army before the war, but in 1914-15 Canadian cyclist and cavalry units were occasionally to visit the isolated village of Imber at its heart.*

At the start of the twentieth century, two barracks had been built four miles apart at Bulford and Tidworth, and rifle and artillery ranges laid out at the expense of a dozen or so farms. Many of the agricultural buildings were soon damaged by practice artillery fire, others being retained for military use, including the storage of range equipment. The latter included Greenland, Keeper's, Newfoundland and New Copse farms, all of which would become familiar to some of the Canadians. Tidworth Barracks comprised eight individual barracks named after British campaign successes in India and Afghanistan.

The area was conveniently close to London, 80 miles away, and the major port of Southampton and was served well by railway lines, including those of the GWR and LSWR on which the Canadians had travelled from Plymouth. The pre-war increase in military traffic had led to the local rail system being enhanced and branch lines built to Bulford and Tidworth; these carried civilian traffic as far as the respective village stations and then extended in to the two barracks. The Bulford branch ran through Amesbury Station, which would become the major railhead for the Canadians and their supplies. A minor line, the Midland & South Western Junction Railway, skirted the Plain's eastern boundary and provided a

---

* The western area around Imber saw increasing military activity, mostly by artillery, during the Great War. In 1943 the village was evacuated so it could be used to train troops for D-Day. After the war it remained in army use and today of the original buildings only St Giles' Church and a few shells stand. The public are allowed occasional access.

ARRIVAL of TROOPS for SALISBURY PLAIN CAMPS.

Amesbury Station was the major railhead for Salisbury Plain and handled many troops and their equipment, as in this pre-war scene.

reasonable link between Southampton and the Midlands and North of England and also connected the GWR and LSWR routes.

The Plain is pleasant enough in good weather, but at other times it is as miserable as most other bleak expanses in southern England. However, being caught on it in snow or heavy rain is not a life-threatening experience, and one is never more than four miles from a village. E. H. Barham summed it up in his *Ingoldsby Legends*:

Oh Salisbury Plain is bleak and bare,
At least so I've heard many people declare,
Tho I must confess that I've never been there.
Not a shrub, not a bush nor tree can you see,
No hedges, no ditches, no gates, no stiles,
Much less a house or a cottage for miles,
It's a very bad thing to be caught in the rain,
When night's coming on, on Salisbury Plain.

There were several military camping-sites, including those at West Down North and South, Pond Farm, Bustard and Lark Hill, all of which were to become all too well-known to the Canadians. Army units had used these sites before the war for one or two weeks at a time, and then only in summer. The visitors were mainly infantry, with Pond Farm being allocated to yeomanry (part-time mounted soldiers).

The only buildings were cooking-shelters, their sides open to the elements, and, at Lark Hill, several aeroplane hangars (which still stand), used until mid-1914 by the Bristol Flying School, whose aircraft were a source of entertainment to soldiers based nearby. The war diary of the 3rd Battalion for 5 November refers to a detachment of 30 men going to 'Flying Shed Camp, for the purpose of assisting in the erection of huts'. The Central Flying School had opened at Upavon in 1912 and there was another military airfield outside Netheravon village, where there was also a cavalry school based at the manor house.

Canadian soldiers had been on the Plain before the war. There would have been some among the King's Colonials or 'Worldwide Empire' regiment at Pond Farm Camp visited by Sir Frederick Borden, then the Canadian Minister of Militia, in mid-August 1909. Officially known as the 4th County of London Imperial Yeomanry (King's Colonials), it had been raised in 1901, recruiting dominion and colonial men living in the London region and, later, other areas, including Oxford and Cambridge. One of its original four squadrons comprised 'British Americans' or Canadians. In 1910 it was renamed King Edward's Horse (the King's Overseas Dominions Regiment) and in 1914 a second regiment was raised, which the next year would form part of the Canadian Cavalry Brigade.

Above: A British soldier posted this card of Bustard Camp two weeks before the Canadians arrived there.

A COOK SHACK.
ADIAN CONTINGENT.

Left: Cooking shelters such as this one were the only structures on the Contingent's camp-sites.

Below: The 'King's Colonials', including a squadron of Canadians, were at this camp at Pond Farm in 1909.

In September 1910 very large-scale manoeuvres were held on the Plain and in counties adjoining Wiltshire; taking part were 26 officers and 528 men of the 2nd Queen's Own Rifles of Canada in its jubilee year. The Rifles operated mainly in Hampshire, at one time 'defending' the historic city of Winchester. The high point came in a mock battle with the East Yorkshire Regiment near Basingstoke, 16 miles to the north of Winchester, where the umpires decreed that the Rifles had 'wiped out' half a British battalion.

The Canadians enjoyed a rapturous reception from the English people but suffered from the 'antediluvian Oliver equipment which ...cut right to the bone'. The Oliver harness was worn on a man and had attached to various items of kit, and was still to prove a problem for the First Contingent in 1914-15.

During the visit several officers fell ill with suspected typhoid, Lieutenant Roy Gzowski dying of enteric fever and being buried in Aldershot Military Cemetery. The month before, Colour Sergeant H. Greet of the Canadian team for the National Rifle Association competition at Bisley had also died from enteric fever, and was interred in Bisley Cemetery.

When elements of the Contingent arrived at Amesbury Station on the Plain in October 1914, H. R. Gordon of the *Toronto Star* was to recall the Queen's Own Rifles leaving there for home four years before, with Kitchener bidding them goodbye. In fact the Rifles had left from Dinton Station, west of Salisbury, and had been seen off by the Duke of Connaught!

Then in 1911 the Royal Canadian Militia Artillery had come to England, following visits in 1886 and 1896. Comprising seven officers and 50 men under the command of Lieutenant Colonel A. F. MacNachtan, the party had spent some of its visit taking part in the National Artillery Association competition on Salisbury Plain, staying under canvas at West Down Camp, where their countrymen (and perhaps some of themselves) would camp in 1914. They were the first to fire for the King's Prize, on 24 August, but, as a portent of three years later, the morning became wet, heavy and misty, which stopped firing for the day. Eventually the Canadians came seventh out of 12 entries, the other contestants being from Britain's Territorial Force. *The Times* stated that the visitors were delighted with the Plain and its 'silent grandeur', finding in its vast expanse a likeness to their native prairies, only improved in respect of easier travelling for horse and man. The delays caused by the weather meant there was no time on the Plain to compete for the Canadian Cup, which had been won in 1907 by a British team visiting the dominion. The competition was rescheduled to take place at Lydd in Kent, where the Canadians regained the trophy, after winning on the Isle of Wight the Londonderry Trophy for heavy guns.

Also in 1911 and using his country's Ross rifle, Private William Clifford of the 10th Royal Grenadiers of

These troops are wearing the unpopular Oliver harness from which items of kit were hung.

Toronto became the first Canadian-born winner of the King's Prize, the international rifle competition held at Bisley. At the outbreak of war he was a staff sergeant and was posted to England in 1915 as a divisional armourer, before transferring to the Royal Flying Corps and being killed in a mission over France in 1917. Another Canadian, Private William Hawkins, won the King's Prize in 1913, again using a Ross rifle.

By 1914 Salisbury Plain had become as evocative a name to British soldiers as Aldershot. Most Regulars, if not based there, would have taken part in exercises and manoeuvres and many Territorials would have attended summer camp under canvas on it.

Many Canadians' memories of the Wiltshire countryside came to be grim, but it is worth recording the contrasting view of Lieutenant Colonel George Nasmith, the Contingent's 'Water Expert', given in his memoirs, *On the Fringe of the Great Fight:*

> one saw a good deal of the Wiltshire scenery in the late winter season. It was a never-failing source of wonder and pleasure to me to see the ivy covered banks, the ivy clad trees and the rhododendrons and holly trees in green leaf in the middle of the winter. In the garden at the back of the famous old Elizabethan house in Potterne – a perfect example of the old Tudor timbered style of architecture – cowslips and pansies were in full blossom, and I was told the wild violets were in flower in the woods. The trim, well kept gardens, hedges and fields of the country side and village were a continual delight to a native of Canada where everything in comparison looks so unfinished and in need of trimming. The winter wheat was as green as the new grass of spring time, and many of the meadows also were fairly green. Some shrubs, and in particular an unknown yellow-flowered, leafless vine, were in blossom. I heard afterwards that it was the Jasmine.

But the Plain is not a good place to train an inexperienced army of 30,000 men in what became one of the wettest winters on record. And, just as British soldiers had found before the war, there was not much for them to do off-duty. The two largest villages, Amesbury and Pewsey, had populations of 1,250 and 1,700 respectively; that of the city of Salisbury was 21,000. There were some 6,730 people in Devizes, to the north of the Plain. The major tourist attraction was Stonehenge, within sight of Lark Hill Camp, and many Canadians paid it a visit. Their horse transport

and artillery were photographed passing very close to the famous stones, a prelude to increasing military activity that threatened the site and became a cause of concern later in the war. Salisbury Cathedral, completed in 1258 after 38 years' work and with a spire 404 feet tall, would also have merited a visit, as would the nearby earthwork remains of Old Sarum, which once had its own, even older, cathedral.

The train journeys from Plymouth took about five hours, transporting the Canadians to Amesbury Station, which had sidings to accommodate military rolling stock, and to Lavington and Patney & Chirton stations on the north side of the Plain. Patney & Chirton, a small station some way from the villages it served, also had a military siding. The men were met, usually at night, by local policemen, postmen or boy scouts and led to their camps. Steam traction engines were on hand to haul wagons containing the men's equipment.

Some men who had de-trained at Amesbury had a reasonably flat march along the main road from London to the South West, forking right just before Stonehenge and passing very close to the famous stones, causing them to ask its origins of their officers – and to receive a variety of semi-informed answers. Those who found themselves at Lavington and Patney & Chirton faced a demanding trudge up a steep escarpment to their camps. The 4th Battalion was particularly unlucky. It arrived at Lavington Station in the early morning and marched the nine miles to Bustard (twice the distance it would have been from Amesbury Station), and then had trouble finding its lines in the dark, no one having been appointed to direct it. It was the last battalion to arrive there, and found that other units had helped themselves to their tents, leaving them short of 35. The 5th Battalion marched through Market Lavington and up 'a truly murderous hill [which] blistered our feet, spoiled our tempers and proved to us in no uncertain manner how stale we had become during our journey overseas,' recalled Sergeant Harold Baldwin. The weather was clear and bright and those arriving in the middle of the day found the heat of the sun on the open Plain uncomfortable. It was not to last.

The 'murderous hill' was Lavington Hill, leading up to the Plain from the village, but equally taxing was Red Horn (known also as Red Hone) Hill, which caused problems not only for men of Lord Strathcona's Horse marching from Patney & Chirton Station to Pond Farm Camp but for a traction engine that could not manage towing three wagons up it, one having to be

Artillery passes close to Stonehenge.

detached. The Strathconas' horses had arrived at Amesbury, which may not necessarily have been a result of confusion, the station there being better suited to off-loading horses than that of Patney & Chirton. When men and steeds were reunited, they trained at Netheravon Cavalry School before it was taken over, first as a temporary hospital and then as a remount depot which received and accommodated animals until they were fit for issue to units.

Herbert Andrews of the Fort Garry Horse recalled being piled into 'packing boxes' at the station at Plymouth and being taken to Market Lavington. Marching from there to his camp, he was struck by the hospitality of the people, the long hill he had to climb out of the village, the hedges and seeing five aeroplanes all at once.

On their journey to the Plain, some 35 men of A Company of the 48th Canadian Highlanders (the 15th Battalion) were taken ill with apparent food poisoning, arriving at Patney at 1am with colic and very severe pains. Blankets were laid in the station building for them, but the unit's surgeon did not consider any cases serious. Some others of the 48th set off for camp as their pipers played (appropriately, given the 250ft-climb ahead) 'We'll take the High Road', their kit on board two wagons drawn by a traction engine. The remainder waited for another traction engine but it turned out to have gone to Lavington Station, six miles away.

Eventually at 3am it was decided to march to the camp, with some of the men carrying 125 pounds of equipment. On the way they met a train of wagons drawn by a traction engine, which Lieutenant Colonel Currie commandeered. He had been told that camp was 11 miles from the station, a march that was completed in just over four hours. Their destination was West Down Camp, which was in two parts, North (in fact seven miles from Patney Station) and South (a further mile).

Artilleryman W. A. Wilson wrote in his diary:

> We ... landed at Plymouth on October 16th and went by train to Amesbury. As our horses had been so long on board they were not considered fit to pull any vehicles and we marched from Amesbury leading our horses to a tented camp at Westdown North, Salisbury Plain. It consisted of bell tents, 13 men to a tent and the horse lines were very muddy.

Shortly after arriving on the Plain, part of his unit moved to Greenland Farm, a mile south of West Down South Camp, whose buildings were used to store equipment for the firing ranges.

The 13th Battalion's destination was Patney Station, from which its members marched with full kit to West Down South. They reckoned the journey to be ten miles, which it covered in three hours and 25 minutes. On their

Patney & Chirton Station had its own military siding for trains carrying troops and stores to and from West Down and Pond Farm camps.

The Canadians' camp at West Down in unusually dry conditions.

march to Pond Farm Camp, a tired Harold Peat and two comrades of the 9th Battalion slipped away and slept in a haystack. Perhaps less weary was Seymour Bannin from Montreal, who had been born in Pewsey. One can imagine his excitement as his train from Plymouth took the line leading to his birthplace and his frustration when it stopped six miles short, at Patney. No doubt he was soon able to visit his old home.

No. 2 General Hospital reached Lavington Station at 12.30am on 17 October and was guided by a policeman, apparently on a tricycle, to West Down North, where at first medical units were concentrated. The facilities were primitive and in those early days urgent cases of sickness and injury were sent by motor-ambulance to the hospital in Tidworth Barracks. No. 1 General Hospital arrived at 2.25am on the 20th, their policeman-guide favouring a conventional bicycle.

The 3rd Field Artillery Brigade arrived at Amesbury Station on 20 October and started to unload its horses before being told to clear the road of guns. Then the men were ordered to unload three railway wagons of infantry equipment, including large packing cases, picks and shovels, and put it into large vans. By that time it was pitch dark. They unloaded the rest of the horses, tying them along the road out of the station and in a nearby field. Several days later, two officers returned to the station with ten teams of horses to collect the Brigade's guns from the jumble of guns, wagons, wheels and harness in the station yard.

No. 2 Stationary Hospital de-trained at Lavington at 1.30am on the 22nd in a steady drizzle and bleak east wind and, rather than march what it understood to be nine miles to camp, decided to rest at the station. Using rubber sheets and blankets, the men slept on the platform, looking very like sacks of potatoes lying together. Five officers occupied a station hut. After three hours of sleep, the cooks served hot coffee, cheese and biscuits to prepare the men for their march to West Down North.

Having handled luggage and stores at Patney Station for two days, Bruce Brommell left for West Down South on a truck of baggage drawn by a traction engine with a dozen drunks on board: 'I held up two myself. About half way the tractor broke down and we had to foot it. Also the drunks.'

One may conjecture when and where these men had become laggards. Captain Fuller's allusion to a 'Drunkard's Special' train comes to mind, but the men must truly have indulged in Plymouth if they were still in the state suggested by Brommell. Perhaps they had taken bottles on board with them, or, immediately on de-training on the Plain, had slipped away to visit the local pubs.

The *New York Times* of 17 October described how the Canadians had arrived on the Plain led by:

> a long transport train composed of wagons drawn by traction engines, then the motor trucks, and lastly the commandeered London motor 'buses. The cavalry and the artillery followed …. Long before dawn the sleepy old villages … were awakened with the clang of hoofs on the hard roads, which, incidentally, have been a revelation to the Canadians, accustomed to their own muddy highways.

This last comment would be one of many quickly to take on irony. The preceding weeks had been dry but this was very soon to change, and the 'hard roads' would soon become as muddy as any in Canada!

The men were singing a medley of tunes such as 'It's a Long Way to Tipperary', 'There'll be a Hot Time in the Old Town Tonight', and the latest American ragtime, including 'This is the Life'. (Other songs popular among the Contingent were 'Hold your Hand Out, Naughty Boy' and 'Henry the Eighth I Am'.) But the people of Wiltshire, apparently expecting a Wild West display, were disappointed that, apart from the 'sombreros' worn by the cavalry, the men's uniforms to the casual eye looked much like those worn by the British. In fact the Canadians' clothes, as with so much else of their equipment, were to prove unsuitable, being too tight, with high, stiff collars and unable to withstand the admittedly exceptional hard wear of the following months; they would be replaced by British uniforms. The 'sombreros' were the stetson hats worn by the 19th Alberta Dragoons, serving as 'divisional cavalry' and providing patrols, orderlies and dispatch riders.

Riding at the head of the supply convoy was a small Montreal newspaper boy who had stowed away:

> … this little chap, in spite of the fact that he was almost lost in the folds of an army coat loaned to him by a good-hearted Sergeant of Highlanders, was nearly frozen, but he insisted on practising the bugle, proficiency in which, he hopes, will give him a chance to go to the front.

Probably this was the 'newspaper boy' noted as a mascot when the Contingent arrived at Plymouth.

The 19th Alberta Dragoons wearing their characteristic stetson hats, photographed on 26 January when they were in the Winterbourne Stoke area on a tactical exercise.

The Bustard Inn was the headquarters of General Alderson and his staff and the most hospitable building on the Plain.

The *New York Times* reporter counted a number of naturalized Americans among the Canadian forces, including a sergeant of a Montreal regiment who claimed to be a veteran of Admiral Dewey's flagship in the 1898 battle of Manilla Bay in the Spanish-American War. A few days later Hughes was to say that 'fully 200,000 Americans have gone to Canada in the hope of joining the Canadian forces', an incredible exaggeration even by his standards.

Reports in local newspapers mentioned that each detachment of Princess Patricia's Canadian Light Infantry was preceded by a small flag with the name of a Canadian state on it. The Pats bragged that they had passed three other battalions on their march from the station.

The *Salisbury Journal* of 24 October declaimed:

The arrival in England of large bodies of Canadian Troops has created considerable satisfaction among the people of this country, by whom the Empire's loyal sons from the great dominion have been welcomed with much cordiality ....

The men ... are splendid fellows. Their physique is of the finest and their hardy and healthy appearance has elicited the favourable comments of everyone who has seen them, especially en masse. During the last few days many members of the contingent have visited Salisbury, where they have created a favourable impression and have been well received. The heartiness of their reception and the hospitality which has been accorded to them has been deeply appreciated by the Canadians, many of whom have relatives in this country .... their sojourn on Salisbury Plain will no doubt be remembered both by the soldiers and the civilians with whom they are becoming acquainted.

The *New York Times* reported that General Alderson would be occupying the only 'saloon' on Salisbury Plain, causing any British reader to pause before realizing that the Americanism referred to the Bustard Inn which was to become the General's headquarters.* There were only a few rooms at the Bustard Inn and these were taken by the most senior staff, with their junior colleagues living in tents close by. At the nearby Bustard camping-site were the 1st Infantry Brigade, the Divisional Mounted Troops and the Princess Pats; two miles to the north west the 2nd and 3rd Brigades were at West Down South Camp; a mile beyond at West Down North were the artillery and the Divisional Supply Column; while two miles further north at Pond Farm Camp were the 4th Brigade, the cavalry, the 17th Battalion (which was not part of any brigade) and the Newfoundlanders.

The Canadians became part of Britain's Southern Command, making Alderson directly responsible to its General Officer Commanding, Lieutenant General Sir William Pitcairn Campbell, and through him to the War Office. At first Alderson frequently communicated directly by cable with the Canadian Government in Ottawa, but on 2 November was told that this was not permissible and that he had to report to Pitcairn Campbell.

The camping-sites had been prepared by men of Britain's Territorial Force who had erected marquees and tents, some of which, including some hospital tents, had no floor-boards. Palliasses (cloth bags 6 feet long and 2 feet wide filled with straw) made reasonable comfortable mattresses, and new blankets were plentifully distributed. A temporary shortage of tents led to overcrowding.

At first the Canadians compared their new home favourably with Valcartier and the earliest arrivals 'one and all voted the place a huge improvement'. But very quickly it was noted that the Plain camps had no lighting, no baths, and a limited water supply and were remote from towns of any size. Within a few days reality swept over the Canadians. On 20 October the weather broke before the last of them reached Salisbury Plain, marking the start of an exceptionally wet winter, with a total of 24 inches of rain – double the average – falling on 89 out of 123 days. Guy ropes of the tents had been pulled taut during the fine weather and as the rain soaked the canvas and ropes they contracted, pulling the pegs out and bringing the tents down upon their occupants. When the tents were re-erected, the British canvas proved of poor quality and let in the rain. Impervious chalk a few inches below ground-level meant that the water could not drain, and scraping the mud from the roads only

---

* The Bustard was a bird native to Wiltshire that had become extinct locally around 1820. Looking like an unkempt turkey, it has a wingspan of 6 feet. There have been several recent attempts to re-introduce the bird to the locality, the latest proving successful.

A cheerful group of men move in to their tents.

exposed the slippery chalk. It is said that snow-ploughs were used, to no avail. On arrival at its camp (at West Down South), the 5th Battalion found that:

its tents leaked incessantly, but … we are healthy and, in consequence, are grumbling all the time. We roundly cursed our officers and anathematized the mud, swore we would mutiny – all done *sotto voce*. But we are very, very happy.

In a report dated 26 October the *Montreal Star* realistically described the Canadians' new home:

… the average Canadian soldier is beginning to feel that Valcartier, rough though it may have been, was not as bad a place after all …. There are not the comforts of Valcartier. The food is even more monotonous, though nutritious. The men are not making any objection. Far from that, they are cheerful and quite contented with their lot …. They do not grumble, not at least beyond the limit which is allowed all soldiers in all parts of the world.

Medical officer George Nasmith reported:

The officers of the headquarter staff were fairly comfortable in comparison to the others. Our tents were pitched in a quadrangle formed by

four rows of trees and scrub, which had evidently been planted around the site of a former house and served to break the high winds. Each officer had a tent with a wooden floor. Mine was carpeted with an extra blanket to exclude draughts and make it feel comfortable under one's bare feet in the morning. The tent was heated by an oil stove which was kept burning night and day; and at night I slept snug and warm in the interior of a Jaeger sleeping blanket in a Wolseley kit. My batman, [Frank] Karner, had made a table from some boxes and boards which he had picked up, I know not where. It is unwise to ask your batman too many foolish questions as to the origin of things – take what he gives you and be thankful.

This table covered with another blanket, served to support a splendid brass lamp with a green silk shade, for which I had paid a fabulous sum in Salisbury town. It also held some books, brushes, and other necessaries. A shelf underneath displayed a little brass kettle and other paraphernalia for making tea, while my other books were arranged in a neat row beneath.

Very soon the newcomers were exploring the villages closest to their camps. This often meant a walk of several miles, though getting away from camp to the

Tilshead was one of several villages to feature in patriotic cards welcoming the Contingent.

warm welcome awaiting them would have made this worthwhile. Mrs George Overs of Barrie received a picture postcard dated 27 October and featuring Market Lavington from her son, Fred of the 7th Battalion, who wrote that:

we visited this place …. We had a very enjoyable time despite the rain. An old lady asked us in for tea, & gave us a great welcome & those who returned from London said they were used right royally.

Ross Taylor wrote to his parents in Lethbridge, Alberta, that the English 'cannot seem to do enough… every lady we met wanted us to come back and have tea with them'.

After handling kit bags all day at Patney Station and sleeping out all night on the platform, Bruce Brommell breakfasted at a house in the village and 'got in bad by offering to pay for it. You simply can't force your money on the villagers'. Some communities made available their public halls for reading, letter-writing and refreshments. Less welcome were local children who, as in Plymouth, continually pestered the men for money.

The Canadians had the advantage of arriving early in the war, at a time when enthusiasm for it was at its highest. Being from overseas they bought an exotic touch to the Wiltshire countryside and photographs of 1914 of Canadian and British soldiers generally show many of the former to be the finer-looking men. There was detailed and eulogistic newspaper coverage of their activities and sterling qualities, and patriotic postcards were published, both nationally and locally. One, featuring the Canadian camp at Pond Farm, was liberally decorated with flags and included the sentiments:

The wish of all at Market Lavington [the nearest village] is that God will guard them, and give them victory, and that all will return safe home to Canada' and 'With the Maple Leaf around the Union Jack are we downhearted? No!!!'.

Once the men had settled in camp, they were given three days' leave, with Scotland proving a popular destination for emigrants from that country, some of whom reported that elderly grandparents had suddenly become ill and needed to be visited. Men going to Scotland and Ireland were allowed an extra day for travelling.

Several soldiers who had migrated to Canada were delighted to find themselves within daily travel of their families. Howard Curtis, initially with the 9th Battalion, then with the 2nd, was able to visit Crockerton, near Warminster, where he met an elderly man who remembered his grandfather. Corporal Arthur Randall of the 14th Battalion was the son of William Sydney and Sarah Rebecca Randall of Wilton, near Salisbury, who must have been delighted with his posting to Wiltshire – but he was to die of meningitis on 29 January 1915. Arthur Edward Chambers of the 11th Battalion had parents living in Gigant Street, Salisbury and had been a stalwart of St Martin's Church in Salisbury before emigrating in 1911. After being transferred to the 4th Battalion and then wounded, he was to die of pneumonia on 28 October 1916 and was buried in the city's London Road churchyard.

One of the first visitors of note, on 24 October, was Field Marshal Lord Roberts, Colonel-in-Chief of Overseas Forces in England, accompanied by Sam

Hughes, who was to return home a week later. Almost all of the men drawn up on parade saw of the old soldier was his car driving past. Aged 82, he was to die on 14 November, having contracted pneumonia when inspecting Indian and British troops in France. The Contingent provided detachments for the funeral and memorial services in London and Salisbury on 19 November. Four guns of the Royal Canadian Horse Artillery fired a salute in Victoria Park, half-a-mile from Salisbury Cathedral.

There were to be many other visitors, including senior officers, British and Canadian politicians, the author Rudyard Kipling, postcard photographers, journalists and civilian gawpers. Many of these served only to disrupt what limited military training was possible. Parents of British-born soldiers flocked to the Plain as soon as they heard that the Contingent was based there, over-crowding the hotels (already very busy catering for British and Canadian officers and their wives) and spending a lot of time trying to track down their sons. Many had headed for Salisbury, not realizing the camps

LARK HILL ON THE MUD

Inked on the back of this card is 'A slight idea of Lark Hill, only slight though'.

were 12 miles and more away and then having to pay sometimes exorbitant taxi fares to visit them. The *Daily Mail* of 9 November cited a case of an officer's sister being asked £5 for a return journey totalling 24 miles. To make the trip by bus cost 4s one way.

On 28 October elements of the Contingent were placed on alert to move to the South Coast after rumours of a German invasion, something that was to be repeated on 16 and 17 December after the German bombardment of Scarborough.

A dismally wet rehearsal with four hours of rain took place on 2 November for the visit on the 4th, in more favourable weather, of George V and Queen Mary. It was perhaps the conditions for this rehearsal that W. A. Wilson misremembered when he described the actual visit:

> King George V … reviewed us in terrible weather with squally rain. We paraded, mounted, at 7.00 a.m.; it consisted of Mount, Dismount, On Cloaks, Off Cloaks. His Majesty arrived at 2.0 p.m. We got back to camp about 4.0 p.m. wet through.

At least Wilson and his colleagues had cloaks, whereas the Royal Canadian Horse Artillery paraded without overcoats and were soaked through. Seven hours to muster men for such an inspection was not unusual, given that the Contingent was far larger than the average division, and its camps were in a comparatively small area. Later in the war, British and Australian units would march many miles, sometimes bivouacking overnight, to attend a Royal inspection.

Though the weather on the 4th started grey, foggy and damp, the sun broke through in the early afternoon. The King and Queen were accompanied by their daughter Princess Mary, Lord Kitchener, Lord Roberts, George Perley (Canada's acting High Commissioner in Britain), and Sir Richard McBride (the premier of British Columbia). The Royal party reached Amesbury Station at 11.30am, and were driven in motor cars to Bustard Camp, where His Majesty judged the Princess Pats to be 'the finest battalion I have ever inspected'. Their commanding officer, Francis Farquhar, had told Alderson on 21 October that his men would be fit for service in 10 days. Given the military experience of the Pats and their imminent deployment on active service before their fellow Canadians, the King would have had good reason to be genuine in his praise. He was to make many more visits to Wiltshire during the war, usually

before a division left for active service, and almost invariably officers have noted the kind remarks that he made to them about the quality of their units.

It had been hoped that the Contingent would march past the King but the recent rain had made conditions too muddy, so the Royal party drove on to West Down North and Pond Farm camps. It is not recorded how the royal limousines with their narrow tyres coped with the roads, the one to Pond Farm Camp being described as a 'mud slide'. (However the camp itself was said to be the least muddy, if most exposed, of the Canadian camps, with the worst mud being at West Down.)

There are several references to the King riding a horse and dismounting to talk to soldiers. Though he toured the Plain by car, it is likely that he was supplied with a steed at each camp and certainly in future visits he usually mounted a horse after arrival by train or car, and riding through the mud would have been preferable to walking through it.

Since no official regulations on how to parade his unit had been published, Major Brutinel of the Automobile Machine Gun Brigade made his own arrangements. Most of the personnel paraded in front their vehicles, but a number were left over and, rather than leaving them behind, he placed them inside the open-top cars, but out of sight. The King wanted to inspect the vehicles more closely and rode up to one of them. When the soldiers rose to their feet and came to attention, his horse reared. The King kept control over his mount, thus avoiding an embarrassing situation. Another version of the story has him walking to the car, fingering the front armour, then the armour of the side panels, and jumping on a wheel to have a look inside the truck, prompting the crew to rise hastily to attention. He said to Lord Kitchener: 'This unit should be very useful, I think.' Lord Kitchener replied: 'I don't think so, Sir, it would unbalance the fire power of a Division.' Later Alderson admitted that Lord Kitchener was right. In 1962 Brutinel recorded his recollections and attributed this incident to the Royal inspection of 4 February 1915. However, the *Salisbury Journal* of 7 November notes:

> at Pond Farm … the King displayed particular interest in the armoured motor cars, one of which his Majesty and Lord Kitchener entered and inspected the armament.

It went on to report that:

The Royal party leaves after visiting the Canadian camps in November.

After the King has left, two officers leave their marks on the planking he stepped on to get into his car.

CHRISTMAS GREETINGS FROM THE CANADIAN ENGINEERS, SALISBURY PLAIN.
REVIEW BY HIS MAJESTY KING GEORGE V.

Troops cheer the King as he leaves Salisbury Plain after his visit.

Scenes of great enthusiasm prevailed when their Majesties drove away in their motor car, a picturesque sight being provided by the Highlanders raising their Glengarries [caps] on their bayonets and cheering lustily. The farewell scene was of a very impressive character. For a distance of two miles from Bustard Camp, the Canadians were drawn up on either side of the road and, as the King's motor car left for Amesbury, the hearty cheers which were raised echoed across The Plain and gave ample proof of the Canadians' appreciation of the Royal Visit paid to them.

Afterwards the King sent this message:

It gives me great pleasure to have this opportunity of welcoming to the Mother Country so fine a contingent of troops from the Dominion of Canada. Their prompt rally to the Empire's call is of inestimable value, both to the fighting strength of my Army and in the evidence which it gives of the solidarity of the Empire. The general appearance and physical standard of the different units are highly creditable. I am glad to hear of the seriousness and earnest spirit which pervades all ranks for it is only by careful training and leading on the part of officers and by efficiently strict discipline and cooperation on the part of all that the demands of modern war can be met. I shall follow with interest the progress and work of my Canadians.

Not for the last time did the Newfoundlanders have reason to feel that their belonging to a separate dominion to Canada was being overlooked. At least the reporter from *The Times* covering the Royal visit did single them out:

A smart Newfoundland contingent which has recently come in has the name of the colony … on its shoulder-straps. The newcomers are usually distinguished from the Canadians by their blue puttees. The type of man is the same – sturdy, strong, and unassuming. They are a splendid body of men.

Complimentary of the Princess Pats the King may have been, but he had his doubts about other units, writing to his uncle the Duke of Connaught that he thought the Canadians were certainly a fine body of men but their discipline was not of the best, there was too much drinking, and some officers were not much good. Nevertheless he felt sure that after adequate training they would give a good account of themselves. No doubt this was not an opinion that the King had formed for himself but was based on briefings from the War Office which, it has been suggested, had been led to believe that the Contingent was fully trained and equipped. Had this been the case, it would have been sent to France in early December.

Their Majesties were followed by other distinguished visitors. Sir Charles Ross was there in late October to lecture on his rifle, and one wonders if misgivings about its practicality in field conditions were voiced, though up to then the Canadians would have had limited opportunity to fire it. On 22 November the British Prime Minister, H. H. Asquith, and his younger daughter made an unofficial visit, lunching at the Bear Hotel in Devizes and visiting Pond Farm and West Down camps.

At Pond Farm Camp on 4 November, the *New York Times* correspondent noted that in great demand were tooth paste and powder, brass polish, patent cough mixtures – and chewing gum, which was not available. Such items were sold in small shops erected in marquees in the various camps. Overlooking the Canadian nurses, *The Times* noted among the 32,000 men only two women, who worked in the 'shop' (presumably the YMCA marquee) at Pond Farm Camp. The reporter also commented favourably on the behaviour of the 'good class of men' at Pond Farm, with rowdyism being almost unknown. They included the Newfoundlanders with their reputation for good discipline and cavalry units of the Permanent Force who were several times employed for policing disturbances among their fellow Canadians. Such deployments reflected both their superior discipline and the fact that mounted soldiers are often better able to control unruly crowds.

On 6 November No. 2 Stationary Hospital became the first Canadian military force to cross the Channel when it left the Plain in pouring rain with 40 tons of goods.

Three days later, No. 1 Stationary Hospital moved from West Down North, taking a train from Lavington to Paddington and then the Underground railway (or 'Tube') to a hospital being renovated at Hampstead in north-west London, its equipment

Traction engines were essential to pull wagons full of stores and materials to the camps, but their ribbed wheels badly damaged the poorly surfaced roads.

presumably going by road. The major aim was to provide it with experience in running a military hospital. On 28 January the building was declared fully equipped and ready for patients, and the next day the Canadians received orders to proceed overseas, embarking at Southampton on 1 February, together with No. 1 Casualty Clearing Station.

On 11 November Lieutenant Colonel Duncan McPherson of the 6th Battalion and Major Norman Edgar of the 5th visited France for about eight days, meeting Prince Alexander of Teck and viewing scenes of recent military action and the German trenches. Before the war the British-born Prince, then a major

in the 2nd Life Guards, had been named as the next Governor General of Canada, but shortly after the outbreak of hostilities he convinced his brother-in-law George V to release him for military service. (The Prince was later to relinquish his German titles and adopt the name 'Cambridge'.)

Following the departure of the two hospital units, most other elements of the Contingent were to remain on the Plain for three months of training hampered by continuing bad weather and mud and interrupted by having to build their own huts and supporting infrastructure.

Chapter Four

Spies, Mud and Gales

As soon as the Contingent arrived in Wiltshire, it began to weed out men who should not have been recruited in Canada because of ill-health or doubts over their loyalty. The immediate concern was identifying those whose behaviour was deemed suspicious and those who had emigrated to Canada from what were now hostile countries. Canada's population of 7,879,00 included almost 400,000 people of German extraction and almost 40,000 who were German born, and there were recent immigrants from many other counties.

The *Toronto Star* told of a private in a Montreal regiment 'said to be of Dutch nationality' asking suspicious questions during the voyage from Canada. When he was arrested, a 'State letter and code' were found on him and he was to be kept in custody until further orders. Louis Keene of the Automobile Machine Gun Brigade heard that one spy, perhaps the same man, caught on board ship had been shot and that one of two men arrested in Devonport had been wearing an officer's uniform. Keane's first story, though repeated by several others in their letters home, would have been mainly fanciful, the second possibly relates if not to a suspect officer then to a soldier dressing up to enjoy some unofficial shore leave.

There were also stories that *four* men had been arrested during the voyage, one of them possessing 'incriminating correspondence and some explosives. They were handed over to the authorities at Plymouth, and there the veil may be drawn.' So was told an YMCA (Young Men's Christian Association) party visiting the Salisbury Plain camps. At Plymouth a man called D'Arcy, apparently of the 13th Battalion and probably Private Alfred D'Arcy, later a lieutenant in the Royal Highlanders of Canada, was marched in handcuffs off the SS *Alaunia* as a German spy but was released later, some mistake having been discovered.

The YMCA party also overheard some Highlanders talking animatedly. 'We've got a German in our corps,'

said one. 'And so have we,' said another. 'They're all right,' said a third, 'but you want to keep an eye on them.'

When more than 30 men of No. 1 Field Ambulance and several of No. 1 Casualty Clearing Station disembarked at Plymouth with ptomaine poisoning, it was attributed to their last meal on SS *Messantic* and was thought to be intentional. More likely it was straightforward food poisoning.

The Contingent's Intelligence summary of 17 October noted that:

> Knowing that a number of aliens had enlisted in the Canadian forces, we began today, the day after our arrival in Camp, to trace them up …. The system we are adopting to discover suspects is to find out from attestation papers the place of birth of individuals and by employing the Intelligence Officer of each Brigade in finding out through Company Officers and selected N.C.Os & men, suspects.

On 30 October German-speaking Major Wilfrid Howell arrived on the Plain 'through Scotland Yard' (the headquarters of the London Metropolitan Police) to assist with the investigation. Next day the 5th Battalion's war diary reported that the:

> Intelligence Department appointed an Intelligence Officer for the Battalion, whose principal duty has been getting information regarding German Suspects & Spies and from the information gathered, this appointment has been warranted, and there is no question that we have several men whose correspondence and actions are very suspicious.

On 5 November the diary reported that 'six Germans and Austrians' were arrested as suspects. The following day more men who had been born in Germany,

Austria and Turkey or were of German or Austrian parentage and 'who are unknown to anyone in the Force' were placed under guard, with civilian clothing being purchased for them pending their return to Canada. Ten days later some forty 'misfits' were taken to Glasgow and put on a ship for return to their places of enlistment. It was recommended that four of them, thought to be 'alien reservists', be interned when they arrived home. The *Toronto Star* put the number at 46, the *Scotsman* said four more and explained that they had been rejected from the Canadian Contingent as unsuitable. They were escorted by the 1st Battalion's Captain Lucius Grover and 17 men. The Department of Militia stated that it would not publish their names to spare their relatives pain.

The *Scotsman* had submitted its report to the censors on the night of the 16th but at first was refused permission to print it. Yet that same day a Glasgow evening paper had told how the party 'of some 45 Germans and Austrians' had arrived by special train from the south amid speculation that they were German prisoners-of-war, enemy aliens rounded up from various parts of the country or 'undesirable' members from the Salisbury Plain contingent. One was said to have been a Canadian detective of German extraction, another a German forced to enlist by his British wife.

On 6 January 1915 a Toronto attorney, Charles Walter, claimed to have been largely instrumental in identifying the returned 'German spies', as he termed them, stating the number was 43, though apparently one of these had been set on by members of his company and killed when he was accused of being a spy.

A member of the 5th Battalion wrote to a friend on 12 November: 'We caught another spy to-day in our midst'. Three days later a man of the 3rd Field Artillery Brigade, the American-born James Strausbaugh, was sent home as an 'undesirable alien'.

Back in Canada, the *Lethbridge Daily Herald* of 17 November was one of several papers to report that a letter received by an Ottawa citizen from a member of the Canadian Contingent told how a sentry on duty by 'one of the big water tanks' had challenged an individual, who shot him in his arm. The sentry returned fire and killed the intruder who was found to be carrying several vials containing cholera germs, intended apparently to contaminate drinking water. The letter-writer added that the authorities had hushed up the affair. One suspects there had been a rumour that grew with each telling, as was so often the case.

The diary of the 4th Infantry Brigade on 6 November notes 'the placing of suspects under arrest'. That of the Contingent for the 21st lists the names of seven men being discharged and returned to Canada as being medically unfit. Also named were 28 others to be discharged, mostly under King's Regulations 377 (2) (c), which related to recruits within three months of service considered unfit for combat, 392 (xi), which concerned misconduct, and 392 iii (e), which referred to a 'soldier of a local battalion abroad considered unlikely to become efficient' because of medical problems, low intelligence or failing to shooting the required 15 aimed rounds per minute on the rifle ranges

The Contingent's daily orders for 24 November names a few dozen men discharged from the 17th of the month under King's Regulations and returned to Canada. The attestation papers of most of these do not seem to exist, but those that do identify some as having alien antecedents or being Americans with German names. Their return to Canada was noted in the press with the information that they had been imprisoned as enemy aliens.

One so-called spy was Victor Cobb of the 48th Highlanders, who described himself as an American from Pittsburgh and was arrested at the end of November wearing civilian clothes in London's Hotel Cecil and with incriminating documents in his pocket. Three weeks later he escaped from detention in Salisbury while awaiting trial for espionage. In February 1915 he was arrested on a charge of fraud while masquerading as 'Lieutenant Jefferson' and jailed for three months for claiming a fictitious commission. When enlisting, Cobb had stated he had served for three years in the United States Army but did not mention his enlistment in the 31st Grey Regiment which his former landlord in Hanover, Ontario said he had joined.

Captain Hubert Klotz of the 3rd Battalion was of German descent but had been born in Hamilton, Ontario and had served in the Militia, this presumably placing him above suspicion. He would be killed at the Battle of Ypres in May 1915.

Most of the incidents described above need to be seen in the context of the near-hysteria about spies and sabotage that was gripping Britain at that time. Shops bearing German names were ransacked and people showing an undue interest in military movements or being seen near a sensitive installation were apprehended. Incidents comparable to those

The George Hotel in Amesbury was popular among officers but in late 1914 employed a German cook.

Right: The German Frederick Rosener took this photograph of happy Canadians at Lark Hill in late 1914.

connected to the Canadians were reported in many British camps in Wiltshire and elsewhere. Photographers were viewed with suspicion, an Australian having been arrested in mid-August for carrying a camera near Windsor Castle's waterworks.

In December the *Daily Express* sent a reporter to the George Hotel in Amesbury, which was said to employ a German chef who cooked lunch for Canadian officers camped nearby. 'I am told you have a German chef here,' the reporter said to the manager, who replied 'quite right, he cooked your lunch'. It transpired that the chef, Peter Kohler, had come to England as a boy and had three brothers fighting for Britain, and at the beginning of the war had been interned but released on the hotel manager's surety. Rather more disturbing was the presence in Durrington, two miles east of Lark Hill, of a German photographer, Frederick Rosener. He had started a photographic business locally in 1913 and when applying for a trading pass to visit local camps had claimed to be a Dane. His pass was withdrawn in August 1914 but he had continued to take photographs

at the camps, including posed shots of Canadian soldiers, some with the names of the subjects added to the prints. In November 1915 he would be charged with being an enemy alien and as such having four cameras without the permission of the registration officer. He admitted to the court that he was a German and said he had tried several times to enlist in the British Army. He was sentenced to six months' imprisonment with hard labour.

On 6 February more 'alien suspects', 14 or 17 in number (depending on which account one reads), nine of them 'enemy born', were returned to Canada. On the 15th they were marched off the SS *Missanabie* at

Halifax, each handcuffed to a soldier. These, added to the men already mentioned, exceed the overall total of 46 enemy aliens given by Colonel A. F. Duguid in *The Official History of the Canadian Forces in the Great War.* The reason may be that some of those sent home following speculation about their loyalty had proved otherwise unsuitable, and those in this latter category were well in the majority.

One imagines that very few of those excluded in this manner from the Contingent were any threat to security. Perhaps one or two 'enemy aliens' were hoping to get to England and then find their way to Germany or Austria to enlist there. Probably the vast majority were well enough disposed towards Canada to wish to fight for it or, at very least, to escape from their humdrum lives.

One of the several Canadian newspaper correspondents with the Contingent on Salisbury Plain was sent home for sending news of possible value to the enemy.

For those soldiers who remained on the Plain, 'mud' and 'rain' soon became ever-recurring words in personal and unit accounts of the Contingent. As George Nasmith observed:

> For a few days all went well; then it began to rain. About the middle of November it settled down in earnest and rained steadily for a month; sometimes it merely drizzled, at other times it poured; but it never stopped, except for an hour or so. The constant tramp of many feet speedily churned into mud the clay turf overlaying the chalk, and the rain could not percolate through this mixture as it did the unbroken sod. In a few days the mud was one inch – four inches – and even a foot deep. Many a time I waded through mud up to my knees.

Captain C. M. Ambrose of Lord Strathcona's Horse wrote of Salisbury Plain:

> In the morn when we arise
> There are but the rainy skies –
> And the mud
> Nine inch deep it lies,
> We are mud up to our eyes,
> In our cakes and in our pies
> There is mud.

There was no exaggeration in the nine inches, indeed, in many places, the mud was deeper. Verses written by another, anonymous, Canadian at this time asked:

> I wonder what our mothers would say if they could see us no
> Covered with mud from head to foot, wallowing

'Motor car v Mud' reads this caption to a *Daily Mirror* photograph. The men are from Lord Strathcona's Horse.

The main road through Lark Hill Camp in 1914.

through the slough
Up to our knees in the slime and slush of
    Salisbury Plain.

The poem then refers to Kitchener of Khartoum, a soubriquet that recognized the Secretary for War's celebrated capture of the Sudanese capital in 1898:

But K. of K. keeps us on Salisbury Plain, and
    we're getting all slack and stale.
Though 'we lack the disciplines Regulars have',
    this idleness we bewail;
The months pass by, and we'll lose the zest that
    we had for a trench to man.

Similar sentiments about the mud are expressed in 'The Lads of the Maple Leaf', a poem that appeared in *With the First Canadian Contingent*:

Ripe for any adventure, sturdy, loyal and game,
Quick to the call of the Mother, the young
    Canadians came.
Eager to show their mettle, ready to shed their
    blood,
They bowed their neck to the collar and trained
    in Wiltshire mud.

In her introduction to the book, Lieutenant Mary Plummer felt that a special (medal) clasp should be

issued for having served on the Plain, such were the conditions. (Hers was an honorary rank that recognized her status in the Canadian Field Comforts Commission, appointed by the Canadian Government to provide extra clothing and comforts for its soldiers.)

George Gibson in *Maple Leaves in Flanders Fields* was eloquent:

The main street of our camp became a running watercourse; the grass disappeared as if by magic, giving place to a chocolate-coloured coagulum which we learnt to know as mud. It entered into our lives; we splashed around in it outside, we found it in our food; it clung to the outsides of our glasses when we went to have a drink; our bodies were plastered in it and our minds polluted by it; it became part of us, eating right into our souls.

The best footgear were 'rubber boots to the knees', and traders hawked these around the camps at scandalous prices.

Jack Seely, formerly Britain's Secretary of State for War, took command of a newly formed Canadian Cavalry Brigade on 1 February 1915:

I went to Salisbury and started off in a motor car

to a place called The Bustard. It could not be reached by car, as the mud was too deep; however I borrowed a horse and managed to ride there. Then I was given the general direction of the Royal Canadian Dragoons and set to work to ride to them. After a time the horse could go no further, being up to its knees and hocks in mud. So I dismounted and walked the rest of the way. Even in Flanders I had not seen such a sea of mud.

Taps were the only washing facilities at some camping-sites.

The men found cleaning up and drying out near impossible. The supply of water to the camping-sites was very limited with, it is said, just two taps at West Down South, and there was very little hot water. Considering that before the war the West Down camps housed hundreds of men under canvas it is a little difficult to believe that only two taps were provided. Be that as it may, part of the contract to build hutments given to the construction company Sir John Jackson Ltd was to improve the water supply. By late November it was near completing a filtering and pumping station on the River Avon near Netheravon. An old corn store in Salisbury, ten miles from the nearest Canadian camp, was equipped with facilities for a hot bath, which were available between 5pm and 8pm on weekdays and on Sunday afternoons at a cost of 4d, including soap and towel.

The Canadians' initial approval of the camps declined rapidly to complement the deterioration in the weather. On 11 November F. A. MacKenzie of the *Toronto Star* reported that he had received many complaints from soldiers about the 'discomfort and misery', though some of their colleagues quickly remonstrated that *they* were not complaining about the conditions:

It is true that they are not such as we should adopt for pleasure in times of peace, but have we not adopted them in grim earnest at a time of imperial danger … We most assuredly say that we are a great deal more comfortable and better off than most troops in England today … we would like to say that Canadian troops arriving in England were given a reception that went to the hearts of us all and particularly those who are Canadian-born and strangers in the country.

Having settled into camp, the Contingent commenced training scheduled to continue for 13 weeks, the period allotted to British recruits. At first, the infantry concentrated on route marches, musketry instruction, foot and arms drill and entrenching. There followed five weeks of training in companies, two at battalion level and two at brigade strength, exercises in the last sometimes falling into confusion because of the large numbers of men involved. The use of both artillery and rifle ranges was limited because of the demand by British troops. Initially the only range was at Shrewton Folly, two miles from the West Down camps, which had 64 targets. Bulford ranges, with 58, became available from mid-December, followed by 40 at Durrington in mid-January. A shortage of live ammunition inhibited artillery training, with a caution on 21 November advising that only small quantities could be issued.

The training was carried out under the direction of Southern Command but was given almost entirely by the Contingent's own officers, the War Office providing just seven instructors. The British Army was having problems finding experienced men for its newly raised 'Kitchener' battalions, and acquired a number of mainly surplus Canadian officers for its own purposes. Some of these would have been older and more experienced than many of their British counterparts who had served only in their school and university Officers' Training Corps .

The British Army laid great importance on rapid rifle fire, to the extent that it was said (perhaps by the British themselves) that early in the war the Germans mistook fire from its rifles for that from machine-guns. So groups of Canadian officers and senior NCOs took a course at the School of Musketry on Hayling Island on the South Coast.

There were rumours that the creation of trenches around tents (for drainage) and out on the Plain (for practice in digging them) were not allowed because they would interfere with hunting. Certainly the well-

Some very hardy Canadians have a bath in January.

Men of the Winnipeg Rifles at bayonet practice.

One feature of the Salisbury Plain were the cattle and here a soldier drives some away from camp. This subject was a curious choice for an official photograph!

Horses suffered terribly on the Plain. Soaked blankets gave them ringworm and 'rug pneumonia'.

established Tedworth* Hunt, with a strong military membership, used the Plain, and pre-war trenching was restricted to very small areas, but the Canadians did dig trenches, notably in the Bustard area. At this early stage in the war, those used for training had to be refilled and the turf replaced. Not to do this would have posed an increasing hazard as more and more were dug. Indeed Canadian units soon found they were digging new trenches on the sites of those created, and filled in, by their comrades. On 3 November three new 'digging areas' were announced, half-a-mile south of Pond Farm Camp, west of Bustard Camp and at Hare Warren (or Warren Hill) south east of Tidworth.

The 5th Battalion's war diary for 24 November includes a small sketch of a trench, 5 feet 9 inches deep, 2 feet wide across at the top and 3 at the bottom, which was filled with stones to promote drainage, with the excavated earth piled up to the rear. On 12 December the diary showed an enhanced structure with soil piled up front and rear and a recess for ammunition. This was dug out of the trench side and surely would have crumbled away in most conditions. Another feature of some the Canadians' trenches were turf roofs supported on logs as a form of concealment. In the next few months, these most basic of designs were to see much development into complex patterns of interlocking and support trenches, where men would spend several days and nights as part of their training. Extensive trench-practice systems were created close to many camps in Wiltshire and elsewhere and traces of them can still be seen, notably south east of Bulford Barracks on Beacon Hill, and below Warren Hill near Tidworth.

A pre-war War Office stipulation protected woodland on the Plain from troop movements, so at first the Canadians were not allowed to cut timber to make shelters for their horses. But photographs do exist of primitive timber shelters and one guesses that these were 'unofficial'. Cynics held that the order was to avoid disturbing game, though widespread cutting of timber would have destroyed many copses. But the fact that woodland, with its advantage of offering cover to troops on exercises, was out of bounds increased the artificiality of tactical exercises.

At West Down South and no doubt other camps, there was a lack of head-ropes, halters and picketing gear, so horses had to be tried to trees and vehicles by any odd piece of rope or strap. The complete absence of shelter and the frequent rain and bitter wind forced the animals to live in a sea of mud, causing gangrenous dermatitis. The few blankets were soaked and plastered with mud, leading to ringworm. Conditions eased with a partial removal to veterinary hospitals at Keeper's Farm (south of West Down South), where cow barns were used for shelter, and to the cavalry barracks at Netheravon. The Royal Society for the Prevention of Cruelty to Animals provided 250 waterproof rugs. It was not until 12 December that horses were permitted to be tethered between trees in plantations, though the 1st Artillery seems to have anticipated this by a day. On the 18th permission was given to use wattle hurdles to provide protection, but these were already very scarce and in demand for laying on the muddy roads.

There were further limitations on what troops might do when training. The War Office leased out much of its land to farmers on the understanding that it might still be used by the military. One outline for an exercise by the 1st Infantry Brigade stated:

> Troops are not to cross any land on which crops are growing, nor must they climb over wire fences. Any gates that are passed through must be left closed behind the troops. They must also avoid disturbing pens which enclose sheep and lambs.

On 8 January orders were issued that pigeons should not be trapped or shot because the Admiralty was using them to carry messages. (It was an offence punishable with a £50 fine or six months' imprisonment to kill, wound or molest a homing pigeon.) Another inconvenience were cattle that appear to have been prone to graze near the tents. A slightly incongruous official photograph shows a heavily kitted solider driving them away.

Private Albert Smith remembered one sham battle in an area that had been cleared of sheep to make way for the troops:

> When we arrived we were ordered to crawl, sprint, and jump down again. The trouble was that the hill was covered with sheep's manure. We were covered with the smelly stuff. As we diligently cleaned and scrubbed our uniforms that night we vowed we would never forget what we came to call, 'The Battle of Lamb Shit Hill'.

---

* 'Tedworth' was an early variation on 'Tidworth' and persists today in the name of the Hunt.

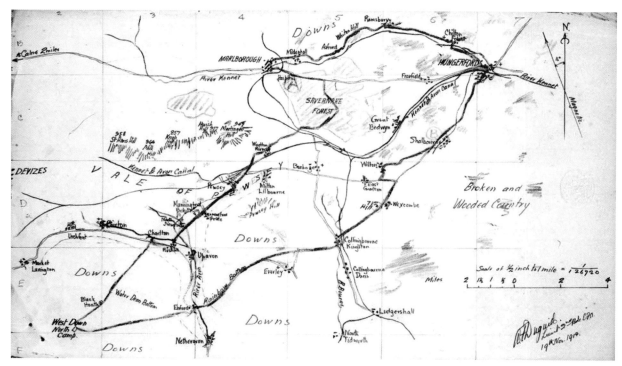

This map sketched by the 2nd Field Artillery Brigade includes the area north and east of the Plain.
It is signed by Lieutenant Archer Duguid, later to become official historian for Canada's forces in the Great War.

Canadian soldiers march across the Plain to be reviewed by General Pitcairn Campbell.

Manouvering increasingly large numbers of troops, especially in misty conditions, occasionally proved too much for the Canadian officers and directing staff. Another problem occurred when one side of the two 'opposing forces' in a battle exercise did not wear distinguishing badges, resulting in nearby troops who were not involved being 'attacked'.

Most of the training confined the men to the Plain itself. The 2nd Field Artillery Brigade appears to have explored further away from its base than most other units, reconnoitering Imber to the west as a possible bivouac site (which was used on 19 November), Savernake Forest to the north east and Yarnbury Castle (an ancient earthwork) to the south west. Patrols reached as far as Hungerford, 25 miles north east of West Down, in a survey of roads and possible billets.

On 27 November the Contingent was reviewed by General Pitcairn Campbell. For the only time on the Plain it was drawn up as an entity. (By the time of a Royal Review of 4 February it had formally become a division and had been reduced more to the size of one.)

Lieutenant Colonel Currie commented:

It was one of the most inspiring sights I have ever seen. There was plenty of room on the plains and after we had performed a number of evolutions we were formed in line miles long and marched some distance, then formed for an attack upon a ridge crowned by a number of tumuli. The earth trembled with the tread of the battalions and the hoofs of the battery horses. Thirty thousand Canadians in battle array is a sight never to be forgotten. Everything passed off well, considering the difficulties with which we had to contend.

Absent was Lieutenant Colonel James Bridges of No. 2 General Hospital, who had received permission to take 14 of his officers and nine batmen to France that day to gain experience working in the hospitals there. The party returned on 8 December.

In late November *The Times* visited the four Canadian camps and in its report of the 28th found it difficult to determine which was the muddiest. It noted that the

Most of the hut building was done by civilian labourers, some of whom were of limited diligence.

men were 'extraordinarily fit', the chief trouble being coughs called 'the Bustard whisper' or the 'Pond Farm particular'. Some men were inclined to overstay their leave, 'for which the character of the roads gives some shadow of excuse', the road to Salisbury being 'a river of mud'. When the Princess Pats' Captain Agar Adamson (who had enlisted at the age of 48 despite being blind in one eye and needing glasses to aid his vision in the other) wrote to his wife about visiting him on the Plain, he advised her that all cars there carried a chain for one of the rear wheels to provide traction.

Nor could the railways offer reliability. The branch line from Amesbury connecting with the main route linking London, Andover, and Salisbury was busy with military traffic at the expense of off-duty soldiers and civilians wishing to use it. British migrants within the Contingent anxious to visit their relatives in other parts of the country faced far from simple journeys, as did Canadian men wishing to visit localities with family links. Frank Betts found himself at Salisbury at 2.30am and had to walk 18 miles to his camp, with an hour's sleep in a haystack on the way.

On 14 August the British Army's Major R. H. O. Armstrong had submitted plans to the War Office for a standard hutted camp that could house one battalion of 1,000 men. The staple unit was a hut (sometimes referred to as an 'Armstrong'), 60 by 20 feet and with an average height of 10 feet, providing sleeping quarters for 24 men and an NCO. New camps began to be built in many parts of the country, with Lark Hill, close to Amesbury and the Canadians' camping-sites, being one of the first, as was Rollestone two miles to the west. There was a need for 3,500 workmen, chiefly carpenters, who came from all over the country. But by mid-November construction was behind schedule because of poor weather and a shortage of workers aggravated by recruitment to the services. There was also a lack of materials such as seasoned wood and galvanized sheets, nearly all the zinc trade being under German control. The mixture of unskilled labour and unseasoned wood led to poor quality work, and soon there was criticism of the attitude of the builders. There were reports of them welcoming the war as the best thing that had happened to them and sleeping when they should have been working. Their pay soared and, with Sunday work, a carpenter was receiving £3 a week and a labourer 35s, plus free accommodation and bedding. In contrast, recruitment posters were offering single men pay in the British Army of 7s a week, with 12s 6d separation allowance for married men with no children.

Sir John Jackson Ltd was the major contractor for building camps on the Plain but could not meet Kitchener's commitment to have all the Canadians in huts before the end of November, so the Contingent had to supply from its own ranks carpenters, bricklayers and unskilled labourers. By 2 January, after negotiations with the labour unions, some 894

The band of the 5th Royal Highlanders of Canada plays as their comrades work in the background.

The Engineers spent most of their time on the Plain building huts and roads.

Canadians were helping, receiving an extra quarter of a pound of meat and an extra 2s a day (paid by the contractor) but, with all parades and drills excused, losing valuable training time. Some of the labour came from the 1st Infantry Brigade under the command of Lieutenant Colonel C. J. Armstrong (who was not related to R. H. O. Armstrong) and from the Contingent's engineers who, of the entire force, lost the most training because they were so busy with construction work. At Rollestone Camp in mid-December, Lieutenant Colonel Edward Shannon was in charge of 810 carpenters, and if most of these were civilians rather than soldiers they would have constituted a demanding command.

The 16th Battalion had:

an eight hour day and [we] go off in batches on fatigue doing all sorts of work: loading junk for the building of hundreds of new huts, truck loads of beams, glass, planks, bricks – the last hell to handle. We have been digging trenches and laying pipes for water – a very mucky job.

Dual control by Jackson's staff and the military proved very discouraging, with small squads being set heavy tasks and large ones jobs that a fraction of their number could handle. There were frequent misunderstandings as to places and times of meetings, and time was wasted wandering from point to point. One group laying stable foundations comprised 12 men in two groups with three officers, two senior sergeants and six corporals.*

---

* In August 1916 Britain's Public Accounts Committee reported critically on the building of camps, particularly pointing to the firm owned by Sir John Jackson, which had won agreements (rather than formal contracts) on the basis of a 5 per cent commission on the actual cost. Sir John asked for a judicial inquiry and a Royal Commission was convened and sat in January 1917. The Commission's report exonerated his company from all imputations but added that the circumstances had enabled him practically to dictate his own terms. It noted that the amount he was entitled to under the agreement for the Salisbury Plain camps was greatly excessive and that the agreement was unreasonable. Sir John's reaction was to reduce his added-on profit claim to 4 per cent, surrendering £30,140.

A further visit by *The Times* produced an article printed on 12 December that was remarkably sanguine. Its reporter acknowledged that the horse lines at Pond Farm Camp were a sea of mud and that the headquarters tents there were:

> in a veritable lagoon of slime, across which no amount of road-making with planks and wattled hurdles and bundles of cut furze-bushes will enable one to reach the tent without getting into mud up to one's boot-laces. None the less there is something invigorating in the thrust and bluster of the wind (though it is rather hard on tents), and the health both of men and horses has been excellent.

This last remark is remarkable for being so positive as to appear disingenuous. True, at this stage there were few reports of serious illness among the soldiers, but they had more than their fair share of colds and other minor problems from the continual wet and damp. And, as we have seen, the horses were suffering terribly.

To add to everyone's woes, there were several gales and violent storms. On 11 November most marquees and all the divisional headquarters tents near the Bustard Inn collapsed, with files and records being scattered far and wide over the muddy fields and roads. Sheets of corrugated iron were blown about where the camps were being built and caused painful injuries. At West Down South two tents serving as orderly rooms were blown down, as was a Harrods mess marquee and a hospital tent, whose 16 patients had to be moved to a canteen hut. The hospital's acetylene gas plant which generated power for lamps was destroyed. Previously it had been found to be 'too delicate for active work', nor had it been possible to find carbide sufficiently fine for the lamps. On the 18th the hospital tent was re-erected, but blew down again within hours, the ground being too soft to hold the pegs,

A gale blew down a tent at West Down North in early December as the paymaster was handing out money to the 2nd Field Artillery Brigade's 5th Battery. The men chased after the notes, gathered them up and decided against returning them, the extent of the ensuing loss not being known. After the YMCA marquee there had fallen victim to the December gale, there was nowhere in which to conduct church services (held in the open air when the weather permitted) and men were given passes to attend those at Tilshead Church. A 'slight blizzard' or, according to the No. 2 General Hospital diary, a hurricane, was reported on 28 December when the 'orderly room' and three marquees suffered again at Bustard, with more

Engineers at work building huts in December 1914.

stationery and records being lost. Yet another gale on 16 January blew down tents serving as officers' and sergeants' messes, the orderly room and quartermaster's office.

Concern remained about the Canadians' efficiency. Lewis Harcourt, Britain's Colonial Secretary, wrote to Kitchener on 16 December to suggest the Canadians were:

> going back on training from that which they received at Valcartier. There they did regular shooting practice and went out for two or three days' manoeuvring under regular service conditions. On Salisbury Plain, they have none of this and, owing to the condition of the soil, they cannot even learn to trench.

The last observation is not borne out by references in unit diaries and memoirs. Harcourt told Kitchener that he 'could not believe that you will ever dare to use them as a single unity together at the Front' and suggested the Contingent be broken up and trained with the better portions of Britain's New Army, something that Hughes had already vehemently opposed.

On 10 November Harcourt had expressed concern about the Newfoundlanders' jealousy of the Canadians and their worries that they might lose their identity and urged that they be separated as soon as possible. On their arrival on Salisbury Plain they had been placed under the command of a Canadian officer, Lieutenant Colonel E. B. Clegg, who re-organized their structure. The men were issued standard British uniforms, including khaki puttees to replace their blue ones, though the term 'Blue Puttee' was unofficially retained as a title of honour for the first volunteers. At some point the idea was put forward that they should join with the 17th (Nova Scotia) Battalion, which was also under strength, a normal battalion comprising a thousand or so officers and men. As the 17th was not part of one of the four Canadian infantry brigades, this seemed a logical step to the War Office but the Newfoundlanders were strongly opposed, fearing that their unit would lose its name, identity and individuality.

Sergeant Owen Steele commented:

> we are very particular here not to be classed as Canadians, for apart from the fact that we are much prouder of our distinction as Newfoundlanders, the Canadians, generally, have been getting a bad name for themselves, wherever they have gone, and this applies particularly to London.

Steele had an uncomfortable fortnight when, having to go to the railhead at Bulford Barracks to collect stores, he borrowed 'knee rubbers' (knee-length boots) from Jim Stacey, giving him his conventional boots in exchange. Stacey then obtained a leave pass for four days but did not return for another ten, during which Steele had a week as orderly sergeant wearing the rubbers.

One verse of a poem, 'The First Newfoundland Regiment' by the Reverend J. V. Hammond of Ayr, reads:

> Five hundred strong they landed and at once
>   began to train.
> With gusto, and, as keen as knives, they drilled
>   on Salisbury Plain
> With swinging stride they marched and made
>   the earth resound again,
> Whilst more and more recruits sped o'er the
>   great Atlantic main.

Poetry was also the medium chosen by Major R. H. Tait when he described the experiences of the Newfoundland Regiment in *The Trail of the Caribou*:

> To Salisbury Plain – that mighty mead
> Of rolling downs and grassy leas
> (Where mud and muck reached to the knees
> Where myriad horse and men were camped
> And countless feet deep furrows tramped).
> The oozing mud and constant rain
> We well remember Salisbury Plain –
> And sagging canvas, dripping wet,
> And other like discomforts. Yet,
> Amidst it all, fond memory clings
> To pictures of more pleasant things.
>
> Here stricter training did begin,
> And sterner army discipline
> Became our lot. And every day
> A new experience came our way,
> Saw rawness from recruit escape,
> And seasoned trooper's form take shape,
> More deft become in art of war,
> Evolving an *esprit de corps*
> That ever gauged the loyalty
> Of that 'Blue Puttee' family.

In November Lieutenant Colonel Richard Burton, a former British Regular brought out of retirement, took over command of the Newfoundlanders. On the 20th they moved from Pond Farm to Bustard Camp, about a mile south east of a former farm-house that was coincidentally named Newfoundland and was used by the army for housing men and stores involved with the ranges.

Whether or not because of Harcourt's comments to Kitchener, the Newfoundlanders left for Fort George, Scotland, on 7 December. They were to be reinforced from home and formed into a complete battalion, continuing to grow in size and to perform magnificently at Suvla Bay, Beaumont Hamel, Cambrai and other significant battles. The action at Beaumont-Hamel was part of the opening day of the Battle of the Somme on 1 July 1916, with 22 officers and 758 other ranks of the First Newfoundland Regiment directly involved in the advance. Of these, all officers and some 658 other ranks became casualties.

Chapter Five
Christmas in Huts and Billets

On 9 November the 4th Infantry Brigade transferred from Pond Farm, the remotest of the camps as well as the one most exposed to the elements, to new hutments at Sling Plantation, a pre-war camping-site close to Bulford Barracks. A week later, Princess Patricia's Canadian Light Infantry moved to Morn Hill Camp, east of Winchester, to become part of the British 80th Infantry Brigade, eventually leaving for France on 20 December. From the start it had been regarded as one of the best, if not the best, of the Contingent's units, Kitchener reckoning that 90 per cent of its men would make non-commissioned officers. Left behind in hospital, temporarily unfit with influenza, was Sergeant Frank S. Brown, author of a number of vigorous and patriotic poems, one supporting Sam Hughes but none appearing to refer to his time on Salisbury Plain. He died on 13 February, his first day in the trenches.

The Divisional Cyclist Company moved from West Down South to Newfoundland Farm, 2½ miles west of Netheravon, on 2 December. Its activities included many rides through countryside that would have been attractive but for the frequent rain that not only soaked uniforms and equipment but made the roads glutinous. The company's longest ride was to Bath via Devizes and back on 11-12 December, a round trip of more than 60 miles. Two machines succumbed to the conditions, their riders returning to camp by train.

Canadians visiting London's Green Park in November would have seen displayed a number of simple huts designed by their compatriot, Francis Aylwin, formerly of the North-West Mounted Police. By the end of the month the Contingent's engineers were erecting these at Hamilton Camp, west of Lark Hill. They consisted of canvas stretched on wooden frames with mica windows and wooden floors, and each could house six men. It was claimed that they could be erected in under two and a half minutes and thousands had been ordered for Salisbury Plain and other military centres. Aylwin had made himself at home in such a hut in sub-

Cleaning up at Newfoundland Farm.

Above: On the left of this photograph, taken in the Lark Hill area in 1915, are primitive Aylwin huts, named after their Canadian designer.

Right: This panoramic map of the Tilshead and Shrewton locality was sketched by the 2nd Field Artillery Brigade.

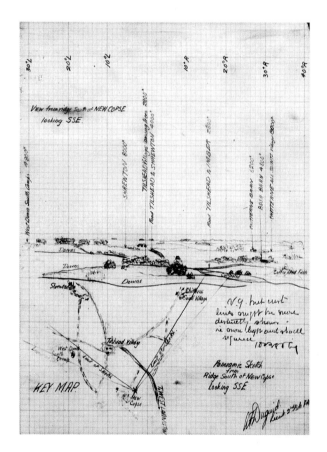

zero conditions in British Columbia, but claims that they provided weatherproof and comfortable accommodation proved unfounded. Photographs of Hamilton Camp taken in 1915 and 1916 show how primitive they were, and their occupants compared them to pig-sties and rabbit-hutches. When a window in one caught fire, the flames spread down the line of huts. The War Office was reluctant to pay Aylwin £40,000 in royalties for the huts and in February 1916 he was declared bankrupt with liabilities of £21,800. Shortly afterwards, the army decided they were not sufficiently weather-resistant and discontinued them, though some remained in use until the end of the war.

By 15 December, 11,000 men were in huts, with another 9,000 expected to move in that week. The number living in a hut increased greatly from the 25 first envisaged, and there are references to as many as 40 being accommodated in each building. On 11 November 66 men of the Reserve Park were compressed into one hut at Sling Plantation (soon to be known just as 'Sling').

The 15th Battalion occupied huts at Lark Hill at Christmas time, as workmen were busy applying finishing touches, 'or as busy as English workmen are accustomed to be,' noted the *Toronto Star* waspishly:

I see a man painting a door. He is very artistic, or very lazy, to judge by the interval between daubs. Three other workmen stand around him watching him, discussing Germany and the rain. It is as good as a comedy to watch the dilatoriness of the four.

Despite initial comments that the new huts were very comfortable and a thousand times better than tents, they were far from ideal, as *Canada in the Great World War* recounts:

> The huts were heated by one stove in the centre. They were invariably overcrowded, and it was a physical impossibility under the circumstances to keep the floors even passably clean. Long-handled brushes of intensely stiff bristles were used twice daily, and fatigue parties with pails and mops were continually on the defensive in an almost hopeless fight. On the boots and clothing of the men, through the doors and windows and through the cracks in the floors the mud intruded. Around the stove in the centre it dried into dust and climbing the walls filled every nook and cranny, and under the influence of the penetrating rain and rising steam formed mud on the walls. Each night the stoves were walled in with fifty or sixty pairs of army boots, piled up neatly, soles inward, drying out. In the morning each man would break off his own pair from the solid mass caked together with dried mud and put them on with sufficient care to preserve the inch-thick deposit without a crack, knowing it to form his best protection against any unnecessary amount of muddy water getting inside.

As the end of 1914 approached, conditions on the Plain continued to deteriorate and it became evident that not enough huts would be ready by Christmas, after which the weather of a worse British winter than usual might be expected to deteriorate further. Kitchener is said to have offered to put the Canadians into the barracks at Bulford and Tidworth, a gesture refused by their officers when they learned this would mean turning out British troops. In the meantime, thousands of men continued to endure the privations of life under canvas. When the War Office realized that the conditions were too unhealthy not only for the Canadians but for British troops, it instituted a massive programme of moving as many as possible into billets, including people's homes. In November there were rumours of a move to Exeter, whose citizens were reportedly saying that 'if the Canadians are sent here, we'll all leave the town', exaggerated press stories and rumours of poor behaviour having caused some apprehension.

In mid-December the 1st Field Artillery Brigade moved to New Copse Farm, 1½ miles north of Tilshead. Nine hundred other artillerymen and 750

horses were put up in buildings in Devizes. The men were addressed by their officers and 'were something more than appealed to so conduct themselves that no discredit should fall upon them or the force they represent'. Judging from later complimentary remarks in Devizes newspapers, these admonitions were heeded. On 17 January, Canon John Almond, a Divisional Artillery Headquarters chaplain based in the town, would note that 'although at first the men had not lived up to their reputation, all this had been altered now they were billeted in the towns and villages'.

A continuing priority were baths, with a number being provided at 20 Northgate Street, Devizes and 'private facilities' in hotels and private houses also being made available. On 7 January the first of a series of concerts for the Canadians billeted in Devizes was held at the town's Corn Exchange.

On the four days leading up to Christmas Day, at a time when 20 per cent of its strength was on leave, the 13th Battalion had to provide 350, 300, 250 and 140 men respectively to dig trenches for water supply. (At this time a Canadian battalion at full strength numbered some 1,150 officers and men.)

On Christmas Eve Canadian soldiers attended a midnight Eucharist in Amesbury Church. Frederick Scott in *The Great War As I Saw It* described how:

> the church windows threw a soft light into the mist that hung over the ancient burial ground. The church inside was bright and beautiful. The old arches and pillars and the little side chapels told of days gone by, when the worship of the holy nuns, who had their convent there, rose up to God day by day. The altar was vested in white and the candles shone out bright and fair. The organist had kindly consented to play the Christmas hymns, in which the men joined heartily. It was a service never to be forgotten, and as I told the men, in the short address I gave them, never before perhaps, in the history of that venerable fane [temple], had it witnessed a more striking assembly. From a distance of nearly seven thousand miles some of them had come, and this was to be our last Christmas before we entered the life and death struggle of the nations. Row after row of men knelt to receive the Bread of Life, and it was a rare privilege to administer it to them. The fog was heavier on our return and some of us had great difficulty in finding our lines.

All work and training was suspended on 25 December, with very little being scheduled for Boxing Day. Over the festive period all ranks were allowed up to six days' leave, with a free ticket to anywhere in the British Isles. But Charles Ogilvie arrived at Amesbury Station on 12 December to discover that he had to pay for his ticket to London, leaving him with very little money to spend in the capital. Many others headed for the delights of London, some stayed with relatives they had left behind when they emigrated to Canada. On 23 December 5,000 of the Contingent were expected in London, replacing 5,000 who had already relaxed there. The 5th Battalion released a fifth of its men at a time between 16 December and 6 January with the periods away overlapping. Other units adopted a similar practice. With its links with Scotland and with that country attaching so much importance to Hogmanay, the 13th Battalion opted for half its men to go on leave at Christmas, the other half over the New Year. Irishmen chose both Christmas and the New Year to visit home, and 'had their way', the implication being that they overstayed their leave without much in the way of punishment, though perhaps there was recognition of their longer journeys.

Many of the new huts were decorated with miniature flags, Christmas trees, holly and mistletoe, and some were facetiously named after famous London hotels. The YMCA distributed fruit and Christmas boxes as gifts of the Canadian War Contingent Association, an organization of Canadians in England and their friends that had been set up in mid-August. Another useful present was 1,000 bottles of cough mixture, recognizing the problems that were afflicting the soldiers.

The Canadian Field Comforts Commission at Amesbury Vicarage received warm clothing, tens of thousands of cigarettes, thousands of pounds of chocolate and many other gifts for distribution. The wife of the commander-in-chief of the British Expeditionary Force, Sir John French, sent a huge bale of warm socks and cholera belts.* The Duchess of Connaught gave every Canadian on Salisbury Plain a box of maple sugar, amounting to a weight of 12,000 pounds, though some accounts say that maple syrup was an alternative. Parcels of gifts continued to arrive throughout January, having been delayed because of blockages in shipping and railway transportation.

The 16th Battalion received 'Xmas cakes, socks, mince pies, sweaters, woollen caps, butter-scotch, mit[t]s, tobacco' and the welcome news from its colonel that it would be 'leaving for France at an early date'.

Those who spent Christmas in camp enjoyed a full festive dinner after which there were self-arranged amusements, though some units were lucky in being entertained by famous London concert and music-hall artists. On the evening of Christmas Day, the 3rd Battalion at Bustard had a bonfire and open-air concert, with the men enjoying a dinner financed by Toronto's city council, a gesture that was repeated on New Year's Day. The 9th Battalion at Sling arranged with a contractor to provide turkey and plum pudding. Another battalion was granted £5 for each of its companies and had oranges and Canadian apples distributed.

Herbert Andrews received a turkey, a box of oranges, a box of mixed fruit, candy, nuts and cigarettes from relatives in England. Having been away on leave over Christmas, for New Year, he arranged with the cook to heat up the turkey and a plum pudding and to make an apple pie. To this was added a bottle of 'Johnny Walker' whisky, available at 4s a bottle.

Troops at Devizes were feted at a reception, dinner and concert given in the town hall by the town's Civilian Training Corps, set up early in the war to teach the rudiments of drill to volunteers who were unfit for the armed services or who wished to make a token gesture without actually joining up. The *Salisbury Times* stated that there were 200 guests from Bustard and West Down Camps but there must also have been men who were billeted in Devizes and its more immediate locality. The menu offered a choice of roast and boiled beef, roast and boiled mutton, roast pork, plum pudding, mince pies, cheese, butter and dessert.

The *Wiltshire Gazette* co-ordinated invitations from Devizes householders for Canadians to spend Christmas Day with them. Initially 90 places were allocated to soldiers from West Down North, 90 to those at Bustard and 20 to Pond Farm men, but eventually firm plans were made for just 86. At noon

---

* There had long been debate about the efficacy of soldiers wearing belts around the stomach as a precaution against cholera, a water-borne disease preventable by purification of water supplies and vaccination. By 1914 the weight of medical opinion was against the practice, one disadvantage being that belts were difficult to keep clean when on active service and harboured vermin. Nevertheless in the winter of 1917 the British Army was to issue them in France to provide extra warmth.

The 8th Battalion, many of whose members came from the 90th Winnipeg Rifles, parade at Stonehenge.

on the 25th two motor lorries bought 60 men to the *Gazette's* offices in Devizes, with the non-arrival of others being unexplained.

The 4th Infantry Brigade was happily spending Christmas Day in camp when, its war diary recounts, it received a 'secret order ... to make ready to proceed to Bumble Green via Effing [*sic*] on receipt of telegraphic word'. The next day the Brigadier conferred with his officers 'regarding arrangements to carry out the secret communication received yesterday'. 'Effing' would appear to be a mis-spelling of Epping, near which Bumble's Green (the correct form) is situated, or it might describe the diarist's subconscious reaction to having his Christmas Day spoiled. But the 4th remained on Salisbury Plain. One suspects a prank, perhaps by someone enjoying Christmas Day just a bit too much and deciding to spoil the 4th's. After enduring awful weather under canvas it had just moved into new huts at Sling, and it would have made little sense to have moved it to Bumble's Green where, presumably, it would have been

back under canvas. Many men were away on leave and others were sick with meningitis, so any transfer at this time would have been chaotic. And 'Bumble Green' itself, though a real place, suggests a joke. The other brigades enjoyed an undisturbed Christmas.

Special permission for a religious service at Stonehenge over the Festive season was given to the '8th Winnipeg Rifles', as they were described in local newspapers reporting on the occasion. More accurately they were the 8th Battalion, most of whose members came from the 90th Winnipeg Rifles.

By Boxing Day 11,133 Canadians were still under canvas and concern grew for their health and that of their horses. At the end of December and early in January billets were requisitioned for as many as possible in nearby villages, mainly those to the north of the Plain and many in the sheltered Vale of Pewsey.

On 28 December Alderson's staff transferred from their tents at Bustard Camp to Elston House near

Canadian transport in trouble in floods at Elston in January.

Horses come to the aid of a stranded car.

Shrewton, where 7 inches of rain had already fallen that month. Alderson himself appears to have remained at the Bustard Hotel. Three days later a further 1¼ inches fell and another half inch the next, with the River Till breaking its banks, flooding the village and trapping the Divisional Supply Column motor lorries. The road by the River Avon north of Amesbury and leading to Lark Hill was blocked by water. Contemporary postcards show Canadian transport struggling through the floods and a soldier, clad only in shorts, diving in to the water at Shrewton.

The Royal Canadian Horse Artillery's billets were in Erlestoke, East Coulston, Tinhead and Edington, westward of West Lavington. In his memoirs Jack Seely claimed the credit for this, saying that one of the first things he did when taking over command of the newly formed cavalry brigade on 1 February was to get the Horse Artillery out of the mud: 'after a good deal of telegraphing, I obtained the necessary permission to move them into billets on the north of the Plain'. However the RCHA batteries had moved into their billets four weeks before Seely's appointment.

Billets for the 3rd Field Artillery Brigade were established at Chirton, Patney, Lydeway, Wedhampton, North Newnton, Rushall, Beech-ingstoke, and Woodborough, with brigade headquarters at Beechingstoke Manor House. John Sutton of the 9th Battery, 3rd Brigade was in billets at Wedhampton, between Urchfont and Chirton, at first above the village stores and then in a local farmhouse. One of his battery officers, Captain James Ross, was housed at Wedhampton Cottages. On 30 December a party of officers and a sergeant major had ridden from West Down North to Patney, stabled and fed the horses in the village and had a lunch of bread, cheese, jam and beer. Then they visited the proposed billets by car, accompanied by a police constable carrying a list of addresses. Early the next afternoon the 9th left camp with its guns piled high with kit, stoves and blankets and marched to Wedhampton, arriving at about 3pm. The horses were stabled in barns and the men in lofts but the villagers soon gladly gave them rooms, beds, baths and food.

The Royal Canadian Dragoons were in billets in Tilshead, Winterbourne Stoke, Berwick St James, Rollestone and Shrewton. The Heavy Battery was at 'Wharton' (presumably Chirton) and 'Marsden' (Marden). On 30 December the 2nd Field Artillery Brigade was ordered in to billets immediately in Market Lavington, Bratton, Easterton, Eastcott and Erlestoke, but when its adjutant tried to get more information from the local police sergeant he found that he was away on a murder enquiry; in the event, only the ammunition column was billeted in Urchfont that day. Finally the 2nd moved into billets on 2 January, though its 6th Battery moved again three days later from Easterton and Eastcott to Urchfont. Some officers established themselves in the Green Dragon Inn in Market Lavington.* Generally the local people seem to have welcomed the arrivals in their midst and part of Market Lavington came to be called 'Canada', with some woodland still known as Canada Woods being approached by a road called Canada Rise.

At Urchfont showers were erected at the Nag's Head so that the men could wash the mud off themselves. One field in the village became known as 'Little Canada' because it was used as a camp, artillery guns being kept in a field west of Cemetery Lane. The YMCA used the Infants' Room at the school without charge but was liable for any damage. Horses were tethered on the east side of the old coach road to Bustard, and 80 years later mushrooms were said to be still more common there than anywhere else on the Plain because of the droppings.

A detachment from No. 2 Field Ambulance appears to have been billeted in Wilton, near Salisbury, in early January, for there is a reference in its war diary for the 5th to 'C. Section at Wilton Town Hall'. (There is another Wilton 8 miles north of Tidworth, which some Canadians visited when making a topographical survey.) Perhaps there was a medical facility at the town hall, as at the end of the month Private Henry Morris was taken there after being knocked off his bicycle in Shrewton.

Canadian medical staff judged pit closets in several villages to be too close to wells providing drinking water, so Lieutenant Colonel James Bridges of No. 2 General Hospital obtained chloride of lime to sterilize the supply.

At the end of December the Signal Company moved from West Down South to billets in Enford, between

---

* The mis-spellings are from individual war diaries, which sometimes give locations that differ slightly from those in letters and printed histories. As with the 6th Battery, there were some movements from one village to other when initial arrangements were found to be unsatisfactory, perhaps because of overcrowding.

Perhaps this Shrewton scene shows 'Churchill' and the child he rescued from a village stream in January 1915.

Pewsey and Amesbury in the sheltered Avon Valley. It had spent several weeks laying communication wires between various points on the Plain, which must have been a thankless task given the muddy conditions. Its diary entries for 8 and 27 January note that the wire between Enford and headquarters at Bustard had been cut, presumably by accident rather than deliberately. As soon as the men had moved in to their billets they found that Enford's public houses had been put out of bounds, and then the rains began to fall more than ever, resulting in the River Avon rising 2 feet and flooding the road through the village.

The Army Service Corps was faced with fresh challenges in its struggle to supply the camps, its motor vehicles sinking up to their hubs in the flood water and its horses floundering helplessly as they struggled with wagons. Lance Sergeant Henry Jones of the Ammunition Park had a narrow escape when he went out on a motor-cycle to help retrieve a truck that had got lost in the floods. Descending in to Chitterne, 4 miles west of Shrewton, he rode his machine into a river that had burst its banks and found himself swimming (in greatcoat and rubber knee-boots) in 8 or 10 feet of water and then being washed about 100 feet downstream. He managed to catch hold of some barbed wire and scrambled out. His machine was 'full of water' and he had to walk 11 miles back to camp.

A popular man in Shrewton was the soldier, named in the press only as Churchill, who rescued a little girl who had fallen into a stream swollen by flood water. He was mobbed by grateful villagers, who took him to the nearest inn and got him roaring drunk. He was probably Arthur H. Churchill of the Royal Canadian Dragoons, who were billeted in the village.

Those units billeted north of the Plain escaped the serious flooding of those to the south. By 8 January the 2nd Field Artillery Brigade's diary reported that:

> already the advantages of being in billets are becoming apparent, the men are smarter & more soldierlike than a week ago, the horses are picking up, and mud has been removed from harness, horse-rugs & vehicles.

On New Year's Day 300 artillerymen moved into billets at Dauntsey Agricultural School, West Lavington, with the approval of its governors, though the headmaster had been visited the week before by officers and a policeman who had said that the buildings could be offered voluntarily or requisitioned. Promptly on the scene were two concerned officials from the Board of Education, which had an agreement with the War Office about the military use of school buildings. They objected to the move and the men had to leave on the 8th, much to the indignation of

The main road through Tilshead. Annotations on the back of this card state that the corporal leaning over the fence is being told by 'Squadron Sergeant Major Bull' to arrest all drunks after 8pm. SSM George Bull was a member of the Royal Canadian Dragoons, with seven years' service in Britain's Royal Horse Guards.

In January the main road north of Amesbury was badly flooded, making it difficult to transport men and materials.

Taking workers to Lark Hill Camp in the floods of January 1915.

On the back of this card of Lark Hill Camp the sender has written that 'the civies in the foreground are called vultures they prey upon the troops', a reference to tradesmen selling goods at inflated prices.

Dauntsey's governors and the local press, the *Wiltshire Advertiser* describing the action as 'high handed'. The *Wiltshire Gazette* thundered that 'those hide-bound, soulless automatons which "run" the Board of Education cannot be too ruthlessly excoriated for their conduct in this matter'. The local Member of Parliament, Basil Peto, raised the affair in the House of Commons on 8 February, when it was explained that the school had been occupied without the authority of the area's General Officer Commanding (Pitcairn Campbell), as required by the Army Council. The men duly moved to billets in Lavington, Potterne and Great and Little Cheverell.

From 7 January, 27 officers, 374 NCOs and men and 425 mounts of Lord Stratchcona's Horse were in billets in Pewsey, with a squadron at Upavon and 70 men of C Squadron at Fyfield House a mile to the east, with headquarters in Pewsey itself, at Bouverie Hall. The village welcomed the men and soon very few householders lacked military guests. At first little training was done, a priority being improving the condition of the horses after the rigours of Pond Farm Camp, but by mid-month there was some infantry drill, exercises in Savernake Forest and firing practice on the Bulford ranges.

Erected in the village centre a year before to commemorate George V's Coronation was the statue of Alfred the Great, who as the 9th century King of Wessex had once owned Pewsey. Very soon it had been dressed as a Strathcona trooper in greatcoat, cap, bandolier and puttees and equipped with spurs and rifle. The regiment's warrant officers and sergeants had their mess at the King's Arms Inn, and a room over the fire station was turned over for recreation. But three senior officers lost all their kit when the vicarage, where they were staying, burnt down on 4 February. Men of the Horse formed a double chain to the River Avon, passing buckets back to the house, and two of the unit's animals pulled the village fire engine to the scene.

Early in 1915 these men had billets in the pleasant hamlet of Fyfield, near Pewsey.

The 1st Infantry Brigade remained in tents at Bustard Camp throughout the winter. Oil stoves provided not only heat but a very heavy atmosphere inside a bell tent containing six, eight or more perspiring men in saturated and mud-plastered clothing and smoking pipes and cigarettes. Within minutes steam rose from the wet clothing and the air became stifling. Then the men would strip and try to rid their underclothing of vermin. Bizarrely the *Manchester Guardian* of 16 November had written that:

a merrier place you would not find than Bustard Camp .... After crossing so many bleak miles of downland, it is cheering to come upon the friendly fires glowing through the haze and the grey tents pressing together, as it were, for comfort.

The canvas accommodation and muddy surroundings would have been very far from comfortable, and the occupants must have envied their comrades inside wooden huts heated by stoves.

Chapter Six

A Question of Discipline

The First Canadian Division, as the Contingent was to become, is generally perceived as being less disciplined than those divisions that followed it, and there is no doubt that there were problems, which are frankly described in many accounts. There are few references in the war diaries of units (though details of individual cases are given in their daily orders), nor in British newspapers, both national or local, which perhaps were concerned at not taking the gloss off the enthusiasm and patriotism of the large volunteer army that had rushed to help the 'Old Country' in its hour of need.

One book, *Canada in the Great War*, multi-authored and published in 1918, put the indiscipline problem into perspective:

> The general conduct of the Canadians thronging these [Wiltshire] villages, if not exemplary, was, at least on the whole, good. Their habitual good nature and open-handed generosity towards the inhabitants were frequently deliberately imposed upon, and in such cases the men were carried beyond any personal intentions of wrong-doing. Cases of wilful damage and misdeeds committed by the more unruly members of certain units were summarily dealt with by the men themselves, the culprit being punished and forced to make restitution. The spirit of rivalry between the various units was keen, and any appeal to the men not to bring disgrace upon the particular unit of the Division of which they were members invariably met with a ready response.

> Slanderous stories of crime and misconduct were spread by unfriendly critics and enemy agents and gained remarkable credence, not only in England, where at that time the word 'Canadian' conjured up a picture of red Indians and cowboys, but at home in Canada where the subsequent contingents then in training were impressed with the necessity of living down the bad name gained by the First Contingent in England. Any city which was of such size as to number among its inhabitants thirty thousand, fit, adventurous, and active men and in which there was no record of crime or drunkenness, would indeed be Utopian. Such a condition is by no means claimed, but drunkenness and lawlessness were the exception and not the rule.

The reference to frequent impositions on the soldiers' good nature is significant. No doubt some Wiltshire folk felt it was the other way around when they had the peace of their villages disrupted by lively young men who were becoming increasingly frustrated by terrible weather and perceived delays in going on active service. Their relative affluence caused resentment and local men would have objected to the rivalry for the affections of girls. But at the same time traders flocked to the camps to sell goods at inflated prices and there was more than a touch of such exploitation among local shopkeepers. Major Frederick Scott, a chaplain with the 14th Battalion (whose poetry celebrates nature, imperialism and the young Canadian soldier at the Front), summed it up well:

> the publicans did their best to make what they could out of the well-paid Canadian troops .... The English people did not understand us, and many of our men certainly gave them good reason to be doubtful.

However Harold Peat of the 9th Battalion noted:

> Personally, I think the English people made too big a fuss over us. The receptions we got at every turn of the way were stupendous; and I am certain a majority of the men had more money than was really good for them. As one young Canadian boy said afterwards: 'Why, they treat us as if they were little tin gods' .... I cannot speak too highly of the treatment handed out to us by the Britishers.

On the matter of indiscipline, George Nasmith observed:

> It was a curious fact that it was the Englishman who had gone out to Canada a few years before and now returned as a Canadian, who was the chief offender in this respect. He had gained a new airiness and sense of freedom which he was proud of, and it brought him into trouble. At one stage it looked as if the force was undergoing a process of decomposition, and would disintegrate. The morale of the men under the very depressing conditions which existed, had almost gone and they did not care what happened them. Privates, perhaps college men or wealthy business men in Canada, frankly said when arrested, that they were quite willing to pay the price, but that they had determined to get warm and dry once more before they were drowned in the mud. It is an easy matter to handle a few cases of this sort, but when you get hundreds of them little can be done, and threats, fines and punishments were of little avail in correcting the existing state of affairs. As a matter of fact, under the conditions the military authorities were hard put to it to control the situation. Each night the motor lorries returned loaded with men under arrest, and each day an equally large number left the camp to undergo the same experience.

There are other references to 'English' members of the Contingent being the prime offenders. As soon as the first Canadians arrived, an immediate problem for the nearby villages was drunkenness, and *The Times* assured its readers that the culprits were mainly men born in the British Isles who had been in Canada for only a few years. The *Toronto Star* of 19 January 1915 stated that the Contingent was composed of 65 per cent 'English born' who had committed 79 per cent of the crimes. One may suspect that the *Star* was committing the ever-common error of describing anyone from the British Isles as English and one may wonder at how it arrived at its statistics.

Some newspaper reports did characterize many of the Contingent as cowboys, rough riders and even 'Red Indians'. But an article in *The Times* of 28 November portrayed the force as being mostly lawyers, farmers, bankers, university undergraduates and business men, accustomed to independence and so having difficulty in understanding that leave to a certain hour is leave to that hour only. 'Practically every gunner and a number of drivers' in the 2nd Artillery Brigade's 5th

Battery were said to have been earning from $1,200 to $3,500 a year before enlisting. George Gibson acknowledged that there were many men with plenty of money but who were unused to discipline. It was unfortunate that a report copied in the *Wiltshire Advertiser* in late October from the *Daily Chronicle* commented on the relative wealth of the Canadians, noting that the $1.25 or 4s 7d daily pay of a private contrasted with the quarter of that amount paid to a British soldier. With little opportunity to spend money at Valcartier and on the transatlantic voyage, some Canadians had accumulated two months' pay. On the first pay-day in Britain some are said to have been paid in gold (sovereign coins, presumably). Nor can matters have been helped when the *Salisbury Times* noted that 'some [Canadians] are reported to have "come over" with hundreds, and some with thousands, of dollars in their inner treasuries'. The Canadians hobnobbed with their British counterparts and treated them to drinks, but the flaunting of newly exchanged pound notes sometimes provoked bloody fights.

An initial problem was changing Canadian dollars into pounds sterling. The YMCA provided a money-exchanging service, one of its offices handling $3,685 in one day and offering to bank the pounds for the Canadians. The *Toronto Star* of 19 October reported that canteens (presumably those in the camps) were accepting dollar bills 'at a sacrifice of four cents'. Village shopkeepers offered 3s for each dollar. The exchange rate was then just over 4s for a dollar, the Canadians' own pay offices converting Canadian dollars to British pounds at the rate of five for one. Soon after the arrival on the Plain, the London branch of the Bank of Montreal sent three officials under armed escort to the camps who exchanged $125,000 over three days.

H. M. Urquhart, the historian of the 16th Battalion, noted that, 'worse, much worse, than either weather conditions, sickness or navvying, to any officer or man was the brand of indiscipline which was placed on the 1st Canadian Division'. He admits that some cases merited the sternest punishment, but most were 'little more than harmless boisterous pranks.' For example, the British provost marshal in London complained that a piper, a company sergeant-major and a private had paraded around the tables of a fashionable West End restaurant and that another private had refused to board a Salisbury train at the capital's Waterloo Station because 'the engine driver did not have a kind face'.

One joke that went the rounds reflecting the

Canadians' relaxed attitude was appreciated by the men themselves:

Sentry: 'Halt! Who goes there?'
Answer: 'First Grenadiers.'
Sentry: 'Pass, First Grenadiers; all's well.'
Sentry: 'Halt! Who goes there?'
Answer: 'What the Hell is that to you?'
Sentry: 'Pass Canadians; all's well.'

Another 'sentry tale', probably apocryphal, was told in the New Zealand magazine *Truth*, of the Irish-Canadian sentry who challenged a tall figure who had jumped out of a car:

Sentry: 'Who are you?'
Answer: 'A friend.'
Sentry: 'Your business?'
Answer: 'Commander-in-Chief, inspecting.'

Kitchener – for the tale says it was he – accepted a cigarette from the astonished sentry, and chatted with him about conditions in the camps.

George Gibson recounted:

On leave one was perpetually having it said, what a fine body of men the Canadians were, but what a pity it was that they had such poor discipline. I think that the very people who said this frequently had very little understanding of the persons they were criticizing. In the ranks of the first division were many men who not only had plenty of money at their command, but who had never in their lives been subjected to any form of discipline or restraint. The Canadian on leave, whether he was a full-private or a General, patronized the finest hotels and dined at the best restaurants. To our rank and file, it was incomprehensible that because he might be dressed as a private he should be excluded from various pleasures which he was in the habit of enjoying at home. In consequence of this our other ranks were much more in evidence than those of other units, and accordingly came in more for criticism.

Well before the Canadians' arrival, the authorities had stipulated that inns in the Salisbury Plain area should close by 9pm because of 'the large number of undisciplined recruits ... at the various camps'. But the problem continued and in the case of the Canadians was at first exacerbated by the fact that their camp canteens were 'dry', that is, they did not serve alcohol.

The one exception was Princess Patricia's Canadian Light Infantry, which had been physically separate from the Contingent during training in Canada and still was not officially part of it, being merely 'attached'. It had had a wet canteen at its camp at Lévis and now had one at Bustard Camp, though it is not known if it admitted men from other units.

Stanley Brittan of the 13th Battalion recorded in his diary that on his first day in camp, 16 October, he went 'down to the village [probably Tilshead, nearest to his camp at West Down South] ... and got terribly drunk'. On the 17th, he 'went to the village again in the evening, but strong guard there'. On the 19th, he optimistically tried the Bustard Hotel, the headquarters of General Alderson himself, but found a guard of about 20 soldiers around it. By then Alderson had received 'serious complaints from local authorities'. He telegraphed Southern Command to stress that 'it is absolutely necessary that there should be canteens for sale of beer in camps', pointing out that men were going to the neighbouring villages, getting 'bad liquor' and becoming quarrelsome. On the 21st, he announced that 'wet' canteens would be allowed. On the 29th there was 'considerable disorder' in the one at West Down North, despite the beer on sale being relatively weak.

Having debated the matter, the Canadian Government acknowledged on 14 November that there had been excesses and disorders among a few men in neighbouring towns and villages where the opportunity to purchase liquor presented itself.

The wet canteens were opened at midday, accounts differing whether it was for one or two hours, and for three hours in the evening. Only beer was sold and non-commissioned officers were always on duty to supervise. The queues outside were discouraging to those ardent advocates of teetotalism, the YMCA officials, though their own recreational and refreshment facilities in the camps continued to be popular. Alderson continued to receive numerous reports of considerable numbers of men on leave (and thus away from the restrictions of the Plain) being drunk and disorderly in London and other towns, but late in November he was able to reassure Sam Hughes that the 'trouble in neighbouring villages has practically ceased since opening of canteens in camp'.

George Gibson enjoyed the beer:

We had our regimental canteens, and they were a great success. In the mud and misery that we were to suffer in the days following, the canteens played a loyal part, and were responsible for very little crime. In any case the beer was good, and when, for the first time, we buried our noses in the dark brown foaming depths of a yard-long tankard, we felt that the British nation was worth fighting for, if it was founded on such good material.

Nevertheless there was some continuing concern about drunkenness among soldiers of all nationalities and among camp-construction workers. The problem was exacerbated by civilians treating soldiers to drinks, but in the Salisbury area it was almost entirely the construction workers who appeared in court, rather than soldiers who were dealt with by their own officers. The Salisbury newspapers contain many reports of men 'employed on the Plain' (as workers on the new army camps) being fined two or three pounds. A rare example of local reportage of drunken soldiers being penalized by the civil authorities was when the *Salisbury Times* recorded that two troopers had been convicted in London and been given small fines. However the authorities in Devizes took a sterner line about disorder by soldiers, and on 13 November Thomas Sharples of the Divisional Ammunition Park at West Down South was frogmarched to Devizes police station after behaving in a drunken and disorderly fashion in the Market Place. He was fined 5s with 4s costs. Superintendent W. T. Brooks urged the newspaper representatives in court to note (in their coverage of the case) that under the Defence of the Realm Act any person selling or giving intoxicating liquor to a soldier on duty in any protected area (such as Wiltshire, with its concentration of camps) was liable to prosecution and to be sentenced to penal servitude for life.*

Following the introduction of restricted opening hours to public houses in Salisbury Plain villages, limitations were brought in elsewhere, including Devizes where pubs had to be closed at 9pm from 26 October and at 8pm as soon as the necessary authority was obtained from the Secretary of State, a move that led to much debate in newspaper correspondence columns. On 12 November all premises licensed to sell intoxicating liquor in the Southern Command area were put out of bounds to all soldiers between 6am and 12 noon, though this was not noted in the 15th Battalion's diary until 19 January. There was also a ban on bottles of liquor being removed from such premises at all times.

On 24 November Henry Staines of the 6th Battalion was found drunk and disorderly at the Railway Hotel, West Lavington, having been bought whisky, but the magistrates took 'no further notice of it', after assurances that the 'prisoner would be proceeded against as a military absentee'. The local courts usually left the discipline of soldiers for civilian misdemeanours to their officers. But the problem continued: in mid-December, three transport wagons left Devizes containing soldiers 'all more or less under the influence of drink'. Perhaps it was these sorts of disturbance that led to the lecture to the 3rd Battalion by Colonel Fawkes of the Royal Army Temperance Union on 14 November.

Lieutenant Colonel Currie of the 15th Battalion reckoned that 80 per cent of the men (whether under his command or in the Contingent as a whole is not clear) were total abstainers. About 10 per cent, chiefly the older men, took an occasional drink, and not more than about three per cent drank to any extent. During its time on the Plain, the Contingent consumed $100,000 of light beer (two per cent strength) from the canteens, with 7½ per cent of the profits being rebated to the men.

Drunken soldiers were hauled back to camp by their comrades taking their turn as pickets, that is, troops acting as guards in towns and villages and outside camps and who perhaps would themselves be over-indulging a day or two later. The penalties included a short confinement to a guard tent, a day's loss of pay, or five or seven days 'confined to barracks' with the appropriate loss of money. Another punishment was clearing mud off the roads.

Shortly after arriving on the Plain to take command of the Cavalry Brigade, Jack Seely came across a Private Shand (perhaps George Shand of Lord Strathcona's Horse) enduring Field Punishment Number One, which entailed being strapped to a wagon wheel. It was a humiliating and controversial

---

* Though in late 1914 Wiltshire was swarming with British and Canadian soldiery, the number of cases involving them that were brought before the courts were remarkably few and any sentences lenient. Researching the establishment in early 1915 of the Canadian Hospital at Taplow in Buckinghamshire, the author consulted copies of the local newspaper, the *Maidenhead Advertiser*. Relatively few British soldiers were based in the locality but featured in a significant number of court hearings, one man being sentenced to a month's imprisonment for stealing a kiss from a girl. But then Maidenhead was a staid town popular with well-to-do Londoners, whereas the Salisbury Plain area had had 15 years to get used to high-spirited soldiery.

penalty and Seely tried it for himself, and then ordered pack drill in full marching order be substituted as punishment. He arrived on the Plain at the end of January and perhaps there had been an outbreak of indiscipline at that time, because the diary of No. 1 Field Ambulance for 1 February cryptically notes that it 'had to adopt severe measures of punishment' at Bustard Camp, which was Seely's initial destination.

Even with the help of the pickets, the local constabulary must have been hard pressed to police the towns and villages. They would have been aided by military police who, of whatever army, were less tolerant than their civilian counterparts and not popular. The Canadians took revenge on them on stormy nights as they patrolled on chalk walks above the mud by creeping up behind them and delivering blows that would topple them into the mire.

Mabel, the wife of Captain Agar Adamson of the Princess Pats, reported that Salisbury looked as if it were in the hands of the Germans:

> A picket goes around every night dragging drunken Canadians out of pubs. The night I was there [8 November], there were 100 arrests, including 22 officers. The fault is with the officers. They have no control over the men, in fact are just as bad. Managers of London theatres have written to the authorities, demanding to know what they are to do with drunken officers; civilians they know what to do with and also the Tommies, but drunken officers they have no precedent for.

In November the General Officer Commanding, Pitcairn Campbell, received a deputation from Salisbury's licensed victuallers to discuss the problem. Somewhat obliquely, he recommended 'the expulsion [presumably from public houses by their landlords] of dissolute women, of whom it is believed a large number are at present in Salisbury'.

Though local newspapers featured few cases of excessive drinking, they did report on other misdemeanours. One soldier in trouble very soon after arrival was Albert Blanchet of the 14th Battalion who was charged with stealing a ring worth 7s 6d on 17 October. He had gone into Messrs Sewell Bros, the pawnbrokers in Milford Street, Salisbury, and tried to walk out with the ring on his finger. A French-Canadian with imperfect English, he had been suspected of stealing $17 from his comrades on board ship. The court dismissed the case against him,

reasoning that he could soon be going abroad to fight for his country, a policy often adopted by the local courts in cases involving Canadians.

On 26 October Sergeant George Hancock and Private Charles Wood of the 1st Battalion appeared before the Warminster magistrates charged with stealing a bottle of gin and a box of cigars valued at 12s 6d from the Angel Inn, Heytesbury, 11 miles west of their camp at Bustard. Wood was found in a garden with his coat on fire and Hancock, 'staggering drunk', darted at a policeman with a pocket-knife. In court he agreed that he had been drunk at 9.30am and the night before. Both men promised to be of good behaviour and were bound over in the sum of £5, the chairman of the magistrates telling them that 'we put it to you as men of honour to play the game', that is, to be fair and honest.

Some officers commanding pickets bought beer for their men when they were on duty with the task of ensuring good behaviour in towns and villages. Another problem was the purchase of liquor from illegal sources, and several British camp workers found themselves in court for supplying drink to soldiers. There was the slightly curious case in early November when Captain Edwin Fisher, adjutant of the 6th Battalion, instructed Private Levi La Rose to buy some whisky. The private acquired it from James Moore, employed at West Down, who had no licence to sell liquor. Fisher told the subsequent court hearing that 'we have had a great deal of trouble through men getting spirits at places other than the bar, and there has been a lot of trouble in the camp'. Moore was fined £3 with costs. What was not clear from the reported evidence was from what source Fisher expected La Rose to obtain the whisky. Lieutenant Colonel Currie of the 15th Battalion ordered his officers not to buy drinks for their men as it was subservient to discipline, except at the regimental canteens when off duty. Such treating reflected the relaxed relationships between men and officers. Harold Peat admitted:

> as far as discipline was concerned, we did not even know it by name. The military authorities could not understand how it was that a major or a captain and a private could go on leave together, eat together and in general chum around together.

English people found such camaraderie unusual. The manager of a Salisbury hotel requested a Canadian private, who had sacrificed a good position to join the army, not to use the reading and smoking rooms when officers were occupying them.

Another problem was that of taking extended leave without permission. The commanding officer of one battalion is said to have called the roll of his battalion and found that 450 men, almost half his strength, were absent without leave; one suspects exaggeration. There was certainly a problem in the first weeks on the Plain, and again it seems to have been those of British origin who were most to blame. Uncertain how long they would be in England, they were anxious to see the families they had left behind. Returning from London on 11 November Charles Ogilvie was asked for his pass at Salisbury Station and was found to be 12 hours late. He was one of 132 late returners who were taken to Bustard Camp and detained overnight without blankets and food in a freezing marquee. The next day his captain 'confined him to barracks' (actually the tented camp) for 48 hours.

Lieutenant Colonel Currie in his history of the 48th Highlanders gives one example of the relaxed attitude to over-staying leave in his account of a man brought before him in the orderly room, the charges being:

That on December 10th, at 2 p.m., Private John B —— of the 48th Highlanders was found loitering in the Park at Bournemouth [a seaside resort 30 miles from the Plain] without a pass. That he became violently abusive on being taken into custody. Witnesses, Police constables J —— and D —— of Bournemouth. Then followed the evidence of the constables taken down in the presence of an officer at Bournemouth, to the effect 'That on Dec. 10th, at 2 p.m., I, Police Constable J ——, together with Constable D ——, was patrolling the Park at Bournemouth when I saw Private B —— of the 15th Battalion sitting on a park seat with two young ladies. As was customary in such cases I asked him if he had a pass. He produced a pass signed by the Commanding Officer of the 15th Battalion, which had expired the day before. When we pointed out that Private B —— was absent without leave, he said he expected an extension by wire that day, from his Commanding Officer. When we told him that it was our duty to take him into custody, he became very abusive, calling us Thick-headed John Bulls, Fat-headed Englishmen, Mutton heads, Blasted Britishers, etc. He had also abused the English people in very violent terms.' The constables had taken charge of him and handed him over to the customary escort sent after him from camp.

Canadian Highlanders Line Up on Salisbury Plain

A fine body of men from the 15th Battalion, but at the second Battle of Ypres 664 members were killed, wounded or captured, two-thirds of its strength.

Private B —— admitted that the charge was true and had nothing to say. He had left England three years ago, and Currie asked him: 'Do you think that three years residence in Canada entitles you to abuse your countrymen, and call them fat-headed Englishmen?' B replied: 'I don't know, Sir.' He forfeited his pay during his absence and was admonished not to use abusive language to his countrymen again.

George Nasmith wrote:

> A fairly large number of the men were given leave, and an equally large number took French leave. The latter migrated in large numbers to the little villages around the outskirts of the plain where they settled down to a few days' comfort before they were rounded up by the military police.
>
> Some went to London, and, worshipping at the shrines of Venus and Bacchus, forgot about the war, and tarried in the fascinating metropolis. Others sought a few hours' respite and forgetfulness in the town of Salisbury, where they hobnobbed with their British *confrères* and treated them to various drinks. At times the British Tommy, stung at the flaunting of pound notes where he had only shillings, smote his colonial brother, and bloody battles resulted in consequence thereof.

But it was generally felt that when the time came for action every man would be at his post and would do his bit. As the weeks on the Plain went by, there was less casual absenteeism but a few cases of actual desertion. But on 13 December two privates, John Ogilvie and William James of the 10th Battalion, were found to be illegally absent without leave and were struck off the strength, as were five more men on the 17th. There were just five absentees when the 5th Battalion marched away from Lark Hill Camp to active service on 9 February.

The Divisional Cyclist Company appears to have been more conscious of discipline than many other units. Its diary is one of the very few in the first week or two on the Plain to name those who were absent, including a sergeant. On 10 November it noted that a roll-call was now to be held every night and a list of absentees forwarded to Divisional Headquarters, a requirement presumably imposed on other units. When in December 'all good conduct men' were issued with weekend passes from noon Saturday to noon Sunday, they were 'required to satisfy the Orderly Sergt. that

they could make all train connections to enable them to return within the appointed time'. When the company spent the night in Bath on 11 December, its commanding officer obtained a certificate from the city's chief inspector of police describing the men's conduct as 'exemplary'.

One Saturday when rioters took over Market Lavington, a hundred men sent to deal with the situation were believed to have joined the rioters, so a squadron from Lord Strathcona's Horse was dispatched with tent-pegs (sharp steel-pointed pieces of wood with small rope handles). Two or three men were posted at each of the four roads leading into the village, where some Canadians were trying to free their comrades from the civilian police station. A troop leader with the Horse, Captain Arthur Critchley (later a brigadier general) and two others, all 6 feet tall, entered one pub and ordered the men out. One demurred and was picked up by the seat of his trousers and thrown out; the others followed. 'They were quite a decent bunch of fellows, really, but simply fed up to the teeth with conditions on the Plain,' noted Critchley.

One report in the *Winnipeg Telegram* 'on the 'Battle of Amesbury' found its way back to Wiltshire. It alleged that 30 Canadians had 'trimmed' 120 British Territorials in a fight that had caused townsfolk to lock themselves in their houses and led the 'Mayor of Amesbury' (a dignitary unknown to the townsfolk) to appeal to the military authorities in Salisbury for help.

Rumours of indiscipline even found their way to Australia, where on 6 January 1915, the Melbourne *Argus* reported that 'there has been trouble with some of the Canadians, and one or two thousand have been hurriedly sent off to the Continent', perhaps a grave distortion of the news that the exemplary Princess Pats, having been deemed suitable for battle, had been sent to France.

In his memoirs Critchley told how Canadian officers were summoned to headquarters (presumably at the Bustard Inn) to be given a good talking to by a British colonel. On 20 November Alderson addressed all officers in the Contingent, emphasising the need for their proper behaviour. Lieutenant Colonel Currie described it as 'a very instructive heart-to-heart lecture which all officers appreciated'. A *Toronto Star* correspondent voiced his own criticism of officers in an article of 27 November which quoted Imperial (that is, British) officers' unfavourable opinions of their Canadian counterparts. The writer believed that only one in ten of those holding commissions in the pre-war Militia took any intense interest in their work, but liked the social distinction that came with rank. He stated that on the outbreak of the war they had flocked to Valcartier with enthusiasm but believing that their status gave them less to do than the men they led. 'The chief thing that must be drilled into the officers … is that they are the custodians of the lives of their men,' he stressed, concluding that there had been 'some straight talks' and less desire to get leave to visit London.

It is worth stressing that there appear to have been no cases of organized disorder within the camps, no angry protests about the conditions and no 'spokesmen' appointed to present formally a list of complaints. In contrast at Codford 11 miles, south west of Lark Hill, British 'Kitchener' battalions were more strident in expressing their disquiet. The camps in the neighbourhood were more sheltered than the Canadians' and closer to villages and railway stations, but men who days before had been civilians (and were often still clothed as such, uniforms sometimes not being issued for some weeks) arrived to find few arrangements for them. There are references to one battalion having to be marched away because it had come close to mutiny. In fact this was the 10th Welsh Regiment, which did leave Codford after a short stay and before the weather deteriorated, but only because it was to form part of a division comprising only Welsh battalions. But the 10th Devonshire Regiment's B Company, who were nearly all Welsh miners who had been working in Devon at the start of the war, did riot and were subdued by a dressing-down from their colonel.

As well as stoppage of pay and other punishments imposed by officers, there are suggestions that some Canadian delinquents were punished by their comrades. The *Toronto Star* of 12 November referred to a rosewood slat removed from a cabin on SS *Tunisian* (one of the vessels that conveyed the Contingent across the Atlantic) being used to punish those who were lax in their duties. Admittedly the context is that of carelessness in executing field manoeuvres, but no doubt men seen as letting down their unit would also have been dealt with unofficially.

The *Salisbury Times* in its issue of 11 December reported that 'drafts of undesirables have been promptly returned to Canada, and the Force now is well behaved, sober and immensely earnest in its work'. Even with the festive season imminent, this optimism seems to have been mainly justified, as senior officers imposed discipline through the hierarchy of ranks and

as military training had its effect. Christmas passed off quietly in the Devizes area with no cases for the Divisional Sessions to hear on 6 January, the chairman finding this 'highly creditable'. Nevertheless Louis Keene described returning to Salisbury Plain after Christmas with 36 men who had formed an escort for 56 undesirables being sent back to Canada. 'It seems strange when men are needed so badly to ship them back because they are a bit unruly or get drunk too often,' he commented. 'Six of them made a dash for it at Liverpool. Three of them got away altogether.'

There remained the occasional crimes that merited court appearances, including the curious one heard on 14 November against Private Philip Dimmock of the 8th Battalion. At 2pm on the 4th, pickets on duty in Tilshead had heard screams 80 or 100 yards from the road behind the Black Horse Inn. There they had found the defendant under the influence of drink and struggling with a married woman, Eva Annie Evans, who was on the ground with a bloody face and disarranged clothes. She had been staying in Birmingham and had arrived at Lavington Station at 4am that morning, reaching Tilshead at 6. Mrs Evans was married to a sergeant in Dimmock's unit and was not present at the first court hearing. Six days later she did appear, only to allege a different assault to that mentioned in the warrant, one that she said occurred between 9 and 10 that morning in the village street when Dimmock had hit her between the eyes without saying anything. A Highland soldier had come to her help. One of the pickets, Private Leslie Campbell, gave evidence about the afternoon attack, but the Clerk to the Court pointed out that there was no corroboration of the first assault and Mrs Evans had not complained of the second, so the case was dismissed.

The same day as the hearing against Dimmock, the 14th, an unfortunate incident took place in Market Lavington, where William Herbert Hopkins and his wife had opened their home, known as the Lighthouse, to provide refreshments for the Canadians. On the day in question, some of their guests had asked for intoxicants. Notices had been displayed saying that these would not be supplied and none allowed on the premises, but these had been torn down. Serving supper to Neil Mackay of the 17th Battalion, Mrs Hopkins asked for a shilling. 'That's all you want,' retorted Mackay. 'It is money that you after.' He threw a half-crown (2s 6d) at Mr Hopkins, knocking a tooth out and rendering him unconscious. None of the other nine Canadians in the room intervened. At the court hearing, two officers expressed the hope that the court would make an example of Mackay as he was 'a bad character'. He was fined £3 with 9s costs, or one month in prison if he defaulted.

On 24 November the 3rd Field Artillery Brigade sent a wagon 'with some detention prisoners' to Devizes, probably to the recently opened military detention centre at the civilian prison in the town. They included Driver Luxton of the 7th Battery who had been court-martialled for some unspecified reason, perhaps to do with the loss of horses.

William Maher of the Divisional Cyclist Company and James Bushnell of the 2nd Field Artillery Brigade, were in court in late November charged with obtaining money by false pretences in the Melksham area of west Wiltshire. They had approached various local people asking for money so that they could get back to camp, receiving various sums of 5s, 2s 6d and £1. The charges were reduced to vagrancy. A Canadian officer told the court that he did not know Maher but could not give Bushnell too good a character, there being a couple of military charges against him. The pair were remanded in custody to await an escort back to camp.

In December Lawrence Carroll and Warren Foley were charged with stealing overcoats from the home of Marcus Bennett, the Bulford Camp photographer and postcard publisher. He had been entertaining several soldiers to dinner and the following morning noticed that his coat, worth £1 1s, was missing, as was a coat and muffler worth 35s belonging to his assistant, Gustave Baker. Carroll, a member of the Fort Garry Horse, explained that it was impossible for soldiers to get drunk in a hotel after 6pm, so he had borrowed the coat to hide his uniform. Both men were fined 30s.

Also in December, Gunner Allan McGregor, who had been in charge of his Battery's pay, had gone missing at the same time that $1,000 of its funds were unaccounted for. He appears to have spent some of the money on high living in London and Paris before crossing to New York, where he was eventually arrested and extradited to Canada. In August 1915, the Canadian Army asked him to be sent to France, where he was court-martialled and sentenced to five years' hard labour.

Another case of the Contingent showing little sympathy for its miscreants was when William Gibbs of Lord Strathcona's Horse was charged with being drunk and disorderly at Urchfont on 7 December. Sergeant Major G. S. Collins had been looking for him after he had gone absent without leave from No. 1

General Hospital and had enlisted the help of a local policeman, whom Gibbs then assaulted. Collins told the court that Gibbs (originally from Devizes) had caused a lot of trouble and his discharge had been approved. He was sent to prison for one month with hard labour.

According to the *Salisbury Times,* 'one of the most audacious thefts which have [*sic*] taken place in Devizes for many years was committed on New Year's night', when Victor Rice, an 18-year-old trumpeter of the Royal Canadian Dragoons, stole a Ford taxi which Alfred Grant of Shrewton had owned for only three days, having paid £147 for it. The worse for drink, Rice had seen the car outside the Crown Hotel in Devizes and 'whizzed away' to Pond Farm Camp, where it was discovered without its registration plates on 13 January outside Simonds' beer tent. At Rice's appearance before Devizes Borough Magistrates on the 21st, a Canadian officer havered about whether he would be disciplined by his unit but then conceded he 'probably' would be. As ever conscious that it was dealing with a soldier who would soon be fighting the Germans, the court fined him £1 and ordered him to pay £10 compensation to Grant, who claimed that it had cost him £1 a day to hire a replacement car. Rice said he would cable his father in Canada for the money, the court then giving him a week to raise it. (After two years service with the Dragoons, Rice appears to have been discharged after suffering shell-shock and neurasthenia, re-enlisting again in January 1918 though then, unusually, his re-attestation papers were not signed by a medical or commanding officer.)

Just after Rice's trial, Alfred Grant had further misfortune when on 27 January he knocked Private Henry Morris of the 7th Battalion's signalling section off a bicycle near the Catherine Wheel Inn in Shrewton. Whether he was driving his newly recovered taxi is not recorded. Morris had been riding on the right, which was the wrong side of the road in Britain, though an officer told the inquest that Morris was from British Columbia, 'the only Canadian state where driving is on the left'! There was a suggestion that Grant had been driving too fast, but the jury recorded a verdict of accidental death, its foreman adding that it was a 'pure accident'.

Reading reports of serious motoring accidents such as this, one is struck by the lack of blame often attributed to either of the parties involved, this at a time when the courts were quite severe with drivers speeding and having no lights on at night and with cyclists riding on footpaths. It is perhaps flippant to add that Morris, aged 34 and with 13 years' service in the Shropshire Light Infantry, had a fine range of tattoos recorded on his attestation papers: an eagle on his right shoulder; lion and star on his right arm; a rose, woman's head, peacock and serpent on his right forearm; a basket of flowers, True Love motto and flags on his left arm; and a butterfly, pierced heart, serpent on a tree, butterfly, pansy and pansies on his left forearm.

With days to go before their departure for France, several artillery men found themselves in court in Devizes for minor theft. Driver William Francis McInnis of the Ammunition Column, 1st Field Artillery Brigade, was charged with stealing a macintosh coat and whisky valued at 20s from the caretaker of New Copse Farm, where his unit was based. Captain Lawrence Cosgrave of the 1st Field Artillery Brigade's Headquarters Staff, (who perhaps resented spending time in court when his unit was busy preparing to leave the Plain) told the court that McInnis was 'a very undesirable and useless man … he would not ask for any leniency.' McInnis was sent to gaol for one month with hard labour, missing the move overseas. Perhaps on his release from prison he was discharged from the army, for on 23 March 1916 he re-enlisted in Pictou, Nova Scotia, noting on his attestation papers that he had six months' military experience. At the same court, Mark Veitch and Lewis

McGregor of the 3rd Field Artillery Brigade, were charged with stealing macintosh coats and other items. Their captain said both were indifferent characters from the military point of view and they each received a month in prison with hard labour. The *Wiltshire Telegraph* pointed out that all three men were 'non-Canadians', that is, had not been born in the dominion. Veitch was originally from Edinburgh, McGregor from Glasgow.

Other cases of pilfering led to Drivers George Haley and James Robert Purcell each being fined £2 with 12s 6d costs after stealing food and kitchen utensils worth 25s at West Lavington.

Given that the Canadians constituted the 'population' of a sizeable town, the incidents mentioned above hardly constitute a crime wave and are not out of proportion to those reported in the local newspapers before the war. Significantly there appears to have been very little violence involving civilians. Comments by soldiers themselves put the matter further into perspective. One NCO in the 13th Battalion replied thus when a relative in Canada wrote to him about the rumours of poor discipline:

In reply to your letter, I will try to give you some dope, taking the points you raise in order. First,

New Copse was one of a number of former farms used by the British Army. Canada's 1st Field Artillery Brigade was based there.

discipline in ours. This is varied. It is not good compared with the Regulars, but it is quite good all the same, and I have never yet heard of a man refusing to obey an officer's order. The Canadians as a whole have a frightful name all over the [illegible] for bad discipline, but that is earned by not saluting when on leave. But after all these things are not the important part of discipline. What is important is to get orders obeyed and that is done very well indeed.

The matter of bad behaviour was to cause some feeling between the First Division and the men of later contingents. The story goes that a newcomer told a veteran that 'we are having a hard time to live down the reputation you fellows left in England.' The veteran replied, 'Oh well, cheer up, you'll have a damn sight worse time living UP to the reputation we have in France.' And on 7 May 1915 Fred Adams wrote home (in a letter published in the *Coburg World* of 28 May):

There are all kinds of fellows over here now to fill up the gaps. Do you know what some of them said? They said that the First Contingent was the riff-raff of Canada and only too glad to join at once. Is that not awful cheek, after what we have had to put up with at Salisbury Plains all winter and after fighting like we have done here. If these standbacks do half as well as the riff-raff did, they will not do bad.

As Corporal H. R. Gordon pointed out:

It is a bit annoying to read that men who have been warm and dry and well fed all winter are better men … than ourselves, who have three and a half months' of mud and water under canvas at Salisbury Plain, and a month's active service under our belts.

Sam Hughes himself is said to have told officers of the Second Division:

I understand, gentlemen, that you are going to live down the reputation of the First Division in England. Well, all I can say is that you'll have quite a time to live up to their reputation in France.

As we shall see, the First Division was to distinguish itself magnificently in battle and indeed did earn an outstanding reputation for determination and valour. As one maxim attributed to it proclaims, 'We lead, others follow'.

Chapter Seven
Equipment and Re-organisation

The raising of the First Contingent in Canada was impressive in terms of its speed, the numbers of men raised and the amount of *matériel* that was assembled for transporting to England. But the months on Salisbury Plain were to test severely not only the soldiers but their equipment. The majority of the men performed well but nearly everything they brought with them proved inadequate. The misguided acquisition of the Burgess-Dunne floatplane described in Chapter One is an extreme example but at least it was not Canadian-made. Many other items of equipment, notably the Ross rifle, were, and Hughes found it impossible to concede that their choice and quality were at fault.

He himself was closely associated with the MacAdam shovel said to have been suggested by his personal secretary, and 'Sam Hughes' was transformed by the troops in to 'Sham Shoes' to describe the shoddy boots issued to the Contingent. With the British army boot deemed too heavy for wear at home, the Canadian Army opted for its own design, produced at a cost per pair of about $3.85, but these soon succumbed to Salisbury Plain's hard roads and thick mud.

During the Canadians' stay in Wiltshire there were several local boards of inquiry into the boots' quality. One, as early as 1 November, was told by a medical officer, Major Ashron Langrill, that they were not waterproof. 'I think that the constant wet feet the men are thereby subject to are the cause of many colds and the frequency of rheumatism, from which the men are suffering,' he stated. On the 19th Alderson wrote to the Department of Militia and Defence to point out that the 'boots [are] not suitable for rough wear in wet weather', having been told the same day that 48,000 pairs of overshoes had been shipped to the Contingent. On 5 December he observed that these did not compensate for the faulty construction of the boots,

Sam Hughes with the combined shovel and shield named after his secretary, Ena MacAdam.

some pairs of which were useless after ten days' wear. At another board on 31 December, Major Ernest Brown of the Canadian Army Medical Corps claimed that a large proportion of his sick parades consisted of men with bad colds caused by wearing unserviceable boots. Captain John Handley, the 13th Battalion's quartermaster, said that a large proportion of the leather was improperly tanned and that 15 per cent of the boots had been returned to stores as defective. The unanimous findings were that the boots were absolutely unfitted for service conditions.

The men of Lord Strathcona's Horse were envied after they acquired high boots and slickers, paid for by a fund organized by Lady Strathcona. On 27 January it was ordered throughout the Contingent that 'every man must be in possession of a pair of perfectly serviceable Imperial [British] pattern Army Regulation boots .... No Canadian pattern boots are to be taken overseas.' Officers were required to certify that every man was in possession of a pair of British boots.

Towards the end of 1914 the French Government had ordered 300,000 pairs of boots from the Quebec Boot & Store Manufacturers' Association. How these came to be regarded by French soldiers is not known, but the Second and Third Divisions were also to have bad experiences with their boots, all of which contributed to something of a national scandal with their poor quality being seen as a blow to Canadian manufacturers' reputation.

The lack of acceptable boots was just a small part of it. A feature of the Canadians' last month on the Plain was the wholesale replacement of their equipment at a time when they should have been putting the finishing touches to their training and when they were preoccupied with floods and illness.

Though it had been condemned after the Boer War, the Oliver harness (which had caused discomfort to the Canadians on their 1910 visit to England) had been issued to all but five battalions. Its pouches held only 80 rounds instead of the 150 of its British equivalent, there was no pack and it cut men under the arms and chin; large brass buckles also made it even more uncomfortable to wear. Alderson had to obtain an issue of the British 1908 pattern harness for seven battalions. In 1915 Hughes authorized $700,000 to be spent on re-building the Oliver harness, to give business to Canadian manufacturers and out of arrogance. Canadian soldiers were sent overseas with it until 1917.

The variety of vehicles made the supply of spare parts a challenge, especially as many had to come from North America. As with the motorized vehicles there were several types of horse-drawn wagon but their parts were not interchangeable. Particularly affected was the Divisional Supply Train, responsible for delivering stores and equipment. A 'Train' did not relate to railways, except that it might collect materials delivered by them, but comprised wagons and motor vehicles. The Contingent's Train had one of the most demanding jobs of any unit on the Plain. Not only was its variety of wagons unreliable but it was very often caught between the demands of the units it was tasked to supply and the inefficiencies of contractors. Its war diary notes many problems obtaining oats, oil and wood, units helping themselves from supplies delivered to railway stations, the ill-health of its horses and the weather. As well as stations already mentioned (Amesbury, Bulford and Patney & Chirton), the Supply Train collected materials delivered to those serving Porton (five miles north east of Salisbury) and Woodborough (three miles west of Pewsey), for example.

One of the Canadians' wagons that suffered so much wear and tear.

On 23 November the Train received a new type of wagon, meaning it now had six makes. 'This is going to make it very hard to replace these waggons on Service,' noted Lieutenant Colonel William Simson in its war diary. Some wagons had been built from parts designed for three or four different types and all were of 'green' wood that was soft and coarse grained. Almost all those that had been put to work on the Plain were now damaged. New wagons were supplied direct from factories in the United Kingdom, meaning that British harness had to replace the Canadian pattern, which was deemed unsuitable and unadaptable. On 2 February it was ordered that no black Canadian-pattern collar harness be taken overseas, though next day this requirement was relaxed in the event of replacement pole-draught harness not being available for the light Bain wagons used as officers' mess carts.

The Reserve Park, with its role in the supply chain, also had a very demanding time, both in fulfilling its duties and coping with poor equipment. A horse-drawn transport company, it was intended to be located about 30 miles behind the front lines, holding two to three days' iron rations and forage to be used in case of contingencies. After a week at Pond Farm Camp it moved to huts at Sling which, being close to the Bulford railhead, was far more convenient for receiving stores. On 30 November Major Charles Adams, its commanding officer, noted in its war diary:

In closing this month, I cannot help concentrating on the discouraging state of affairs, which finds us, at the end of nearly four months of mobilization, without having yet received the most necessary articles of our equipment, and with some of the articles which we have received, so utterly useless for the work in hand, poor horses, worse waggons, ill-fitting clothing boots of inferior quality; and many things besides too numerous to mention in such a report as this.

Originally the Contingent had been equipped with enough motor transport for a normal-sized division, whereas it had 11,000 more men, not to mention units that were 'attached' to it. Sixteen lorries had been loaned to Sir John Jackson Ltd, and all its 24 Gramm lorries had been laid up, suffering from considerable engine trouble and several having broken crank shafts. Of the 25 Jefferies lorries on the establishment of the Ammunition Park, 19 had developed faults in their driving gear, with replacement parts having to be ordered from America. (As its title suggests, the Ammunition Park was responsible for transporting and storing ammunition.) On 31 December the Contingent was ordered to leave behind in England its motor lorries for the use of the Second Contingent then training in Canada but expected shortly to come to England. They had been used to full capacity and arguably beyond it, taking into account the conditions.

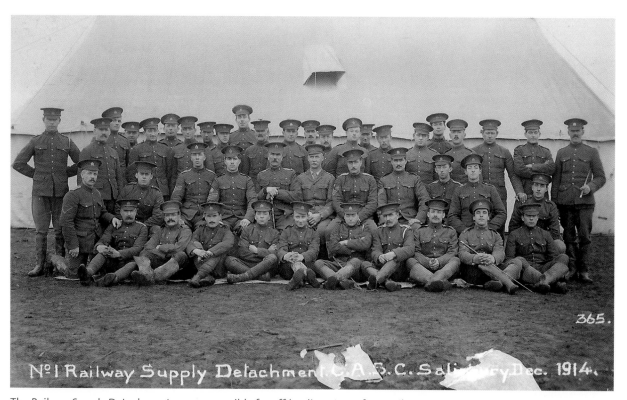

The Railway Supply Detachment was responsible for off-loading stores from railway wagons on to road transport.

Sling Camp, newly built and offering far more shelter than tents.

Two vehicles were bought and registered locally in December, an Indian motor-cycle for the Ordnance Corps at Bulford and a Ford car for Lieutenant Colonel Frank Meighen of the 14th Battalion at West Down South Camp. Whether the Ford was an official or personal purchase is not known.

As late as 23 January, General Alderson was noting such inadequacies as no travelling field-kitchens, too few machine-guns, infantry lacking telephones, and only 48 out of 600 replacement bicycles to hand, the original machines having been condemned. And the Canadians' ammunition had been stored out in the open all winter.

Back in Canada, Hughes was being kept informed of the wide-scale replacement of equipment by telegrams from Colonel Carson, who had led the Contingent's advance party and was now established at the White Hart Hotel in Salisbury as his special representative in England responsible for maintaining supplies. On 9 January Hughes sent Carson a telegram whose tone, even allowing for the economy of words customary in such communications, betrayed his exasperation about criticism of the MacAdam shovels and insisting that an order for British shovels must be cancelled and the Canadian model used:

See general Alderson and if necessary Earl Kitchener but I will not permit this improper interference. British entrenching tool absolutely

useless for any purpose ours is perfect for protection and with handle attached is excellent for shovelling.

Most of the men who had to use the object disagreed. Donald Fraser was forthright:

Another huge farce was the entrenching tools of Col. Sam Hughes. Absolutely no person with a grain of sense would have passed these tools as practical. Their defects, their uselessness were obvious. Whoever was responsible for the issue must have had a childish idea of the requirements of the fighting man or he must have been financially interested in the matter. Most soldiers take the latter view.

This motor-cycle looks clean enough to be a soldier's pride and joy and would have proved useful for getting away on leave, as well as going out on fatigue duties.

The heliograph was used for long-distance signalling. It reflected sunrays from a mirror which was moved by a small key.

An alarmed Carson telegrammed the Department of Militia and Defence on 10 February, by when the Contingent was in France:

> Alderson states our wagons and harness condemned by order of War Office and replacement by general service wagons with breast collar harness .... Alderson states our [MacAdam] shovels tried as shields but not found satisfactory. [British] trenching tools issued our troops. Could not carry our shovels in addition so they are left behind.

Nevertheless on 2 March Hughes recommended the purchase of handles (each weighing eight ounces) for the 25,000 shovels at a price of $3,800. (In May 1917 the shovels, which had cost $1.35 each, were sold as 50 tons of scrap for $1,400.)

Thirteen days later, Carson, still indignant, told Hughes that the replacement motor lorries supplied by the War Office comprised six different makes, in his eyes making nonsense of the lack of interchangeability cited by the British authorities as one reason for the Contingent's original vehicles being unsuitable. He may have had a point, but at least spare parts would be available from depots in England and on the Continent supplying and servicing British vehicles.

On 28 March a letter to Carson signed by Alderson, whose command had come out of front-line trenches the day before, sought to justify some of the decisions that had been taken about the original equipment. It pointed out that the MacAdam shovels were too heavy, each battalion would require three wagons to transport them, and there was no chance of getting these. Word had got back to Hughes, probably via Carson, that equipment had been abandoned in the camps on departure from the Plain, and Alderson acknowledged that harness had been left around. He pointed out that at Lark Hill replacement wagons and harness had been received only at 10pm the day before they were due to be at Amesbury Station at 3am for entraining. A marquee in which the new harness was being prepared had blown down so, Alderson pointed out, it was no wonder that the old harness had been abandoned.

Hughes continued to take badly the replacement of so much of the equipment whose acquisition he had encouraged and influenced, and in 1916 claimed that in many cases they had been supplanted by inferior articles. A court of inquiry appointed by the Militia Department found that the original Canadian boots were of unsuitable style and shape for active service. It absolved Canadian manufacturers of fraudulence and negligence, though acknowledging that the boots could be improved. Some 22 companies had shared the first orders for boots and one, Ames Holden McCready Ltd, placed an advertisement in the *Calgary Herald* of 21 May 1915 stressing that the 32,217 pairs it had supplied to the First Contingent had proved satisfactory, despite being 'baked on hot stoves, grilled on steam radiators and roasted before open fires'. Hughes was exonerated because the boots were made to a pattern accepted by his predecessor, Frederick Borden. After more criticism on a number of issues, he sent a letter to the Prime Minister, Sir Robert Borden, claiming there was a conspiracy against him. When Borden demanded his resignation, Hughes obliged.

The Canadian's field telephone sets proved too fragile and had to be replaced by a British pattern. Only on 15 January were telephone and telegraph communications established between the various camps, following several attempts to lay wire between them. Until then, communication had been by map, flag and heliograph (when there was any sun) and motor-cyclist.

About the only items of equipment that did not have to be replaced were officers' side-arms and the artillery (British-made 18- and 60-pounders), which were repainted in camouflage, 'all splashed over with daubs of paint of various hues, and the effect is certainly somewhat weird'. British ammunition did not suit the Colt machine-guns, whose tripods proved unsatisfactory.

Assessments of the Contingent invariably and with good reason take into account the terrible weather and poor accommodation that its members suffered, but little has been noted of the affect on morale of having so much equipment that was manifestly inferior. However there were some who were suspicious of the wholesale replacement. Frank Iriam of the 8th Battalion recalled in his memoirs, *In The Trenches, 1914-1918*, that the Contingent's commanding officer was British, as was a majority of its members:

> It was easy to get complaints enough from the rank and file to make a strong showing .... Poor old Sam Hughes protested at the time in no uncertain voice but he was drowned out and swamped out as thoroughly as our equipment that was stored in a basement warehouse in Salisbury in readiness for the annual flooding of the Avon. That is as regular as the tides and well known to the Imperial authorities .... We were re-equipped for overseas almost wholly with English made goods. I would like to know the personal history of the committee of inspectors who went the rounds with Alderson and clinched the deal at Salisbury Plains.

The Canadians' uniforms also had to be replaced, though it is doubtful whether any clothing could have survived the harsh conditions. As Iriam observed:

> We were put on cross country foot races, a run of six miles with whole companies and battalions in the run, up hill and down dale in the winter rain through wet grass and pools of water. We would finish the run steaming hot, soaking wet with sweat and rain water, ending up in tent where you waded in soup ankle-deep to the door. No fires here, no change of clothes, no rub down, not even dry blankets. We would squat in the slithery mud smooched floor and get busy with a knife scraping the mud from our clothing to make it presentable for the next parade.

The 13th Battalion was affiliated to the Black Watch, so shortly after arriving in Wiltshire Captain Charles Smith was sent to Scotland to obtain kilts, glengarry caps and badges of the approved pattern and to convey his greetings to Black Watch officers at their regimental headquarters. As it happened the Scottish regiments themselves were short of tartan material, a matter that was raised in the House of Commons in early January. It is not known if Captain Smith returned with the items he sought, but he was presented with 120 copies of the regimental history. Later the Marchioness of Tullibardine (whose family was closely linked to the Black Watch) offered to equip the 13th with khaki hose tops.

The 16th (Canadian Scottish) Battalion's comprised four Militia units who had assumed Scottish Highland links and each had its own tartan. The adoption of a single tartan for the battalion had been a contentious issue at Valcartier and continued to be so on the Plain. After much debate, known as the 'Battle of the Kilts', officers of the 16th voted on 21 December by 21 votes to seven to adopt a plain khaki kilt (as was already being worn by some other Canadian Scottish units), though one swore he had lived in a Gordon kilt and he would die in one. The khaki kilts would not reach the 16th Battalion until June 1915 and were greeted with such contempt that the whole issue was withdrawn. The matter remained unresolved until 1917 when the entire battalion received kilts of the Mackenzie tartan.

In England the Canadians were issued with cloth lapelettes or small shoulder straps to indicate to which branch they belonged: blue for the infantry, scarlet for the artillery, yellow for the cavalry, and blue with a yellow loop for the engineers, for example. The straps were to become a privilege of the First Contingent, an

Canadians of the First Contingent wore cloth lapelettes or shoulder straps to indicate to which branch of the army they belonged.

order of 24 September 1918 stating that:

> Coloured shoulder straps are permitted to be worn by warrant officers, non-commissioned officers and men of the original 1st Canadian Contingent, who have been returned to Canada from overseas.

Louis Keene found the new uniforms much more comfortable than his original one. Instead of the hard cap there was a soft one that was:

> something like a big golf cap with the flap on to pull down over the ears. These are much more comfortable. They have one great advantage over the old kind we can sleep in them. We can now lie down in our complete outfits even to our hats.

At the start of the war Keene had been producing drawings and cartoons for a Montreal newspaper. A cartoon showing a stoical Canadian soldier splashing through the mud on Salisbury Plain appeared in the *Red Cross Magazine* of September 1918. His book, *Crumps*, is an excellent account of his experiences in the Great War.

Just before Christmas, the Canadian War Contingent Association in London asked the public to donate socks, body belts, mufflers, gloves, mittens, cardigans and sweaters and sleeping caps for the men on the Plain. On 21 January an appeal was launched in Devizes for 500 pairs of mittens for the Canadians 'who are shortly going to the Front'. Only 200 pairs were forthcoming, partly due to a rumour that the Canadians did not want them. However in February Agar Adamson wrote to his wife that he had 'had got some beautifully lined mitts from Britain today for the whole draft' which he was commanding at Tidworth.

One issue among many men was the names of the units in which they were serving. Many rued the absorption of their local Militia units into sometimes anonymous battalions, and there were attempts to retain the original identities of some of the former in new titles. The 7th Battalion was often referred to as the 1st British Columbia Regiment, reflecting the locations from which its members came. Divisional orders for 11 November announced that the 15th Battalion had been officially recognized as the 48th Highlanders of Canada, whose members constituted by far the majority of the unit. The 16th had wanted to adopt the name 'Princess Mary's Highlanders', but when the War Office did not approve of this its officers on 14 December decided on the name '16th Battalion Canadian Scottish'. Had Alderson had his way, the unit might have been known by a mere number. On 4 December he had announced he intended to do away with all distinctive battalion badges and substitute numerals for them. All commanding officers protested strongly, and Lieutenant Colonel Currie of the 15th

Battalion warned that it would be up against public opinion in Canada. Alderson dropped the idea. On 16 December the 3rd Battalion won approval to be known as the Toronto Regiment.

The Contingent continually changed shape and size, with several units leaving, the largest being the Princess Pats, which anyway was not officially part of it. Various small groups and individuals also joined it. One independent detachment, Elliott's Horse, raised by a wealthy King's Counsel, R. P. Elliott, had arrived too late at Valcartier to join the Contingent and had come to England at his expense, despite being told that mounted men were not wanted. After being stranded in London and replacing their four original officers, the 80 men were authorized to become part of the force at the request of the acting High Commissioner for Canada, George Perley. But the Army Council pointed out that this was not to be taken as a precedent and that no other men were to be enlisted in England. When the Horse arrived on the Plain, its members were distributed between the Royal Canadian Dragoons and Lord Strathcona's Horse and, later, King Edward's Horse when it became part of the Canadian Cavalry Brigade.

On 29 October, Lieutenant Colonel Charles Nelles of the Royal Canadian Dragoons asked permission to recruit 23 'good men' who were offering to enlist in Britain. Approval was given by Alderson, only for the War Office to reverse his decision on 12 November, causing the general to protest, pointing out that his

men and officers were being permitted to transfer to the British Army. Indeed, on 5 November Kitchener had suggested to Alderson that 300 Canadians be supplied to the British forces, given that there was an excess of officers in the Contingent. Following a further protest from Alderson, the Army Council modified its previous decision, conceding that special cases might be considered. On 12 January he submitted a list of 14 *bona fide* Canadians he wished to recruit but this brought a reply from the Adjutant-General that

> Lord Kitchener has always been opposed to your recruiting Canadians in this country for fear of our being inundated with men from the Colony, and by so-called Canadians in England. The very suggestion that higher rates of pay could be obtained in England than our regulars get would have a very disturbing influence on our recruiting.

In the event 15 special cases were subsequently approved. In early January a shortage of about 30 artificers, shoeing-smiths and farriers was identified and at Alderson's request non-Canadians were enlisted to fill these vacancies.

Despite the War Office opposition, a number of units managed independently to take on men from various parts of Britain who attested locally. Those joining the 2nd Battalion had numbers 8671 to 8680 allocated to them, the majority having no Canadian connection apparent from their attestation papers. They included

The sergeants of the 2nd Battalion.

Albert Scurr, with no military experience, and Herbert Jackson, who had three years' service with the Lancashire Territorials, who attested as late as 14 and 17 January respectively. Basil Green, a British immigrant and member of the 100th Winnipeg Grenadiers, was on leave in England when war broke out and joined his comrades from the 100th, now incorporated into the 11th Battalion, at Pond Farm Camp.

An unusual late recruit was Nathan Agranovitch of Winnipeg who had been working in Australia for two years before the outbreak of war. Having arranged to meet his father in Turkey, he was on the SS *Zieten en route* from Australia when war was declared. The German cruiser SMS *Königsberg* intercepted the *Zieten*, and all its passengers from belligerent nations were disembarked at Mozambique. With the help of the British High Commission, Agranovitch made his way to England, but was without means. In a letter dated 14 January 1915, no less a person than Lieutenant Colonel Sir Edward Ward, Kitchener's representative in matters concerning the general comfort of the Canadian Contingent, explained Agranovitch's situation to the commanding officer of the 2nd Battalion, noting that his father was a successful businessman in Winnipeg who earned an annual income in the 'thousands of pounds'.* Agranovitch was accepted as a recruit and attested with the 2nd Battalion on 15 January 1915 at Bustard Camp. When the 2nd sailed for France on 7 February, he remained behind and was transferred to the 9th Reserve Battalion at Tidworth. There he ran into problems for refusing to be vaccinated against typhoid, despite having agreed to this on his attestation papers, but was eventually posted to France as part of a reinforcing draft.

In November, the Contingent was re-organized with the aim of transforming it more into the size and shape of a British division. There were several changes of mind, with battalions converting from having eight companies each to four and back again, the argument for four being that they were easier for a battalion commander to control than eight dispersed across a battlefield. The sequence went something like this, though there are variations in different accounts:

> 20-22 October: Each battalion's eight companies merge into four. This formation was used for

Lord Roberts' inspection on the 24th. The 15th Battalion's diary for 3 November refers to it being manoeuvred that day for the first time in four-company formation.

6 November: The Army Council decided that overseas contingents should have an eight-company formation.

17 November: The Contingent started to revert to this. The 15th Battalion's diary for the 19th refers to orders being received to revert to eight-company formation, something its officers regretted, as they had become proficient in the new drill. On 23 November the 14th Battalion's diary optimistically noted that all battalions were 'definitely organised on 4 (*sic*) company and platoon basis', the compiler perhaps being understandably confused about the number of companies.

10 December: Alderson was told that the Army Council had decided on a four-company formation.

14 December: The Army Council reversed this decision.

15 January: The 3rd Infantry Brigade diary notes orders to revert to a four-company formation, the Contingent as a whole starting to do so the next day.

In the end, most battalions lost 11 or so officers each, leading to a surplus that caused General Alderson considerable concern, as some officers and NCOs who were mostly surplus to requirements had already been transferred to Britain's New Armies. The 10th Battalion's roll in early 1915 comprised 1,080 men and 44 officers, but because its establishment was 929 men and 34 officers it had to give up a significant number. However, it did acquire from the 6th Battalion (which was replaced in the 2nd Brigade by the 11th) the 32-man band of the 106th Winnipeg Light Infantry. The 6th itself disbanded, transferring some members to other units, including three officers and 100 men to the Remount Depot at West Down South, followed by 346 all ranks on the 31st. Its Fort Garry Horse element was re-established as a mounted unit, training starting on 22 January.

---

* Sir Edward should not be confused with Lieutenant Colonel Walter Ward, who was Chief Paymaster and Officer in Charge of Records at the Canadian Pay Office in London. In the same office was Captain C. Warne Ward, a relative to Walter, perhaps his son.

The 4th Brigade was disbanded (or 'ceased to exist' as its diary for 18 January sadly notes). Three of its battalions and the 17th Battalion of Nova Scotians became reinforcing units at the Canadian Training Depot, which had been established at Tidworth Barracks under the short-lived command of Colonel W. R. W. James, a former governor of St Helena.* After first acquaintance Captain Agar Adamson of the Princess Pats wrote home that he thought James was 'a nice dugout [brought-out-of-retirement] man who is determined to take it easy'. The Pats were now in France but had left behind some instructional NCOs under Adamson to handle replacement drafts from Canada at Tidworth. But Adamson's subsequent letters show that he changed this opinion. When he suggested to James that 500 reinforcements from Canada who had arrived at Tidworth on 1 February be armed with the Lee Enfield rifle rather than the Ross, he was told that his suggestion was out of order 'as the men are members of the 12th and the 12th do not wish your advice'.

On 8 February Adamson wrote to his wife about being 'so pushed about by that silly ass James', who was proving obstructive to the extent that Adamson and Francis Farquhar, the Pats' commanding officer, met with Pitcairn Campbell, the upshot being that the Pats became independent of James. When on parade its men gave Farquhar three cheers, James was so angry that he ordered them put under arrest, a decision later cancelled. It may be significant that James was given an appointment in France on 24 March after only a couple of months at Tidworth.

Movements of men within the Contingent continued up to its departure from Wiltshire. A visit to Tidworth by the 16th Battalion in search of replacements yielded no results. A second visit produced some men originally intended for the Princess Pats who refused to wear the 16th's kilts and were returned to Tidworth, which declined to accept them. Then, because the Pats were now part of a British division, the War Office said its drafts were under its control and could not be used to reinforce other Canadian units. So the men returned to Tidworth, before finally being allocated to the 16th. They had been on and off battalion and company rosters five times!

In early December the 9th Battalion had been told that it would not be going to France as an unit, Captain John Parks breaking the news to his men of D Company with tears running down his cheeks. The 9th's Harold Peat was one of 300 of its men drafted into the 3rd Battalion, where he thankfully exchanged his 'Oliver torture' harness for the more efficient British system.

---

* A new 4th Infantry Brigade comprising battalions raised in Ontario became part of the Second Division.

Chapter Eight
Sickness and Death

Death came to the Canadians very soon after they started to arrive on the Plain. On Sunday morning, 19 October, the body of the 14th Battalion's Private William Hartley from Quebec was found lying on a heap of weeds by the side of the road near Shrewton. His commanding officer said he had been 'affected' by the voyage from Canada. Hartley appeared to have fallen over onto the weeds and turned his face into them, obstructing his nose and mouth and causing his death from asphyxia. He had been on the Plain only since the 16th and perhaps had been stressed by the near-three-hour march from Patney Station which, the battalion's diary noted, had proved 'very tiring for the men as they are soft after nearly 3 weeks on board ship'. Hartley was buried in Maddington Church. The 14th Battalion's war diary records him as having died on the 17th and implies that the inquest took place that same day, which would have been

remarkably prompt. Local newspapers and his gravestone give the date as the 19th.

Then on 20 October the 9th Battalion's Sergeant Ernest Lock, a former Royal Marine who had emigrated to Canada, died of natural causes after a game of football a few days before his 28th birthday. He was buried in his home town of Bristol.

Another early casualty was Gunner George Read of the 1st Field Artillery Brigade, who died on 24 October. On the 25th, Private William Ogden of the 7th Battalion (though described in the *Salisbury Times* as being of the 11th Battery, 4th Brigade) was killed at Pond Farm by an gunshot accidentally fired by Private Gavin Wilson from a rifle into which Ogden had mistakenly inserted a live cartridge. And on the 29th Private Samuel Smith of the 13th Battalion (or the '13th Brigade, 3rd Battery', as the

Pond Farm Camp in late 1914.

Salisbury Times, still struggling with unit titles, put it) fell off an armoured car of Automobile Machine Gun Brigade No. 1 near Shrewton crossroads, falling on his head and dying instantly.

At West Down North on 28 October, Gunner Percy Sawyer of the Headquarters Staff, Divisional Artillery, was killed by a runaway horse, having been dragged behind it by a rope attached to its neck strap and then kicked in the head. A medical officer, Major John McCrae, examined Sawyer and found he was dead. Part of his scalp had been completely removed from his skull, the base of his skull fractured and he had suffered a brain haemorrhage. He was buried in Tilshead churchyard.

For future generations John McCrae would be the most famous man in the Contingent. He was a highly talented physician who in August 1914 was crossing the Atlantic to holiday in Europe. When war broke out his ship was diverted to England. Having served with the Royal Canadian Artillery during the Boer War, he tried to enlist in London but was rejected because of his age of 42. An appeal to an old friend who was Director of Artillery with Canada's Permanent Militia led to an offer of an appointment as brigade surgeon to the 1st Field Artillery. He returned to Canada to settle his affairs and sailed with the First Contingent. After the second Battle of Ypres he wrote the poem that was to make him famous and to inspire the adoption of the poppy as a symbol of sacrifice, its first lines being:

> In Flanders Fields the poppies blow
> Between the crosses, row on row
> That mark our place; and in the sky
> The larks, still bravely singing, fly
> Scarce heard amid the guns below.

In January 1918 McCrae died the day before he was appointed Consulting Physician to the First British Army with the temporary rank of colonel.

Away from the Plain, Alexander Ogilvie of the 4th Battalion was found in a dazed state at King's Cross Station in London on 30 October. Thinking he was drunk, a policeman took him to the police headquarters at Scotland Yard, where he died. *Angina pectoris* was diagnosed, with no evidence that he had been drinking. He was buried in Aberdeen, Scotland, where his wife was living. Then on 13 November the body of Gunner Theophilus Walter Burdock of the Royal Canadian Horse Artillery was taken from the River Avon at Batheaston, just over Wiltshire's border with Somerset. It was wearing plain cloth trousers and army-pattern vest, pants and boots. Burdock had been under arrest from 21 to 27 October for being absent without leave, and was again absent on the 30th. The coroner's jury's verdict was suicide whilst temporary insane. He was buried in Batheaston Churchyard.

On 30 October the *Toronto Star* reported the death in France of Private William Cockhill of Montreal who, it said in one article, was a member of the First Contingent. But an accompanying column cast doubts on this and suggested he had been a civilian, perhaps one of those who had responded to calls for gentlemen chauffeurs to volunteer themselves and their cars to make British Expeditionary Force officers more mobile. Certainly no William Cockhill appears in official Canadian military records.

Walter Pendleton of the '1st Montreal Heavy Brigade' (actually the 1st Heavy Battery, Field Artillery), cut his throat at West Down North on 7 November after behaving peculiarly for a couple of days. The verdict on his death was 'suicide whilst of unsound mind'.

On 2 December Private Hugh Peden of the 16th Battalion was acting as an advance guard on a route march between Amesbury and Shrewton when he was involved in an accident with a lorry that had 'turned', apparently sharply, to avoid a stationary traction engine. The lorry driver said he had had so many trips to make that it was impossible to go slower. Peden later died at the Canadian hospital at Bulford Manor.

Seven days later, Private Charles Matthews of No. 2 Field Ambulance fell down a disused well 300-feet deep at Easterton Hill Farm. He had been on tactical operations and at 5pm had moved a door covering the well to help keep the wind and rain out of a dismantled house where officers were to sleep. There was 50 feet of water in the well, which was 4½ feet across. With the help of the Devizes construction company Rendell, the body was recovered with a grappling iron. At the inquest a police sergeant said there were 'several other practically open wells at dismantled farms on the Plain', leading the coroner to advise that areas used by the King's troops should be inspected for such hazards by a responsible officer. Matthews was buried in Tilshead Churchyard.

When Sapper George Burnett of No. 3 Company, Field Engineers was buried in Durrington Cemetery on 8 December after dying from pneumonia, his family from Manchester was present and his comrades collected £35 for his widow, Ellen.

On 23 December three senior officers, Colonel Richard Turner of the 3rd Infantry Brigade (who had won the Victoria Cross and Distinguished Service Order in the Boer War) and Lieutenant Colonels Burland of the 14th and Currie of the 15th Battalions were being driven in a car from Salisbury to Lark Hill Camp when the steering-gear malfunctioned and the vehicle turned over. Currie was thrown against the windshield, shattering the glass but suffering not a scratch. Turner, and Burland were buried under the machine. They were dragged out of the wreck and another car was commandeered to take Turner back to Salisbury, where his collar-bone and several ribs were found to be broken. The 14th's Lieutenant Colonel Frank Meighen assumed temporary command of the brigade until Turner returned on 13 January.

Lieutenant Ross Briscoe of the 9th Battalion was accidentally shot during rifle practice at Sling on 6 January. He had been standing in a pit behind the targets and so was at risk from deflected bullets. He had been warned about this in December, the prescribed position being in a pit in *front* of the targets.

On 26 January George Dean, a bugler of the 17th Battalion, was killed at High Post, between Salisbury and Amesbury, when a Canadian car drove into him at high speed. Dean was just 4 feet 11 inches tall and 15½ years old. Perhaps he was the 'mascot newspaper boy' who had stowed away on the troop convoy from Canada and who wanted to be a bugler. If so, his ambition had been quickly fulfilled, for Dean attested on 24 October at Pond Farm Camp, when he said he had been born in Manchester, England. Sadly no family tribute was carved on his gravestone, as was customarily done, and he may have been a 'Barnado' orphan sent out to Canada.

Another, unnamed, young bugler was aged 14 or 15 years and was said to have paid his way over from British Columbia, having belonged to a Militia unit there. In England, he was put in the care of Sergeant C. Austin Bell of No. 3 Company, Field Engineers, who reported on 7 February that 'we had some time getting his papers through headquarters, but they just came through today'.

Captain Henry Cook of the Pay Corps shot himself in Kew in south-west London on 3 February, when staying with his sister. Based in the Pay and Record Office both on the Plain and in London, he had become ill and gone to his sister's to recuperate. (The Chief Paymaster was based at 36 Victoria Street, London, with a pay depot at Osborne Terrace,

Windsor Road, Salisbury and a field cashier at Bustard.) The inquest was told that he had seemed to dwell on the war and was disappointed that he was not going to the Front. A verdict was returned of suicide during temporary insanity.

On 16 February Trooper Alfred Ellis of the Army Veterinary Corps fell into a small reservoir near the road when walking back from Tilshead to his base at Keeper's Farm. Ellis had tried to escape the mud on the road by walking off it. The water was between 7 and 12 feet deep and was protected only by a low wire fence. The coroner's jury returned a verdict of death by misadventure, noting that the reservoir was insufficiently fenced and a danger to children as well as soldiers. Incidentally Ellis was a late arrival in England, having attested in Montreal on 24 October and sworn his oath of allegiance on 3 November; originally he had come from Runcorn in Cheshire, where he was buried.

Accidents apart, ill-health was to be a major scourge of the Contingent, resulting in many deaths, notably in early 1915. As in the case of British recruits, medical inspections had been rudimentary and failed to detect many health problems that should have precluded military service, resulting in some soldiers being discharged shortly after they had started training at Valcartier. Others made it to Salisbury Plain before their problems became apparent.

Two such belonged men to the 10th Battalion and were recommended for discharge on 27 October, E. Mantel suffering from epilepsy, William Clarke from chronic heart disease. It was thought that they had been rejected at Valcartier and had stowed away or were shipped across in error. Yet Clarke's attestation papers show that he passed his medical examination, such as it was. No attestation papers for Mantel have been traced.

It had been intended that sick Canadians would be treated at Tidworth Military Hospital and Salisbury General Infirmary, but these became filled with wounded from the first Battle of Ypres. The Contingent's Director of Medical Services, Colonel Carleton Jones, had been led to believe that a hospital was being built near Stonehenge but found no trace of it. This would have been Fargo Hospital, planned just over a mile from the ancient monument as part of the development of Lark Hill Camp, where construction work had been underway for just a few weeks.

So at first the Canadians had to make do with using tents as hospital accommodation before conditions deteriorated and the number of patients increased, forcing the taking over of buildings as temporary hospitals. A few acute cases were handled by civilian hospitals, and the records of Sarum Isolation Hospital show that Robert Berry of the '1st Battery, 1st Brigade, 1st Ontario' and Newfoundlander John Ellis were both treated in December for diphtheria. Actually Berry belonged to the Ammunition Column of the 2nd Field Artillery Brigade! The hospital had only recently been built two miles north of Salisbury and close to the ancient earthworks of Old Sarum.

Apart from coughs and colds, some admittedly severe enough to merit hospitalization, the Canadians suffered remarkably few serious illnesses when in tents, even though many of these were of poor quality canvas and some at first had no boarded floors. Of 58 Canadian graves in Wiltshire dating from October 1914 to April 1915, eight are of soldiers who died before 1 December. Most of those who died later would have been living in huts. As early as 3 December it was noted that men still under canvas were healthier than those who had recently moved into huts. Causes of death were not always specified in reports, though pneumonia and meningitis were cited several times, with the latter killing 28. Typically the rumour machine exaggerated the number, one man writing home on 11 January that there had already been 300 deaths and the *World* weekly periodical claiming that 500 Canadians had lost their lives because of exposure to the weather.

Ironically it was living in huts that contributed to a sharp increase in sickness. As we have seen in Chapter Five, at night the men got the stoves red hot and went to bed with the huts overheated. When the fires died down, the huts cooled and the men awoke at three or four in the morning cold and shivering. The heat also shrunk the floorboards, which were not jointed, so gaps quickly opened. With the huts being built on brick pillars 2 feet high, the wind blew up through the boards, making matters even worse. The men of the 1st Infantry Brigade who remained under canvas throughout the winter suffered less ill-health than their comrades in huts. On 8 November Lieutenant Colonel Simson thought the huts at Sling 'much better' than the mud of Pond Farm Camp, but by the 22nd he had noticed that the sick parades had become much longer.

The most serious problem was a meningitis epidemic among the Canadians, thought to have originated at Valcartier and to have been made worse by overcrowding on board ship and in tents and huts, with 28 cases proving fatal. The situation was exacerbated by the move in to huts each accommodating 40 and more men in close proximity. By 2 November, No. 2 General Hospital's tents at West Down North had 109 patients and was appealing for more marquees; three days later, it was looking after 230 men. Two manor houses at Figheldean (pronounced 'Filedean') and Ablington were taken over as convalescent homes. Figheldean House, the residence of the officer commanding the Royal Engineers on Salisbury Plain,

Patients at Figheldean House, which the Canadians used as a temporary hospital for two months in 1914-15.

was in use from 7 December to 14 February and provided 50 beds. On 4 November permission was given for No. 1 General Hospital to take over Bulford Manor, with the first patients moving in on the 6th. Next day the first men moved into Ablington House, also owned by the War Office. A tent ward remained at West Down North, mainly to cater for cases of venereal disease, whose treatment was seldom sympathetic.

By 10 November it had become necessary to place the Rose and Crown Inn at Bulford out of bounds, suggesting that patients at Bulford Manor had been taking advantage of it. That same day, a cryptic entry in No. 1 General Hospital's war diary noted 'Rules adopted to prevent premises being injured or filled with tobacco fumes at all hours'; presumably this related to Bulford and Ablington Manors.

Netheravon Cavalry School became a temporary hospital for sick Canadians.

Men of No. 1 Field Ambulance were sent to Lark Hill to open a 20-bed hospital on 20 November. That day there were 150 men in the hospital at Bulford Manor; three weeks later there were 780. It had rained every day in the interval and there was a great deal of influenza and bronchitis. A field opposite Bulford Manor was being used as a tent hospital for increasing numbers of VD cases. Some new cottages about 200 yards away were also taken over. On 1 December, 22 patients were invalided back to Canada via London and Liverpool, followed by 24 more on the 15th, these leaving from Avonmouth. By the 17th there were 281 patients in the modest tented facilities at West Down North and on the 21st 1,001 men were noted 'in hospital' at Bulford Manor. The riding school at Netheravon Cavalry School was considered for hospital use but its indoor riding area was so vast that it would have needed innumerable stoves to warm it. But authority to take over all of the Cavalry School, including the former manor house, was given on 16

December, enabling 342 beds to be provided. When the Canadians handed back the accommodation in mid-March, a Royal Army Medical Corps colonel refused to accept it until the guardroom had been holy-stoned to snowy whiteness.

Medical officer George Nasmith went to London to see an expert bacteriologist on meningitis and to arrange to start a laboratory with the aim of seeing what could be done to locate 'carriers' of the disease germ and so keep it from spreading. On Christmas Eve he was able to borrow Dr Joseph Arkwright of the Lister Institute (a leading biomedical organisation) and the necessary apparatus to equip a laboratory. To transport it all by rail cost £780 in excess baggage. At Salisbury the connecting train for Bulford was held for five minutes until the equipment could be transferred to it.

Professor D. N. Ellis and Dr Rankin, the provincial bacteriologist for Alberta, who were working at the Lister Institute, visited Bulford and in March 1915 accompanied No. 5 Canadian Mobile Laboratory (the result of Nasmith's efforts) to France with the ranks of captain.

Nor was illness confined to the soldiers. On 30 December a YMCA worker telegrammed his superior in Bristol about the situation in the YMCA tent at Sling: 'Serious epidemic in Camp all workers ill Would like to discuss closing Tent   Can you come over'.

Honorary Captain George Ingles, the 3rd Battalion chaplain on attachment to No. 1 General Hospital, died on New Year's Eve of meningitis, thought to have been caught during his visits to patients. On 2 May 1915 a tablet to his memory was unveiled in Bulford Church. Meningitis was also to kill Lieutenant Colonel Frank Strange, the Contingent's senior ordnance officer and the highest ranking of its members to die on the Plain. He had been a member of the advance party that had left New York on 23 September. He was buried locally, but after the war his remains were repatriated and re-interred at Kingston, Ontario.

On 14 and 15 January the Canadian Sir William Osler, of the Queen's Canadian Military Hospital and an authority on diseases of the heart, lungs and blood, visited Bulford Manor to provide expert advice. The Queen's Canadian Military Hospital was near Folkestone, at Beachborough Park, whose owners had placed their house and its staff at the disposal of the Canadian War Contingent Association in mid-

October. It initially had 50 to 60 beds and a staff of Canadian nurses who had been in England at the outbreak of war, under the supervision of Miss Amy MacMahon of Toronto. Sir William, the Regius Professor of Medicine at Oxford University, was appointed its physician. The first patients had been wounded Belgian soldiers.

On 25 January the number of hospital patients among the Contingent was 1,210, including 17 officers.

The meningitis outbreak served to educate officers and men about the need to observe simple precautions to prevent the spread of disease. In mid-January senior officers planned a ball to acknowledge the hospitality and good will shown to the Canadians, but local health officials asked that it and other dances be cancelled. At the month's end, they requested local girls to refrain from kissing Canadian (and presumably British) soldiers. Happily there had been no fresh cases in the last week or so, though occasional infections were to continue. Men were cautioned not to place their mouths under water taps and from 22 January drinking vessels in canteens had to be placed in a solution of pomegranate of potash.

The Contingent had arrived in England with 65 per cent of the men inoculated against typhoid, and it was Nasmith's ambition to get them all treated before the departure for France. He began his education campaign at the Bear Hotel in Devizes, the headquarters of the Divisional Artillery, where Lieutenant Colonel Henry Burstall ordered his officers to help in every possible way. Nasmith warned of the danger of using impure water, described typhus fever and how it was conveyed by lice and stressed the necessity of anti-typhoid inoculation. His first talk was to about 700 artillery men in the company of Lieutenant Colonel Edward Morrison, commanding officer of the 1st Artillery Brigade, and Major John McCrae. On parade next day, 370 uninoculated soldiers were treated, the few who refused being withdrawn from those soon to leave for France and sent to the base depot at Tidworth.

Nasmith continued his talks, touring the Plain and addressing the men in farm yards, village squares, churches, schools, hay-lofts, and open fields. By the time the Contingent left for France 97 per cent of its members had been inoculated

With the Contingent's dispersal at the turn of the year to villages around the Plain, two sections of No. 2 Field Ambulance moved in to the Manor House,

Market Lavington on 3 January and prepared it as a clearing hospital. From 17 January daily entries in the unit's war diary were made at Littleton Pannell on the outskirts of West Lavington, suggesting further accommodation was taken over. In late January the daily tally of patients ranged from 19 to 48.

Late in January and in to February there was a great number of cases of enteritis, attributed to food poisoning or unclean cooking utensils and treated with castor oil.

The Red Cross hospital at Braeside in Devizes also took in Canadian casualties. In mid-January it had visits on successive days from two former governor generals of Canada, Earl Grey on the 17th and then the Marquess of Lansdowne and his wife. It had accommodation for 54 men, mostly British soldiers, though at the time of the visits patients included four Canadians.

Lax discipline among the VD patients in the Bulford hospital tents led to 100 men of the Fort Garry Horse being deputed to act as guards on 15 February, with another 40 joining them on the 17th. An inquiry recommended the replacement of the medical officer in charge by a stronger man and the issue of hospital clothing, presumably the blue uniforms worn by British soldiers to identify them as patients. On 24 March, 40 men, upset at a change-over in their medical attendants and their confinement in fine Spring weather, staged an 'incipient mutiny', quelled by guards with fixed bayonets.

Of the 4,000 hospital admissions during the Canadians' 14 weeks on Salisbury Plain, 1,249 were cases of venereal disease. There were 23 cases of insanity, some of which were transferred to the County Asylum at Devizes. Possibly one of these 'lunatics' was the man who startled Richard Grant of the 1st Field Artillery Brigade, who had been injured when unloading a gun at Plymouth and had spent six weeks in that city's hospital before moving to a hospital tent on Salisbury Plain:

> where I reclined with forty other patients, and directly opposite our tent was another in which were confined under guard a number of patients who were subject to fits, some of a very serious nature ... one night, when just dozing off, I was frightened into wakefulness by a scream. A man, who turned out to be an escaped epileptic, was standing in the doorway screaming, his eyes bulging out of his head. He had escaped by

striking the sentry over the head with the fire brazier, used to keep the sentry warm. Staring wildly about the room for a couple of seconds, he made a leap for the nearest man and bit him in the arm; he then jumped at the next patient, biting him; I was the following recipient of his devotions, getting a bite on the wrist ... By way of diversion he then took hold of the beds and started upsetting them, rolling the patients out on to the floor, causing a tremendous amount of pain and suffering to the men upset who, some of them, like myself, had casts on their limbs. In the midst of his mad capers the guest and orderlies rushed in, but before he was subdued he managed to fasten his molars in the arm of the guard.

On 16 December the Contingent's Clearing Hospital moved to Taplow (25 miles west of London and 65 from the Canadian camps), where medical facilities were being created in covered tennis courts measuring 122 by 80 feet and on a bowling alley next to Taplow Lodge, about a mile from Cliveden (pronounced Cliv-d'n) House. Its owner, Waldorf Astor, had offered this large mansion to the British Army, which decided it would be too difficult to adapt, and he had then approached the Canadians. Work on converting the lodge in to a hospital had started in November 1914. Extra piping had been installed to augment the heating and there was an operating room with x-ray facilities. The initial aim was for 100 beds but then Charles Hodgett, London Commissioner of the Canadian Red Cross Society, had become involved and the plans were expanded. Taplow Lodge was turned into staff accommodation, whilst nurses were also accommodated in Cliveden House itself.

The local newspaper, the *Maidenhead Advertiser*, advised on 20 January 1915 that 90 NCOs and men of the Canadian Army Medical Corps, mainly from Nova Scotia, were on site, under the command of Lieutenant Colonel Frederick Ford, who was soon to leave for the

Front. Twenty nurses were expected soon. The *Toronto Star* of 11 February reported that the:

> Cliveden base hospital would open on Monday the 15th with 125 beds, which will be subsequently enlarged to 1,000 beds. No more splendidly placed and equipped military hospital exists anywhere.

The Duchess of Connaught's Canadian Red Cross Hospital at Taplow.

Lieutenant Colonel Arthur Gorrell, Ford's successor, said that 'you can tell the people of Canada that this is the finest military war hospital in the world. There is nothing to beat it as a temporary hospital anywhere.' The Canadian Red Cross provided equipment costing $10,000. The first 70 patients, including 14 Canadians, arrived on 14 March. It became the Duchess of Connaught's Canadian Red Cross Hospital and the base of No. 15 Canadian General Hospital.

The Canadian cemetery near Cliveden House contains 42 burials of the 1814-1918 war, of which 28 are Canadian, one being a member of the First Contingent, Sergeant Frederick Slater of No. 1 General Hospital, who died on 27 April 1915. The site, much developed, became a major Canadian hospital in the Second World War.

Chapter Nine
Welfare and Recreation

Salisbury Plain in winter had very little to offer some 30,000 men living in crowded tents and huts, especially if some of them were used to the attractions of city life. There were those who might take pleasure in the countryside but this certainly was not at its most appealing in the dreadful winter of 1914-15. Access to villages and their public houses was severely restricted and the only place nearby of any size was Salisbury, which was 12 miles from the nearest camps, with no convenient rail service.

But it was somewhat unfair of the 5th Battalion's Harold Baldwin to report an:

> entire absence of amusement except what we manufactured ourselves and some tolerance may be vouchsafed us .... If these boys let loose occasionally, they also held the road to Calais, and many forget this when criticising the men, who not only facing hell in France and Flanders, but cheerfully forewent almost all the advantages that later contingents enjoyed while in training.

This overlooks the very generous efforts made by the British people, notably those living close to the camps, and the Young Men's Christian Association and other organizations. The YMCA had been founded by George Williams who, when working for a drapery wholesaler in London, became concerned about the welfare and spiritual well-being of those around him. In 1844 he helped start a bible-study group which formally became a society that addressed the concerns of young men working in cities. Public lectures and education classes were given and reading rooms and refreshment areas helped young men to adjust to urban life. Very soon the YMCA spread outside London and then to the USA and Canada. Before the Great War its marquees featured at many camps, both for Canadian Militia units and on Salisbury Plain, offering food, drink, free writing-paper and pastoral support. Nearly every wartime base and airfield in Wiltshire had a YMCA hut.

Six Canadian YMCA secretaries (local organizers within the Association) accompanied the Contingent, continuing their peacetime role of providing pastoral care but in uniform and with the honorary rank of lieutenant. On arrival in Wiltshire they had found that their British counterparts had established facilities in each of the camps allocated to them, supplying stationery, reading materials and refreshments, but with no scope for athletics and not much entertainment.

The soldiers quickly came to appreciate the YMCA. On 10 November, just four days before he died, Lord Roberts expressed his gratitude, noting that when he had inspected the men on Salisbury Plain on 24 October they had told him that they did not know what they would have done without the facilities provided by the Association.

The YMCA marquee at Pond Farm Camp was more than 160 feet long and able to accommodate at least 1,500 men. Following the departure of most soldiers from Pond Farm at the beginning of 1915, it was moved to Bulford.

YMCA representatives visiting Salisbury Plain in late October were about 5 miles from Bustard Camp when they gave a lift to a man who had been kicked four times by a horse. They were delighted when they discovered that he was a member of a church in Toronto and knew John McNeill, the 'Scottish Evangelist', who preached at Cook's Presbyterian Church there, and Griffith Thomas, Principal of the city's Wycliffe College. On arrival at Bustard, the YMCA representatives heard how 'a little Russian Jew had spoken to the men about the things of God'. They said he was Private H. Zussmann, who also knew McNeill, but his name does not appear in Canadian attestation papers nor in the *List of Officers and Men Serving in the First Canadian Contingent*. There were thought to be at least 250 Jews among the Contingent, some of Russian and Romanian origin, who were

CHURCH PARADE LARK HILL CAMP SALISBURY PLAIN 497

Church services were held outside when the weather permitted.

Comrades worship together. Six months later, many would be dead.

visited by the Reverend Michael Adler, who had been appointed Honorary Chaplain to H.M. Forces in 1906 with responsibility for Jewish servicemen.

Charles Alexander, another well-known evangelist, spent five days touring the camps accompanied by a colleague, two soloists and a pianist. He was an American who had led missions in many parts of the world, including to Canada in 1911. He, with his wife Helen, founded the Pocket Testament League to motivate Christians to read, carry and share the Word of God and during the war he extended his missions to military camps. At West Down South he attracted an audience of 1,000 men, each receiving his little combination Gospel and hymn-book. Though Testaments had been given to the men on departure from Canada, these were found to be too large and there was demand for smaller versions. Alexander cited Stonewall Jackson, the American Civil War general, as a famed soldier who was 'one of the godliest men you ever saw', and then invited his audience to stand up for the Lord. They sang the vibrant marching chorus, 'Give your heart to Jesus', Alexander urging the men to 'sing it in this country, right into France, and on into Germany', a patriotic sentiment that was loudly cheered. There followed an address about the Pocket Testament League, with the promise of a special League Testament to those who pledged to join. The signed acceptance of a Testament entailed its recipient undertaking to carry it and to read at least one chapter each day.

At a similar event at Bustard Camp, when the 1,300 men said to be present were asked if they were willing to accept Christ, it seemed to an YMCA onlooker as if the whole audience responded. Led by Mr Alexander, they declared 'I accept Jesus Christ as my saviour, my Lord, and my King'. The same observer claimed that in its four days on the Plain, visiting British as well as Canadian camps, the YMCA delegation had distributed 6,000 copies of the combination Gospel and hymn-book, 2,000 soldiers had become members of the Pocket Testament League, and 400 had formally 'declared for Christ', accepting Him as their Lord, Saviour and King. By Christmas, it was claimed, 10,000 of the British and Canadian troops on the Plain had joined the League.

YMCA events often included the men singing favourite songs such as 'Home, Sweet Home', 'Annie Laurie', 'Till the Sands of the Desert Grow Cold', then hymns such as 'Onward Christian Soldiers' and 'God Be With You Till We Meet Again', with a talk by the local YMCA secretary in between. There were excellent speakers among the men themselves, including the Reverend Dr John Pringle, a Presbyterian clergyman from Seattle aged 62 who was chaplain to the 17th Battalion. (Though on the 17th's roll in November 1914, he did not formally attest until 25 January the next year.)

Entertainment came from a number of sources. *With the First Canadian Contingent* records how:

> During January a London friend, who is untiring in her work for the Empire's soldiers, wrote asking … if a concert party to give four concerts would be appreciated by the Canadians …. Her kind offer was, of course, jumped at, and never, I think, have performers had a more appreciative audience. Four ladies came down … two concerts were held at Netheravon Hospital in the afternoon and two at Lark Hill in the evening. Those big huts, packed with a thousand men, were a wonderful sight.

The Canadian Field Comforts Commission was organized by two Toronto ladies, the Misses Mary Plummer and Joan Arnoldi, who had proceeded overseas with the First Contingent with the ranks of honorary lieutenants and were responsible for the distribution of gifts received from home. They established its depot at the vicarage in Amesbury, from where all sorts of parcels holding all sorts of items to make the men's lives easier were delivered to the camps. After the Canadians' departure from Wiltshire, the Commission continued its work from Shorncliffe in Kent after it became the main Canadian depot in Britain. Shorncliffe was on the edge of the port town of Folkestone, from where ships conveyed countless soldiers across the English Channel to Boulogne and on to the battlefields.

Salisbury Council House was made available to the soldiers on Sunday afternoons, with entertainment, a buffet, orchestra and writing tables provided. Then there were the self-made amusements. An officers' musical quartet was well received by an audience of 3,000 in Bournemouth, and George Gibson, in *Maple Leaves in Flanders Fields* (in which he fictionalizes the names of locations and individuals) told how the officers in one battalion mimicked:

> Zeppelin raids, when the airship, consisting of two chairs and a section of table, floated round the anteroom. The intrepid aviators, hovering on their giddy perch, dropped bombs, consisting of empty beer-bottles, on the heads of notabilities

thousands of feet beneath them. Or it was a shipwreck, when the sun-grilled mariners navigated the vast unending waters of the mess-room floor on an upturned table, searching for a sail through a telescopic whisky-bottle, and clamoured vainly for drinks. There the ancient mariner shot the albatross which flapped down from the top of the piano. We tied it to his neck, and ate it finally at mess on the morrow under the heading of pheasant !

There were sordid dramas from real life, when little Alice, dressed in a table-cloth and her mother in curl-papers, waited for the drunken father outside the gin-palace door. Then there was the poisoning act, when the foully wronged heroine, Lieutenant Lindsay, caught the villain, Lieutenant Montgomery, in the act of inserting No. 9 pills [laxatives] in her whisky-and-soda; and rushing to the windows, discovered the lights of her lover's (Lieutenant Madden's) motor-car coming up the drive. The car was a soap-box and the lights one candle. It acted quite well, as the lamps in the anteroom were all turned out to make this seem more realistic.

Then there were other nights when we went over to the Jocks on the top of the hill, and danced reels to the music of the pipes; or the Saskatoons gave a dance, and we did the light fantastic until an early hour in the morning, and rolled on to parade without troubling our beds at all.

A library was opened at Sling Camp on 25 November, probably the 'Overseas Contingent Library' to which Queen Mary sent presents of books, *The Times* book club providing another 500. By mid-December there were four libraries serving the camps, offering 60,000 books.

There are few reports of athletic competitions within the Contingent but its members took part in rugby matches and other sporting events against British units. A hockey team was formed, managed by Lieutenant Geoffrey Taylor of the 48th Highlanders and including several well-known players. On 12 December the Canadian cavalry valiantly took part in a somewhat one-sided game of rugby against the 5th Gloucestershire Regiment, the team members being handicapped by not having played together. That same day another rugby team lost 11 points to 13 against the Universities and Public Schools Brigade, comprising battalions of the Royal Fusiliers. Over the Christmas period, a Canadian eight competed in several rowing races on the Thames at Richmond, and a football team went to Glasgow on New Year's Day and played 'a very strong game but were up against new rules that penalized them, so they did not win'.

In November the Sergeants' Mess of the headquarters staff at West Down participated in a 16-a-side shooting match against Devizes Working Men's Club. Embarrassingly no doubt, the working men won by 432 points to 410, three of them recording higher scores than the Canadians' best performer, Sergeant

There were few sporting facilities so the Canadians had to improvise.

Graham. Perhaps this was Drum Sergeant James Graham, on the staff of the 16th Battalion, then at West Down South. He had been clerk of the court at Vancouver's Supreme Court and had seven years' military experience.

Later that month, the Canadians took part in a drill competition against the New Zealanders at Sling Camp. These comprised some 250 men who had been in England when war broke out and who had enlisted in their country's army. They included five All Black rugby players, an English rugby international and three Rhodes scholars and were helping to build a camp intended for Australian and New Zealand troops on the way from their home countries. When the Canadians' experiences on the Plain persuaded the authorities to divert the convoy to Egypt, the New Zealanders left to join them on 12 December. Quite what military training they had received in between erecting huts is not clear, but their drill was considered much smarter than that of the Canadians, whose 'hesitation, slight though it was, became shortly obvious', noted *The Times*.

A popular occupation in the tents and huts was the gambling game craps, the leisure time being too short for poker. Men were astonished to find that they could not buy craps dice in London and had to draw their specification to have them made.

In early November Burroughes and Watts, the Toronto billiard-table makers, offered to supply four tables via their London factory. The Canadians accepted the offer but pointed out that they would not be able to use them for a month until huts were erected. They would have had only a few weeks' enjoyment of them, if that, but no doubt the tables were much appreciated by the many units of several nationalities based on the Plain in the years ahead!

Vitally important to morale were communications with home. A proportion of soldiers' mail was delayed or never delivered because of uncertainties as to where it should be addressed and where the intended recipients were. Sometimes the address details were insufficient or difficult to read, and some cards and letters had to be stamped 'Not Known' by the Canadian postal staff. On 21 September James G. Stephen's wife had posted a card to him at 'Army Reserve Camp Quebec', leaving staff there to identify him among the 30,000 or so men at Valcartier. Miss A. Ford conscientiously addressed her card to 'Earnest Smith. 4th Sec No 1 Co. 7th Batt. Valcartier Camp. Quebec', and 'Bella' wrote to 'Pte. W. McLagan

C.A.S.C. No. 4 Valcartier Quebec'. In all these cases, the intended recipients could not be traced and they never received their mail.

Such mail appears to have been forwarded from Valcartier in the assumption that the addressees were on Salisbury Plain, though not all of their names appear in the Contingent's *List of Officers and Men* compiled in November, nor in attestation papers. Fred E. Livingstone's brother sent a card to him at Valcartier, asking 'did you get my litter [*sic*] and baby picture'. Another hand has crossed through the outdated address and added 'Salsbury [*sic*] Plain England', where Fred was 'Not Known'. He was a member of No. 2 Stationary Hospital, which arrived on 22 October and left for France on 6 November. Little wonder then that the card never caught up with him.

This card was posted to Fred E. Livingstone's brother and forwarded to Salisbury Plain but he left for France on 6 November and never received it.

When the Contingent departed from Wiltshire, the undelivered mail appears to have been abandoned, some items perhaps finding their way into the hands of local people as souvenirs. A batch of postcards stamped 'Not Known' from Canada was auctioned in the Devizes area in the early twenty-first century.

On 16 October it was officially directed that mail for the Canadians should be addressed to 'Canadian Contingent, Salisbury Plain', though two days earlier the *Portage le Prairie Weekly Review* had published advice that it should be made out to 'Canadian Expeditionary Corps, Salisbury Plains, England', and the *Toronto Star* on the 17th advised that it should be sent to Headquarters at Bustard Camp! As early as 21 October there were discussions between the Canadian and British post offices on the best methods of sending bulk mail. Letters for Contingent members were handled in England initially, and apparently cumbersomely, by the General Post Office's South Western District Office, which forwarded them to the War Office in London where they were sorted and returned to the GPO for distribution. But on 18 November one man was advising that his address was 'Canadian Expeditionary Force, War Office, London', so perhaps the system had been changed.

One postcard, sent from Inverness in Scotland on 30 September, was addressed to 'Canadian Expeditionary Force. Field Post Office, Salisbury' because, its sender explained, 'it was on the stamp [postmark] of the P.C. [postcard] you sent'. Unfortunately the 'Not Known' stamp has obscured the addressee's name. Other cards bore merely the name of the soldier and 'Salisbury Plain, England'.

There was also some confusion about the postage rates for the Canadians' mail. A GPO circular of 3 November confirmed that their letters and parcels were subject to ordinary postage rates, and advised that special overseas rates would not apply until the Contingent joined the British Expeditionary Force on the Continent. On 23 November a British Member of Parliament received confirmation from the Postmaster General that correspondence to and from 'colonial' troops attracted the same concessionary rates as that for British troops. Next day the GPO advised that mail from Canada should be addressed to 'London, England, Canadian Expeditionary Force, Salisbury Plains', thus ensuring that postal officials would not challenge it being sent at concessionary rates, as might be the case with items directly addressed to individual camps. One may imagine the impracticability of communicating this guidance and that concerning addresses to families and friends living the width and breadth of Canada.

Having noted that the French and Belgian authorities were not charging duty on tobacco sent to the British Expeditionary Force, R. M. Coulter, Canada's Deputy Postmaster General, queried the position regarding his countrymen in England. The GPO referred the matter to the War Office, which on 12 December advised that all dutiable packages for individuals and specific units should be sent to the appropriate commanding officer, who would sign for it and superintend its distribution free of duty. This exemption did not extend to parcels sent to Canadian soldiers serving with the British Army, which must have led to further confusion when Contingent members transferred to that force or within the Contingent itself. Private H. Salder of the 3rd Scots Guards based at Wellington Barracks in London was charged 14s 6d for a package from

Canada containing tobacco, confectionery and woollen comforts sent to him as a Christmas present.

Before the war Tidworth and Bulford barracks had their own post offices which handled incoming and outgoing mail, the latter being franked with the relevant barracks postmarks. Temporary post offices were set up on all the summer camping-sites later used by the Canadians and these applied postmarks naming the appropriate camp to outgoing mail. The Canadians had their own postal service and a postmark of elegant design was applied to official and some private mail. A crude postmark, inscribed 'DIV'L ARTILLERY H Q.', was used on mail sent by senior staff billeted in the Bear Hotel in Devizes in early 1915.

This postmark was applied to mail sent by Canadians billeted in the Bear Hotel in Devizes.

The Wiltshire postal services, coped well with pre-war peaks in mail at the summer camps but struggled to deal with all the correspondence generated by the tens of thousands of soldiers in the Salisbury area in the winter of 1914-15, the situation not being helped by some of their own staff having joined up. On 3 December Mr Coulter reported to the GPO complaints that he had received of late and non-delivery of letters to the camps. It was alleged that mail was taking two weeks and more to be transported from Montreal to Salisbury Plain and, understandably perhaps, some mail for the Contingent's No. 2 General Hospital was being sent to the British unit of that name in France. The Post Office acknowledged that the 'complaints are numerous ... too numerous', but its enquiries suggested that much of the delay was due to the Canadians themselves after mail had been delivered to their base post office in Salisbury, where it was sorted for delivery to different units. The poor weather had not helped, and it was stated that a Lieutenant Caldwell was facing a court-martial on 12 December after bags of registered mail had been left unopened for several days. Caldwell, a former railway mail clerk, enjoyed the distinction of being listed twice in the *List of Officers and Men*, as Lieutenant Bruce M. Caldwell of the Divisional Headquarters Postal

Detachment and as Honorary Lieutenant B. McG. Caldwell of the Postal Corps.

Major Wheeler of the Home Depot section of the War Office said there was no evidence of mail taking 16 to 19 days to cross the Atlantic, the average being 9 days. It was suggested, apparently by a British sergeant attached to the Canadians to help with their mail, that, with many of their units being recruited from specific areas, post for a particular battalion could be bagged locally in Canada. This idea appears to have adopted for on 11 November Alfred Williams, the Salisbury postmaster, noted, inaccurately, that

> the Contingent consisted mainly of the Queens Own Regiment and the 48th. Highlanders from the 3rd and 15th. Battalions respectively.

> It would greatly assist matters here if representations could be made to divide [in Canada] the correspondence of these two Regiments.

Around Christmas, locally posted letters were delivered late, by a week or more, or even up to a month in some cases. Some, perhaps much, of the delay was within the camps themselves, with units moving from one to another and men entering and leaving hospital. At Christmas time Salisbury Post Office usually took on 60 extra staff but that year could only find 20, such were the competing demands for labour. It handled 10,000 parcels for the Canadians alone.

In a letter published in the *Wiltshire Advertiser* on 17 December, Devizes Post Office warned that its staff was depleted and that on the 22nd, 23rd and 24th collections in the town would be brought forward by an hour, and in rural areas by 30 minutes. Christmas correspondence should be posted not later than the morning of the 23rd.

Much of the soldiers' outgoing mail consisted of picture postcards, which had been introduced in the 1890s and by the early 1900s had become very popular.

Several photographs of the January flood were taken from this spot in Elston. This one shows the sort of old cottages that intrigued the Canadians.

This lorry visited Lark Hill to supply the troops with some welcome home produce.

They proved a particularly convenient way for soldiers to communicate with family and friends. Local photographers did a roaring trade by selling images of camps, individuals and groups of men. In 1914 three were particularly prominent on the Plain. There was T. L. Fuller of Amesbury, some of whose photographs appeared in *With the First Canadian Contingent*, and his rival (for whom he had briefly worked) Marcus Bennett, who had a hut-studio in Bulford Camp. Albert Marett of Shrewton was well placed to photograph Canadians billeted locally and struggling through the flooded village roads of January 1915. Marett was a professional photographer who appears to have had some minor local competition from W. Ross, also of Shrewton, who published a few postcards of similar scenes and other military activities early in the war. The national publisher, Raphael Tuck, also produced at least four sets of six postcards featuring the Contingent, confusingly with different cards bearing the same reference numbers. Thus it is possible to find today contemporary postcards of many of the units camped on Salisbury Plain and in some cases to identify the men featured.

Around the turn of the year, the Canadian Government arranged with the Canadian Pacific Railway Telegraph Company a weekend cablegram service between soldiers, sailors and nurses in Great Britain and their relatives for 5 cents a word.

One or two short clips of moving-film depicted the Canadians on the Plain, and photographs and drawings, sometimes over-dramatized, appeared in magazines such as *The Graphic* and *War Illustrated* and in newspapers. The *Manchester Guardian* on 4 January 1916 rather naughtily printed two photographs of the Canadians struggling in floodwater as if they had been taken recently, rather than a year before.

The 2nd Battalion produced its own magazine, the *Bulletin*, the second issue being a Christmas number. Containing illustrations of camp life, it was edited by Signaller Charles Crean of C Company and was published by the printers of the *Salisbury Times*. Another publication was the *Strathconian*, printed by C. H. Woodward of Devizes. The title page of the first issue had a colour illustration of the Lord Strathcona's Horse 'ribbon', a long poem entitled 'The Call' and an account of the voyage across the Atlantic on the SS *Bermudian*.

Harrods of London provided the catering for most of the officers' messes at 5s 6d a head a day, of which the individual paid 1s, the Canadian Government the rest. The company had been told to allow for 800 officers, when in fact there turned out to be some 1,500. On 20 October the 14th Battalion officers' mess met with a Harrods representative and as early as that concluded that the arrangements did not seem likely to be satisfactory. In the event the company had problems with transport, weather and staff unwilling to remain in camp, and reckoned to have lost several thousand pounds on the contract. On 23 June 1915 its managing director wrote to the British Government about £6,857 owing from its dealings with the Contingent. The response is not known, but on 23 May 1916 the company had a meeting with a Major Alexander concerning a messing account of £834 11s 0d and 'Officers Drinks, Smokes etc' to the value of £1,513 3s 1d. Harrods agreed to accept £500 in settlement of the messing account, provided the difference be added to the amount of the outstanding balance of the money not paid by officers, which would be referred to the Canadian Government

Other ranks endured a monotonous diet of food prepared in very difficult conditions. Each man was allocated a pound of bread, a pound of vegetables and a pound of fresh meat or bacon, with extra rations for those helping to build the huts. He was also given 4d a day to buy food over and above the military ration. This would buy 'a thick and meaty sandwich, a cup of strong hot coffee, and a hunk of raisin dabbled bread'. Brussels sprouts featured frequently, perhaps an unfortunate choice given that the men were sleeping in very confined quarters. Two or three times a week, Miss Nellie Crees of Etchilhampton Manor, two miles from Devizes, and Miss Florence Meek of Bayswater, London, motored to the camps to sell fruit, cakes and sundries to the men. By 12 November they had raised £40, which they gave to the Prince of Wales's National Relief Fund.

Perhaps these two ladies are Miss Nellie Crees of Etchilhampton Manor near Devizes and Miss Florence Meek of London who sold fruit to the men. The car was registered to a Devizes trader.

On 26 January Sir Hiram Maxim, inventor of the eponymous machine-gun, visited the Plain to present the Canadians with six and a half tons of pork and beans in 10,200 cans. He had intended to make the gift before Christmas, when it was reported to have consisted of 25,000 tins with the contents prepared in a new way to make them 'more appetizing and delectable', but he had had to postpone his visit, perhaps because the cans had been lost for three months.

Whatever the response to evangelism may have been and however welcome the YMCA facilities were, many of the soldiers were eager for female company. On 22 December *The Times* reported on the war's effect on Salisbury. In July, it noted, the city had been:

> a cathedral town with a theological college, excellent fishing, two markets a week, old curiosity shops, old-fashioned comfortable hotels, and a quiet, steady retail trade.... The metropolis of 100,000 soldiers, the distribution centre of vast daily supplies of food and stores, the recreation ground of troop upon troop of high-spirited young men, the temporary home of thousands of imported workmen – that is what Salisbury has become.

The Canadians, remarked *The Times*, were:

> eager to motor over miles of ruined roads for a little change and select female society .... The hotels overflow with officers on leave, especially Canadian officers and their wives.

The latter's presence proved a distraction, with their husbands often visiting them in their lodgings miles from camp and having to be rounded up by orderlies if an exercise was called at short notice. Among the wives noted by Agar Adamson of the Pats were those of his senior officers, Mrs John McKinery ('full of South African money obtained from mines and feathers, but with a very limited range of conversation'), Marguerite Gault ('very nice generally, sings a bit, is very much in love with her husband, wears a new dress every night for dinner') and Lady Evelyn Farquhar ('a bit of a dragon, full of ability, upper gum and seasickness').

Just before Christmas, according to the *Daily Dispatch*, there was resentment among some Contingent officers at the 'presence of this supplementary feminine-brigade' in the Salisbury area. Doubtless the officers in question were those without wives though the

Dispatch journalist mentioned one who, after a week, had sent his wife off to her family in Scotland as the Plain was no place for womenfolk.

Early in the war local newspapers published few accounts of cases involving prostitution and brothels. This may have been out of a sense of delicacy, either for the sensitivities of their readers or due to a reluctance to disparage by association Britain's gallant allies. But as early as 24 October Kitchener had felt it necessary to issue a national appeal to the public to help soldiers keep 'thoroughly fit and healthy'; they should not be treated to drinks and the public should 'give them every assistance in resisting temptations which are often placed before them'. Rather more explicit were several correspondents to *The Times*, including one whose letter was published on 30 October:

> May I appeal to the womanhood of those girls and women who are haunting our camps to abandon their evil course, and to help, not hinder, our soldiers in their noble and arduous life of self-sacrifice.

But Wiltshire girls were far from immune to the charms of the Canadians and inevitably liaisons occurred, especially with many young local males having joined up. There were a few weddings, the first being that of Lieutenant Jack Williamson who met Charlotte Suzanne José, a young French girl, in Plymouth and within a week had married her. The 7th Battalion's Victor Baker got to know a Belgian refugee girl at a hostel in London and, despite a serious language difficulty, proposed to her on their second meeting. They married in the presence of Baker's father, who was training with him. After a few days' acquaintance Sergeant Mannering Jones applied for a special licence to marry Miss Thomasson of Brixton, 'a pretty cenematograph [*sic*] actress, whom the war has driven into a doll factory'. On 7 December the 12th Battalion's Captain Harry Caulfeild married Geraldine Marguerite Boyd. Gunner Gilbert Lee of Headquarters, 1st Divisional Artillery, wedded a widow, Mrs Ann Osborne, 'of French extraction' and from Philadelphia, at St John's Church, Devizes on 12 January. When the next day Lieutenant Kenneth Edmiston of the 19th Alberta Dragoons was married at Netheravon to Mary Allen of Ottawa, some of his comrades provided a travelling escort and others formed an arch of swords outside the church.

One Canadian billeted at Lydeway (three miles south east of Devizes) wedded a woman who turned out to already have a husband. There was also a problem at the marriage of a Canadian soldier in Reading in January, when a man in a civilian clothes grabbed the girl and dared the Canadian to marry her. A fight was narrowly averted. It transpired that the civilian had 'walked out' with the girl, but they were not engaged.

The *Salisbury Times* of 1 January asked rhetorically (if ungrammatically): 'How many of the present people, especially female, of Salisbury, will shortly find its way to Quebec or Winnipeg or Toronto?' But there is little evidence of this happening 'shortly'. Indeed, any woman marrying a Canadian would have had a long separation before the war ended and they could make a home together, were she not widowed first.

One Urchfont girl, Emmy Gillett, wedded a Canadian soldier and went back to Canada with him. But then he disappeared, leaving Emmy with a new daughter and frostbite but no money; the Salvation Army helped her and her baby to return home. A history of Market Lavington tells how Sapper James Augustus Williams of the 3rd Tunnelling Company married a local girl, who in February 1916 was expecting his child. He overstayed his leave, resulting in a police constable calling at his wife's house in Church Street on 9 March, eight days after he was due to report to go overseas, leading to his reporting for duty later that day. Village anecdotes such as this often need to be treated with caution, but James Augustus Williams was a Nova Scotian member of the 17th Battalion who in 1914 had been at Pond Farm, not far from Market Lavington. Originally a collier from Glamorgan, his coal-mining skills would have fitted him for a transfer to a tunnelling company.

Some four per cent of the Contingent contracted venereal disease. Given that infection can often be carried in the body for several months before its symptoms appear, one can only speculate where and how the disease was contracted. Perhaps it was on a last fling before embarking from Canada, during a snatched opportunity in Plymouth (whose vice trade was well used to dealing with the needs of sailors), on leave in London or in the relative backwaters of Wiltshire.*

---

* Of 332 Australians with VD transferred from Fovant Camp, west of Salisbury, in the last six months of 1917, 218 reckoned to have contracted the disease in London, 10 locally, 103 elsewhere in the United Kingdom and one didn't know.

The Royal Canadian Dragoons near their billets in the Shrewton area in January 1915.

When the Royal Canadian Dragoons were billeted in the Shrewton area, William Lighthall witnessed the procuring success of his comrade 'Archibald', a British immigrant and bigamist who deprived his colleagues of any spare cash in the crown-and-anchor (dice game) sessions that he ran. Lighthall:

> noticed a furtive gathering around the kitchen door [of a house near Shrewton church] …. we looked through the kitchen window and there saw the reason for the crowd. Stretched out on the kitchen table, stripped bare as the day of her birth, lay a daughter of joy serving the line of eager applicants who had paid a fee to Archibald at the door. And above – the church organ played a moving hymn to lead the devout to their weekly prayer meeting.

A few weeks later, a constant stream of invalids attended sick call and deeply regretted their participation in Archibald's lates[t] financial venture.

Archibald, like many of the Canadians, had become lousy and, after sleeping with the vicar's daughter, passed on his lice to her and her family, claimed Lighthall, who added (and one does wonder about much of this tale):

> He also passed on something far harder to get rid of and the unfortunate damsel soon found she was pregnant – made so by a man who had one wife in Canada and another in England.

Of course Archibald himself was soon to leave Wiltshire and his newly acquired responsibilities, if indeed he was the type to recognize these.

Another Canadian, named by Lighthall as Reggie Tyner (possibly Henry R. Tyner of the Dragoons' B Squadron), proved popular with Shrewton's young ladies and one evening received a perfumed note suggesting a rendezvous at Fern Cottage. He arrived expectantly, only to find *four* girls, each having had a *billet doux* full of protestations of affection and suggesting that she meet Reggie there. Watching on from cover were his comrades, who had written the notes and who were delighted when the four ganged up on him and nearly tore off his clothes.

Archibald was not the only person to exploit the sexual needs of the Canadians. On 2 November Charles Thurlow, an engine driver of 27 Sheep Street, Devizes, appeared in court charged with living wholly or in part on the immoral earnings of his wife, Minnie. She was known to be a prostitute and soldiers had been seen visiting the house in the evening and at night. Henry Trout, the appropriately named owner of a fried-fish shop at 115 Sheep Street, testified that he had enquiries for Number 27, mostly from Canadians. Thurlow claimed that he had been offering the men merely refreshment but he was sent to prison for two months. Superintendent Brooks stated that this was 'a case of a class that fortunately very rarely comes before a Bench of magistrates in this county [of Wiltshire]'.

Perhaps this was so, though barracks such as Bulford and Tidworth would have provided a market for prostitution and there must have been houses similar to Thurlow's in nearby towns, though there were few related court cases reported in the pre-war local press.

On the same day that the *Wiltshire Advertiser* was wishing the Canadians well as they left the Plain, it was recounting a 'terrible story of immorality, which is, of course, not suitable for reproduction in these columns', though again there were reassurances that such cases were very rare in the district. A young widow, Mary Ann Watts, of Church Lane, Urchfont, was charged with keeping a disorderly house there with her sister, Nellie Stokes, aged 20, who was similarly charged. The police had been observing the house since 25 October (shortly after the Canadians had arrived at Pond Farm Camp, three miles away). A soldier had been seen wearing women's clothes, in the company of Nellie Stokes in a soldier's uniform. Lieutenant Frederick Green, of the 2nd Field Artillery Brigade, billeted in the village, said that he had arrested a man there on 19 January and that NCOs had complained about the house. Watts was sent to prison for three months, Stokes for one, both with hard labour. A further consequence for Watts was the suspension of payments of 11s a week that she had been receiving from a Workmen's Compensation Award following the death of her husband. The pair must have thought it very fortunate when so many potential customers moved into the locality but, with the village having a population of fewer than 800, surely must have realized that what they were up to would quickly become common knowledge.

At the same time, Private George Henry Phillips of the 17th Battalion was arrested at Wilton, having run away with a young girl whose parents then applied for a warrant. The Salisbury court remanded him in custody to await a military escort.

Many other liaisons did not require being arranged by a pimp or madam. As is remarked in *The Gentlemen of the Party*, A. G. Street's factual wartime novel of the Fovant area (west of Salisbury and which from 1915 had three military camps), 'girls were at a premium, and many of them loved too well, only to find when trouble came that their lovers were overseas'. One of the book's characters remarks (in Wiltshire brogue) that:

half the [village] 'oomen to-day be hoors .... there's one thing what 'ave got cheaper. An' that's 'oomen. They do vling it at 'ee, wi out waitin' to be askcd. Dirty bitches.

Street, a local farmer, himself wrote that:

the newspapers might print articles telling how splendid the girls were, and in many cases these articles might be justified. But in any camp district during that hectic period of history, 1914 to 1918, the older men and women knew that the girls, both native-borne and war-imported, were anything but splendid.

For many of the soldiers who enjoyed the attentions and favours of local women, whether given commercially or freely, the experiences would have been the last (perhaps even the first) of that type before death and mutilation on the battlefield.

Chapter Ten

Leaving for France

Rumour has always been a part of military life and this was certainly the case among the Canadians. One myth was that things were going so well in France that the War Office dare not publish the details for fear of deterring recruiting. There were the Angels of Mons which were said to have appeared in the sky to hearten British troops in Belgium. Russian troops with snow on their boots had been seen coming south from Scotland. Japanese, Indian and Australian soldiers had crossed Canada on their way to Europe. The Australians were going to join or replace the Canadians. Somewhere on Salisbury Plain the war was being run by Allied generals in a deserted farmhouse or deep-dug cellar.

In fact Japanese officers were to visit Wiltshire to witness how Britain trained its army, Indian troops would be based in the adjoining county of Hampshire and from 1916 many of the Salisbury Plain camps would house Australians. Though when Colonel Henry Chauval of Australia had visited the Plain in October 1914, he had found nothing had been done to build huts for troops on their way from Australia and New Zealand who were due to replace the Canadians. An army doctor reported that to 'house Australian troops in tents in mid-winter on this windswept area after [a] long voyage in troopships passing through tropics and sub-tropics would be criminal'. Representations to Lord Kitchener led to the troops heading for Wiltshire being diverted to Egypt and then to Gallipoli. As for the 'deep-dug cellar', in the 1960s and 1970s there would be speculation that under Salisbury Plain there was a secret underground bunker that would become the Government's headquarters in the event of a nuclear war. It actually was in Wiltshire but near Corsham, 15 miles to the north west of the Plain.

The recurring topic was when the Contingent would be sent overseas, exactly where, and in what form – as an entity or divided up. On 22 November the 14th Battalion drew 310,000 rounds of ammunition, and bayonets were ordered to be sharpened, causing the men to think that a move to France was imminent. In fact the ammunition was for the rifle practice to which the British Army attached so much importance, and the bayonets should have been sharpened on board ship on the voyage from Canada but there had been a lack of emery stones.

Some amateur strategists among the Canadians suggested that the Middle East was another option. Lieutenant Ian Sinclair of the 13th Battalion heard a rumour 'that we were going to be sent to the far east somewhere. Headquarters sent down a supply of summer uniforms'. There would be several instances later in the war of British troops in Wiltshire being issued with tropical kit, only to have their orders changed and being sent to mainland Europe. Lieutenant Colonel Adam Shillington wrote to a friend in Ottawa that the War Office was considering sending the Canadians to Egypt, a story that appeared in the *Toronto Star* of 18 November, There had been one or two semi-official suggestions, one from Hughes' representative, Colonel Carson, about such a move. 'All ranks our contingent anxious to get there,' he wired Hughes on 7 December. People in Canada receiving letters from Contingent members would pass on such speculation to newspapers, their apparent incaution being offset by there being so many conflicting stories that they would have been of no use to the enemy. Covering several options, Private Hugh Brewer of the 14th Battalion wrote:

> There are four or five rumours as to our destination. One says Ostend, another Egypt, and another that we are moving to huts at a nearby camp, and still another that a detachment of 500 or 1,000 is going into barracks at Bristol.

The *Toronto Star* of 31 December announced that the Contingent was 'busy completing final preparations' and that leave would end on 7 January. But on the 5th it quoted a letter from 'an officer with the troops' claiming that the Contingent's artillerymen and cavalry had been sent to the South of France to complete their training!

On 7 January Carson reported to the Canadian Prime Minister, Sir Robert Borden, that he had been asked by the British Government whether Canada would agree to having selected battalions or brigades sent to the front. The intention seems to have been to place them temporarily with British units to get them familiarized with trench warfare. But Hughes opposed the notion, insisting, as he had always done, that the Canadians should go into action as a division.

But one thing was certain: the Canadians would be moving soon. General Alderson told the 15th Battalion's sergeants' mess on 9 January that he expected to be eating dinner in France in three weeks, a statement that was published in the *Toronto Star* on the 18th. Next day, a *Star* headline proclaimed 'CANADIANS BEGIN TO SET OUT FOR FRANCE' but cautioned that it must not be taken for granted that they were leaving for the firing-line:

> There are good grounds for believing that the movement is in part due to the desire to get the men from the present wet surroundings, and it is suggested that a large part of the contingent will simply be transferred out of England and undergo a further period of training.

Perhaps to improve security or to minimize distractions, tradesmen were banned from the camp lines from 10 January onwards, as were visitors except on prescribed days. Then all men helping construct the camps were ordered back to their units, except for the 250-strong working parties from each battalion of the 4th Infantry Brigade, which was not going overseas.

On 17 January Earl Grey inspected troops at Devizes. At the following service at St John's Church in the town, he revealed that the men 'would undoubtedly be sent to the Front in a very short time'.

The Contingent officially became the First Canadian Division on 26 January, though the 1st Infantry Brigade's diary for 27 November had already referred to the '1st Division Canadian Contingent'.

The *Wiltshire Telegraph* of 30 January noted:

> In these days of rigid press censorship we must not state here the date... of departure ... It can be said with impunity, however, that the day ... is

at hand, and that it is doubtful whether they will be with us when the next issue of the *Telegraph* goes to press.

However on 6 February the Division was still on the Plain: 'nothing definite is known, probably not to the officers themselves,' conceded the *Telegraph* inaccurately. But on 3 February the *Red Deer News* of Alberta had printed a report dated 30 January announcing that the departure for France would begin 'the next Tuesday'!

On 31 January Honorary Captain Hugh McCullough, the paymaster for No. 1 General Hospital, was robbed of $1,500. Other reports made the theft to comprise £34, important documents and IOUs, which appear to have been kept in his room at Bulford Manor. The items were never recovered, any investigation presumably being rushed as everyone prepared to depart. One guesses that it was this loss that led to McCullough being replaced on 4 February.

On 1 February the Agricultural Education Committee of Wiltshire County Council sent its travelling farrier school to Devizes to hold a class for 25 people, nearly all Canadians, taken by F. Bazley, a Devizes member of the Royal College of Veterinary Surgeons.

That day the motor-ambulance wagons and workshops and sanitary section were ordered to move at midnight to embark at Avonmouth at noon the next day. Also on the 1st, the 3rd Battalion's stretcher-bearers had to be segregated because one of them had contracted meningitis. An outbreak of measles within the 16th's ranks on 10 February was to raise fears that they could not leave for active service; fortunately only two huts were affected and just 40 men were left behind. On 2 February various advance and billeting parties left for France.

The King inspected the Canadians again on 4 February. By now a military railway had been laid from the Amesbury-Bulford line through Lark Hill and two miles beyond to Rollestone Camp. The royal train, consisting of a locomotive, a wagon and coach, followed by a second locomotive lest the other break down, steamed to a temporary station close to Bustard Inn, near where the Division was drawn up on Knighton Down. Compared with their first Royal inspection back in November, the men looked less like a newly formed civilian militia lacking some of their kit and marching somewhat raggedly but more like a well-trained army.

On 4 February 1915 the royal train conveys George V past cheering Canadians lining the new Lark Hill Military Railway.

Canadian cavalry assemble for the Royal review of February 1915.

Harold Baldwin described the occasion:

> Morning broke with the usual drizzle of rain, which happily stopped later on, giving us instead a very fine day. We filed out to the parade ground, a distance of about two miles. The Highlanders had arrived before us and a splendid sight they made. Standing at ease on the slope of a gently rising hill, their khaki aprons having been discarded for the occasion, they made a wonderful splash of colour on the dull landscape. Tall, lithe fellows for the most part, they looked the *beau idéal* of the British soldier. There seemed to be an air of dashing gallantry about them that was irresistible. Making the air hideous with their terrific skirling, the pipes droned and squealed their defiance of everything non-Scotch. The pipes were decorated with long coloured streamers of the same pattern as the kilts and plaids of their owners. The pipers themselves were men of unusually fine physique, and surely Scotland and Canada would have felt proud to have seen the brave sight.

> In spite of our dislike for the pipes there was an indescribable lilt to the music that seemed to get into our feet, and shoulders were thrown back and two thousand feet swung as one. In this fashion we arrived on the ground allotted to us for the parade. After the usual movement for placing troops in review order we stood in ranks in platoon formation, two by two, one behind the other.

Having been assembled with plenty of time to spare, Baldwin and his comrades were able to take in their surroundings, with line after line of infantry, a massed band contributing to a feeling of elation, and a huge Union Jack flying over the reviewing platform. To his rear, reminding him of 'the wrath to come', stood stretcher-bearers.

> At last the puffing of a train was heard and we knew that our royal visitors had arrived. The King, Lord Kitchener, and other prominent soldiers and statesmen stepped off the train. The band crashed out the first bars of the national anthem, a quick command to us, 'Present arms', a movement, and all was still except for the rolling of the anthem across the plain, and then silence once more.

> The King shook hands with the officers and the inspection began. This was the second time I had seen his majesty, but in spite of the fact that I am a loyal Britisher, I was much more interested in the martial figure by his side; this was the man who at that time held the defence of Britain's military forces in the hollow of his hand. I had read that Lord Kitchener was an inscrutable man, never known to smile; it was a fiction; he smiled genially at us all. But those keen, dark eyes did not miss one single detail of the men in front of him. My sensation as he passed in front of me was that he was looking straight through me into the man at my rear. No word of approval or otherwise did the renowned soldier utter, but I think he was pleased by the stalwart physique and the soldierly bearing of the boys.

The Royal party then took its place on the saluting platform and the march past began, led by the artillery thundering down the slope to slow gradually to a walk past the platform.

> Next the cavalry, the men with their swords at the carry, trotted by. A gallant sight they made with their Stetson hats [worn by the Alberta cavalry units] and long yellow cloaks [of Lord Strathcona's Horse]. The coats of horses perfectly groomed shone in the sun like satin and made a picture that was never surpassed by anything of the kind in the days when 'Knighthood was in Flower.'

> Then came the first battalion of infantry and before I could notice more we, ourselves, had started to march past. The band struck up a martial air and four thousand feet, keeping perfect time, made the ground echo with their tread. My own battalion swung past the royal party with a lilt in its step that thrilled one through and through, and at the order 'Eyes right' every head turned like clockwork.

The King left this message for the Division:

> Officers, non-commissioned officers and men: at the beginning of November I had the pleasure of welcoming to the Mother Country this fine contingent from the Dominion of Canada, and now, after three months' training, I bid you God's speed on your way to assist my army in the field.

> I am well aware of the discomforts that you have experienced from the inclement weather and abnormal rain, and I admire the cheerful spirit displayed by all ranks in facing and overcoming all difficulties. From all I have heard, and from

H.M. The King at the Saluting Base, Salisbury Plain

George V's second visit to the Canadians was shortly before they left for active service.

what I have been able to see at today's inspection and march past, I am satisfied that you have made good use of your time spent on Salisbury Plain. By your willing and prompt rally to our common flag, you have already earned the gratitude of the Motherland.

By your deeds and achievements on the field of battle, I am confident that you will emulate the example of your fellow countrymen in the South African war, and thus help to secure the triumph of our arms. I shall follow with pride and interest all your movements and I pray that God may bless you and watch over you.

The artillery in Devizes had had the choice of marching ten miles through the dark to take part in the review or camping overnight nearby. It opted for the latter and arrived on the parade ground at 9.30am, half an hour after men of No. 2 and No. 3 Field Ambulance, who had risen early and marched 11 and 8 miles respectively. The Royal Canadian Horse

Artillery left Erlestoke at 6.30am and after a 13-mile journey was in position by 10.15.

On 3 February, days before the departure for France, holes were being drilled in the bottom of the Ross rifle magazines in an attempt to prevent jamming, this being the latest in a series of modifications. Two days later the War Office rejected Alderson's request that the Ross rifles used by his artillery and cavalry be exchanged for Lee Enfields. At the Battle of Ypres in April many Canadians were to throw away the former and pick up the latter from British casualties. Despite vociferous criticism of the Ross by those who had to use it in battle, Hughes staunchly defended it, insisting that the problems were minor and often the result of improper use.

With departure now certain, personal kit was carefully checked and weighed. That of officers was strictly limited to 35 pounds, but some bedecked themselves with automatic pistols, binoculars, water-bottles, periscopes, wire-cutters, torches, haversacks, amputating knives, can-openers, corkscrews, oyster knives, range-finders, cameras, compasses, flasks, marling spikes and other trinkets. Progressively they had to discard items until they satisfied the officer in charge of the scales, the discarded items being placed in a Surplus Baggage Depot.

A man's kit comprised trousers, drawers, an undershirt, a shirt, two towels, one balaclava, three pairs of socks, a pair of boots, a 'house-wife' (or sewing kit), a greatcoat and a hold-all containing soap, razor and so on. Strapped to each man was a blanket, rubber sheet, mess tin and haversack containing a day's ration. A rifle and 150 rounds of ammunition brought the weight to almost 80 pounds.

Because of War Office reluctance, the YMCA secretaries were not at first to accompany the Division to France, but Canadian commanding officers agreed that they should go, resulting in four of the honorary officers travelling with them, a fifth being too ill to do so.

After weeding out its unfit members, the 14th Battalion found itself 100 men short and received a draft from the 17th to make good the deficiency. They turned out to be in little better state than those who were to be left behind, and their paperwork and clothing were also in very bad shape.

At last, after weeks of speculation and rumour, the Canadians finally moved. The *Salisbury Times* of 5 February noted that:

> parties of Canadians have left Amesbury and other places, and others have arrived to take their place. Large numbers of horses have been arriving by rail, for service with the Canadians on the Plain.

The arrivals were reinforcements from home, 131 officers and 4,061 men having sailed from Canada in January to join the Division.

In its issue of the 5th, the Devizes-based *Wiltshire Advertiser* wrote:

> The Canadians are going, and the whole town will regret their departure, for they have ingratiated themselves into all hearts by their good-nature, light-heartedness and kindliness. Much activity was noticed early in the week among the troops, and though the date of their departure and ultimate destination is, of course,

unknown to us, their visit is apparently drawing to a close…

> Though among a large body of men there are sure to be a few delinquents, these have been small in number, the majority of the men behaved themselves, and the Brigade as a whole showing a remarkably clean sheet…

> The first Canadian Volunteers have impressed us with particular pleasure.

In its next issue, published on the 11th, the *Advertiser* noted that the 'Canadians had moved into another district' and expressed the hope that other Canadians would replace them.

The first unit departed by train for Avonmouth on 7 February, a typically wet day. This port was not the first choice but, as with the Contingent's arrival, there were fears of submarine attacks on the routes out of Southampton. The stations used were the same as in October, with the addition of Bulford, conveniently placed for those troops at Sling Camp. Over four days 90 special trains left the Plain's stations. On the 9th at modest Patney & Chirton, 11 departed between 5.55am and 1.55pm, all a few minutes ahead of schedule. Generally the departure from the Plain and the embarkation to France appear to have been well organized, though the 15th Battalion's train was 30 minutes late arriving at Amesbury.

Compared with the excitement that greeted the Canadians' arrival, their departure passed unmarked in the national press, it having been realized that publicizing major troop movements was useful to the enemy. Not even was the King's visit of 4 February mentioned in the Court Circular published in *The Times* and it was not until 18 February, after the Division had arrived in France, that the *Toronto Star* was able to publish its account of the review. Harold Peat recalled marching 'in the utmost secrecy' to the station, where the trains had their blinds drawn.

After the Division had arrived in France, the Topical Press Agency of Fleet Street, London, did issue photographs showing the 2nd Battalion marching through a village, purportedly as it left for active service. But the 2nd had proceeded in the dark from Bustard Camp to Amesbury Station in two parts at 9 and 11pm, and would not have needed to pass through a town or village. In fact the photographs show the battalion marching north through Shrewton, probably returning to camp after one of the several route

The 2nd Battalion marches through Shrewton shortly before leaving the Plain.

marches they made in the last half of January.

As units marched from Lark Hill, they saw vulture-like flocks of civilians waiting to cart whatever they could find from the vacated hutments. There would have been much surplus kit and many comforts that could not be taken on active service. Later in the day, a Canadian fatigue party from Tidworth moved about collecting and burning rubbish and sorting out articles to be returned to the stores, including rolls of blankets, oil stoves and rubber boots. Also left behind were pianos, a Ford car, gramophones and rifles.

Louis Keene walked through the lines of other battalions which had left, and:

saw fold-up bedsteads, uniforms, equipment, books, buckets, washing-bowls, cartridges and stoves of every conceivable kind and shape: hundreds, from the single 'Beatrice' [used for heating a small room and cooking] to the big tiled

heaters. Some tents were half full of blankets thrown in, others with harness. All the government stuff is collected, but private stuff is burnt.

At New Copse Farm, now empty of soldiers, a civilian, George Baker, helped himself to 33 bags, each containing 80 pounds of oats, and other military property. He claimed he had been told to clear up the place by an officer and, with no previous record, was not convicted but had to pay 16s in costs. A police superintendent told the court that a large number of empty oat bags worth 1s each had been taken and asked that these be returned to police stations. In late March, Edward Hale of Coulston (where the Royal Canadian Horse Artillery had been billeted) was charged with stealing two abandoned Canadian bicycles, but the case was dismissed.

Some units were left behind. The Automobile Machine Gun Brigade (the usefulness of whose armoured cars Kitchener had doubted) moved to Wilton, near

Salisbury, on 12 February and then on 17 March to Ashford in Kent, where it assumed a home defence role. In early November their vehicles' design, only two months before thought to be 'of the most modern type', had proved flawed, when the similar open-roofed armoured cars of other makes in France had proved vulnerable to fire from above. The brigade was re-united with the First Division in France in mid-June 1915, when it was re-designated the 1st Canadian Motor Machine Gun Brigade.

At least its vehicles had been useful on the Plain, in contrast to the Contingent's sole aircraft. After its departure from Canada the Burgess-Dunne never flew again. It lay on the docks at Plymouth until it was taken to the Central Flying School at Upavon on the northern edge of Salisbury Plain, where it was broken up for scrap. Nevertheless the Burgess-Dunne is regarded as Canada's first military aeroplane and as such is commemorated on a 46-cent postage stamp issued in September 1999 to mark the 75th anniversary of the Canadian Air Force.

A curious four-line 'news brief ' had appeared in the *Toronto Star* of 1 December 1914:

Canadian aviator corps organised at Salisbury Plain. Commanded by Capt. Jauney [sic] of Galt, Ont. Nearly 600 applicants for posts in corps.

The only foundation for this story was Captain Janney's grand plan for a Canadian Aviation Corps of eight aircraft, five horses, ten trucks and 46 men. With an advance of money from the paymaster, Janney disappeared, apparently to look for a suitable site for a Corps aerodrome. Having heard nothing of him for some weeks, Alderson struck the Corps from his establishment. The *Toronto Star* cryptically remarked on 11 January that:

Unless the aviation men with the contingent make much more progress with their branch than they have done hitherto, they will be of little use to the troops. Whatever the cause of the inaction the aviators seem to have had no opportunity to attain efficiency.

One imagines that the absence of any aircraft was a major cause of the inaction! Whatever the case, Militia Headquarters instructed the First Contingent 'to sever Lieutenant [sic] Janney's connection with the CEF' and on 23 January 1915 he sailed for Canada, later to become a sub-lieutenant in the Royal Canadian Navy Volunteer Reserve. Lieutenant Sharpe, his colleague in

persuading Hughes that an aeroplane be purchased, went on to train first as an observer with the Royal Flying Corps, then as a pilot. He became the first Canadian service aviation casualty when he was killed in a flying accident on 4 February 1915. A third member of the Canadian Aviation Corps, mechanic Sergeant Harry Farr, was discharged from the CEF in May 1915 'in consequence of Flying Corps being disbanded' He joined the Royal Naval Air Service, winning the Distinguished Service Cross and Distinguished Flying Cross.

The Canadian Army Hydrological Corps at Bustard Camp became No. 5 Canadian Mobile Laboratory, moving to France on 21 March to investigate and control disease. No. 3 Depot Battery remained briefly in the Devizes, Market Lavington and Beechingstoke area. A medical supplies base depot was maintained at Southampton. For a short time No. 1 Advanced Depot Medical Stores remained at Amesbury Vicarage, having transferred there from West Down on 17 December. The unit moved again on 27 April to Shorncliffe. The medical base depot may have tarried at Southampton for longer, perhaps even for the war's duration, given that port's convenience for ships from Canada. No. 1 and No. 2 Veterinary Corps also stayed behind at Netheravon for a short time, and the Remount Depot must have felt it isolated in the all-but-empty camp at West Down South before it moved to Netheravon.

Also remaining behind on the Plain was No. 1 General Hospital, which remained in charge of the Division's sick at Bulford and Lavington Manor. It finally left Wiltshire on 13 May, its members going to Shorncliffe or to the Continent on active service; 118 of its VD patients were transferred to the military hospital at Shorncliffe. On the 11th the last staff to leave placed wreaths on the graves of their colleagues before departing from Southampton two days later. 'Clear and goodbye to SALISBURY rain,' noted its war diary.

No. 2 General Hospital also remained in Wiltshire to bring its complement up to strength. In late February Lieutenant Colonel Bridges visited three London stores to obtain quotations for stores (the nature of which is not specified in the unit diary), accepting the tender of £5,146 7s 8d from Harrods, delivery to be in seven days. The unit left for France on 13 March.

The 9th, 11th, 12th, and 17th Battalions stayed in England as reserve battalions to form an Infantry Training Depot at Tidworth, providing replacements for casualties. In early February these battalions had

ROLLESTONE 1914

The Royal Canadian Horse Artillery at Rollestone Camp.

supplied 1,077 men to bring up to strength those units about to leave on active service.

The 17th had had an unsettled life. At Valcartier it had lost some of its men to other battalions and despite receiving new drafts had sailed a quarter under strength. It was for this reason that it was never one of the four infantry brigades. With a strong Nova Scotian identity, it had been as opposed as the Newfoundlanders to a merger that would have resulted in a full battalion. Now it was to lose other detachments to other units. Lieutenant Colonel Struan Robertson, its commanding officer, was deeply opposed to it being broken up. His unhappiness had started in Valcartier, when he complained that his men were being mistreated and there had been no transport available for last-minute drafts that would have brought the battalion up to strength. Asked to resign, he refused, leading to his replacement by his second-in-command, Major Daniel Cameron, who held the same opinion as Robertson and even had a sign on his tent saying 'Politically Unfit', acknowledging his discord with authority.

The formation of the Canadian Cavalry Brigade was announced on 31 January 1915 under the command of a British officer, Jack Seely (with the temporary rank of brigadier general). His appointment in preference to a Canadian caused some annoyance, inevitably and particularly to Hughes The new brigade comprised the Royal Canadian Horse Artillery, Royal Canadian Dragoons, Lord Strathcona's Horse and 2nd King Edward's Horse. This last unit had been recently created in England and, like the original regiment, included many soldiers from various parts of the Empire. The Dragoons stayed on in billets in the Shrewton area until 1 March, as did the Horse Artillery at Tinhead, Edington and Bratton. The brigade then concentrated at Maresfield Park, Sussex early in the month. On 2 March, Lord Strathcona's Horse left Pewsey in six special trains 'to the great regret of the inhabitants generally, for they had been held in very high esteem'. The Brigade reinforced the First Canadian Division after the second Battle of Ypres.

The First Canadian Division's order of battle dated 10 February listed 623 officers, 18,013 men and 4,968 horses. As has been noted, as well as several smaller units, the original expeditionary force had already lost the Princess Pats, on 16 November and the Newfoundlanders on 7 December. Between 18 October and 15 February 131 officers and 1,013 men had been struck off the Contingent's strength, some because their 'services were no longer required', usually an euphemism denoting un-suitability or worse. Reasons for the officers' being removed comprised:

services no longer required	13
at own request	1
permitted to resign	21
medically unfit	1
returned to Canada	59
appointed to British forces	31
died	5

Reasons for 'other ranks' being struck off strength comprised:

unlikely to become efficient soldiers or unfitted for their duties	93
undesirable or because of misconduct	153
physically unfit	161
services no longer required (including 46 enemy aliens)*	53
commissioned into other forces	242
deserters	94
invalided to Canada	126
died	63
special cases	25
reasons unknown	3

One may conjecture about the deserters. Some British immigrants, perhaps disillusioned with Canada, saw enlistment as giving them a free ticket home. Others, realizing that the war was not going to be over quickly and that it had turned into a very nasty affair, did not fancy active service. Perhaps a few preferred to serve with British units and had enlisted with them. Just before the Canadians' departure, John Thompson of the 4th Battalion was charged with desertion after a policeman saw him wearing a plain jacket with khaki trousers and arrested him. He had been absent without leave for 15 days and was remanded in custody to await a military escort.

Little has been recorded of the weeding-out of unsuitable officers, though on 9 December Howard Curtis of the 9th Battalion wrote to his mother: 'We are getting some new officers in our battalion, including a colonel and paymaster. I hear there has been some swindling going on'. Though the war diaries of many of the Contingent's units have survived, that for the 9th for this period has not; it may have shed a little light on this. Duguid's *Official History* refers to one infantry commander being replaced though illness. Lieutenant Colonel Frank Osborne and three lieutenants of the 9th did receive 'special permission' to return to Canada, but whether there was some ulterior reason behind this is not known. It may well have been that their departures were innocuous enough but were attended by unfounded rumour and speculation.

The war diary of the Divisional Supply Train makes a rare reference to an officer being punished. He was Lieutenant Geoffrey Lafferty who appeared before General Alderson on 11 November, having twice been charged with drunkenness. He was ordered home to Canada. And the Signal Company's diary for 4 January notes that a Captain Fox had been absent for four days from his post at Bustard Camp, where perhaps he was responsible for maintaining communications between the headquarters there and other parts of the Contingent. Frederick George Fox did not attest until 15 January, a fortnight after he became absent. He was a 32-year-old architect from Norwich, England with two years' service with South Africa's Kaffrarian Rifles, who had been appointed a captain, initially as a supernumerary. Perhaps on his belated return to duty after his Christmas absence it was realized that he had not yet formally enlisted as a soldier and thus was not subject to military discipline.

The Canadians had brought with them to England, or acquired whilst in the country, a number of animal mascots. One may wonder why some were adopted in the first place, given that they would have been out of place on active service. There was the Nova Scotians' bloodhound, Duneau Harrogate, presented by Miss Brogden of Carmarthen. After arriving at Plymouth the Newfoundlanders were given a black cat with a pink, white and green ribbon around its neck, the colours being those of an unofficial flag adopted by the earlier inhabitants of Newfoundland. An Alberta cavalry unit

---

* This statistic contradicts those given in newspaper reports quoted in Chapter Three. The list is a simplified version of that given in appendix 119 to Duguid's *Official History.*

had a husky (or 'Eskimo dog'), and Mac, a large dog of uncertain breed, was the mascot of the 'Canadian Highlanders'. Possibly this was the 15th Battalion, but the 13th and 16th Battalions also included Highland Militia units. Certainly the 15th had a dog mascot called Bruno. The Princess Pats boasted a massive 17-hands mule dubbed 'Kaiser'. The 5th Battalion's mascot was a goat, Sergeant Billy, who was taken to France and was wounded at Ypres. He received several medals, was disciplined for charging an officer, saved another from a shell by butting him, went missing, was gassed at the second Battle of Ypres, and suffered wounds and shell-shock. After the war he lived in Regina until his death, after which he was stuffed and displayed at the Saskatchewan Legislative Building.

Left behind in Britain in the care of the Zoological Society were several bears, the most famous being the original Winnie-the-Pooh, later the inspiration of much-loved stories written for children by A. A. Milne. Shortly after the outbreak of the war Lieutenant Harry Colebourn, a veterinary surgeon with the Fort Garry Horse, was travelling by train to Valcartier. Changing trains at White River Bend, he saw a trapper with a female bear cub whose mother had been shot. Colebourn bought the cub for $20, naming her Winnie, after Winnipeg, his home town. When he joined the 2nd Infantry Brigade she became that unit's mascot and went with it to Salisbury Plain. There she was a firm favourite with the soldiers and slept in Colebourn's tent. One account says 'under his bed', which is fanciful given that most soldiers made do with blankets and bed-boards, though low-slung camp beds could be purchased.

Left: Sergeant Billy', the mascot of the 5th Battalion.

Below: The original Winnie-the-Pooh and Lieutenant Harry Colebourn.

The Camp's Mascot

On 9 December 1914 Colebourn passed through London and, mindful that shortly he would be in France and thinking the war would soon be over, left Winnie at London Zoo, where she became a firm favourite with visitors and keepers, being very tame and well behaved. After the war Colebourne returned to reclaim Winnie, but left her there after seeing how well loved she was. In 1924 Milne visited the zoo with his son, Christopher Robin, who became enchanted with Winnie. Two years later Milne, having changed the bear's gender, published the first Winnie-the-Pooh book.

In 1996 Canada Post produced a souvenir sheet of four stamps commemorating Winnie, one showing Colebourn bottle-feeding the original bear cub. A statue of the two stands in Assiniboine Park, Winnipeg.

Many members of the First Contingent went on to distinguished careers but perhaps there is irony in the contrast between the two who are today its two best-known – one among the most popular of children's characters, the other John McCrae, inspiration for the poppy's iconic and poignant imagery.

Chapter Eleven
After the Departure

Five months after the Canadian Contingent had begun to assemble at Valcartier, it moved to the front line in France as the First Canadian Division, just before the first British Territorial divisions. (Individual Territorial battalions had been there for some time.) The Territorials had had the benefit of pre-war training, though in Kitchener's eyes this had been insufficient to make them suitable for immediate deployment on the outbreak of hostilities. The first of his own New Army divisions, formed from recruits at the same time as the Contingent, left for active service early in May 1915. The first Canadian unit to serve in France was No. 2 Stationary Hospital which landed on 8 November, followed on 21 December by the Princess Pats, who entered the front line on the night of 6-7 January 1915. Already part of British regiments fighting both in France and Flanders were individual Canadians, including university students and Royal Military College graduates, who had been in Britain when war broke out.

Between 17 February and 2 March, each of the First Division's infantry brigades was attached for a week to a British division holding the line in front of Armentières to receive 48 hours of individual familiarization and 24 hours of training in platoons. On 28 February the Canadians began to relieve the 7th British Division and on 3 March took over 6,400 yards of line, forming the left wing of Sir Henry Rawlinson's 4th Corps.

For a week the Canadians accustomed themselves to the routine of trench warfare, then on 10 March took part in an attack aimed at capturing the village of Neuve Chapelle. At 7.30am their artillery shelled enemy positions followed by their riflemen and machine-gunners opening fire. After hard hand-to-hand fighting the village was captured, but then the assault stalled until orders for it to continue were implemented at 5.30, as dusk was falling. Overnight the Germans were able to bring up reinforcements and prepare new defences so that by the 12th the British

The 48th Highlanders in trenches at Neuve Chapelle.

and Canadians had to establish a new defensive line on ground that they had gained.

The Canadians' introduction to the front line ended on 27 March when they were relieved and went into reserve, having experienced what was little more than a tactical exercise, albeit one in which they suffered 100 casualties and which confirmed fears about the unreliability of the Ross rifle. Between 14 and 17 April the Division took over from the French 4,500 yards of poorly prepared and waterlogged line near Ypres, scene of one of the earliest battles of the war. On the 22nd, after a preliminary German artillery bombardment, the second Battle of Ypres started in earnest, with the Germans using for the first time chlorine gas, contrary to the Hague Conventions and affecting first the French troops, then the Canadians. (The Germans had fired gas-filled shells on the Eastern front in January, but these were lachrymatory, not lethal.)

When the Allies' line broke, General Sir Horace Smith-Dorrien rushed Canadian units into the gap. They had been issued with cotton pads to be wetted and tied over the face if a gas cloud approached. These were to prove ineffective, and those Canadians still able to fight struggled with their Ross rifles, which were jamming from rapid firing and the mud. But they held the line. A few members of the 15th Battalion's right-hand company who had survived the chlorine fell back, with the Germans breaking through. In the subsequent action Lance Corporal Frederick Fisher used his Colt machine-gun to cover the retreat of a battery. The first Canadian to be awarded the Victoria Cross, he was killed the next day. Sir John French, the Commander-in-Chief of the British Expeditionary Force, was to comment:

> In spite of the danger to which they were exposed the Canadians held their ground with a magnificent display of tenacity and courage; and it is not too much to say that the bearing and conduct of these splendid troops averted a disaster which might have been attended with the most serious consequences.

Then the 10th and 16th Battalions counter-attacked to drive the Germans out of a wood. With no reconnaissance having been done beforehand, the 10th ran into a strong hedge reinforced with wire. The men were forced to break through the obstacle with rifle butts in the face of German machine-gun fire. Both battalions then charged into the wood, throwing the Germans out and reclaiming four captured British guns, but suffering more than 75 per cent casualties. Fierce counter-attacks forced them to retire but only after they had bought time to close the gap in the Allies' line.

The Germans launched another gas attack on 24 April directly at the Canadians who, after withdrawing from their first line of trenches, stood their ground and inflicted heavy losses on advancing infantry. For a week British and Canadians troops fought tenaciously, eventually preventing a German break-through. The 7th Battalion's Machine Gun Officer, Lieutenant Edward Bellew, though wounded and cut off from his unit, kept his last gun firing until he ran out of ammunition. Having destroyed it, he met his opponents with fixed bayonet until overwhelmed and captured. He was awarded the Victoria Cross. VCs were also awarded to Company Sergeant Major Frederick Hall after he was killed when rescuing wounded comrades from no-man's land and to a doctor, Captain Francis Scrimger, who on the 25th saved patients from a farm building that was being shelled.

Eventually Smith-Dorrien ordered a withdrawal to the edge of Ypres. The battle continued for three more weeks, ending with the city being saved. With the First Division being withdrawn on 3 May, the only Canadian battalion involved in the later stages were the Princess Pats, now part of the British 27th Division. On 8 May they came under heavy enemy fire that caused so many casualties that orderlies and batmen were ordered into the support trenches. With a company of the 4th Rifle Brigade, they repelled repeated attacks.

The Canadians' fortitude and discipline early in the battle had saved the situation: Ypres had been held, but at great cost. During its time in the line from 15 April to 3 May, the First Division's killed, wounded and missing numbered 208 officers and 5,828 other ranks. The Pats had 678 casualties in their longer period in action.

The second Battle of Ypres was the worst battle the First Division would fight in the course of the war and gave birth to a formidable reputation. It justified the keeping together of Canadian units as an entity and enabled them to claim their place along the best divisions of their allies. Sir John French wrote to Alderson:

> I wish to express to you and the Canadian troops my admiration of the gallant stand and fight they

The *Montreal Star* of 26 April 1915 proclaims the valour of the First Canadian Division.

have made. They have performed a most brilliant and valuable service. Last night and again this morning I reported their splendid behaviour to the Secretary of State for War and I have a reply from him saying how highly their gallantry and determination in a difficult position are appreciated in England.

The King sent his own message of congratulation:

During the past week I have followed with admiration the splendid achievements of my troops … and the gallant conduct of the Canadian Division in repulsing the enemy and recapturing four heavy guns. I heartily congratulate all units who have taken part in these successful actions.

One Canadian wrote from France:

You will remember – who could every forget – what they used to say about us in England, about our discipline, our this and our that, until one wondered if we had any friends in the country. That reputation preceded us here, I know, but in less than a week all was changed, and on more than one occasion I have heard Staff officers say, 'I wish to God we had a few more like the Canadians'.

Andrew Iarocci in *Shoestring Soldiers – The 1st Canadian Division at War 1914-1915* has sought effectively to refute a traditional perception that the First Division was an amateur and ill-prepared force when it entered combat and has analyzed the training that it received before doing so. He has argued that it throughout its first year of combat it was an effective fighting organization that made a vital contribution to the Allied cause, not that this has been much doubted. The camaraderie between officers and men that was so alien to the British Army stood the Division in good stead on the battlefield, where it showed a high level of discipline. Many officers were determined to make their men efficient. Iarocci points out that the conditions of Salisbury Plain were far from ideal for training but were not dissimilar to service conditions in France and Flanders, and though the training itself was disrupted by weather and fatigues it did not cease. Duguid in his *Official History* observed that 'few of those who served on the Western Front in the next four years were called upon to suffer such prolonged and unavailing misery as was endured on Salisbury Plain'.

The Contingent's period of training on the Plain lasted

two or three weeks longer than the average for a British battalion, but this included the protracted move from Plymouth. Nor did any other unit in training in Britain have to contend with so much illness, spend so much time building its own huts and put up with such bad weather.

The time on the Plain had enabled unsuitable officers and men to be weeded out and equally unsuitable equipment to be replaced. The proportion of unacceptable personnel was relatively small. Looking at the numbers discharged for reasons such as 'services no longer required' or 'undesirable', one may roughly estimate that two per cent of the officers were deemed completely unsuitable, with a somewhat lower proportion of enlisted men. A few discharges were for compassionate reasons, such as that of the 5th Battalion's Frank Bucknan, who was released when his father fell seriously ill in Springsides, Saskatchewan.

Back on Salisbury Plain after the departure of the bulk of the Division, the remaining Canadian units, with the exception of the Cavalry Brigade, were placed under the command of Brigadier General James MacDougall, Alderson's military secretary and a long-serving member of Canada's Permanent Force. At Tidworth the 17th Battalion was comfortable in the former married quarters in Jellalabad Barracks, as was the 9th in Bhurtpore Barracks, and the 11th and 12th in Candahar Barracks. These were not so crowded as the Lark Hill huts and had running water and fireplaces. The immediate countryside was more pleasant, too, and the barracks were very close to Tidworth village, with another village, Ludgershall (served by a railway station) and the market-town of Andover not too far away. One problem appeared to be delays in receiving pay, some men saying that they had not had any for 38 days and that they could not afford to buy even soap. However it was noted that almost every other man was smoking cigars and some were enjoying 'half dollar lunches', while British cavalrymen nearby were making to do with cigarettes and threepenny meals.

Herbert Andrews of the Fort Garry Horse was one of those who stayed on the Plain for a short while after the First Division had left. He had visited Lark Hill on 27 January to find the camp was full of rumours about it leaving for France and that there was a rush to get into the units that were going. Andrews tried to get moved to one of these, but three days later was marched to West Down South to help look after the mules at the Remount Depot. With 25 men to handle 50 mules, this proved not too demanding but, with the

Candahar Barracks in Tidworth, which the Canadians occupied briefly in 1915.

animals standing in mud to their fetlocks he and his colleagues moved again on 9 February, to Bustard Camp. On the 15th a fatigue party went to Lark Hill, to find that the Canadian lines were empty apart from, it would appear, 'No. 1 Butchery'. The Butchery's organization had been approved on 16 January, with 19 NCOs and men selected from the Infantry Training Depot at Tidworth. After what must have been some forlorn weeks at Lark Hill it moved to Tidworth on 14 March, eventually joining the Divisional Supply Column in France in May.

The Remount Depot moved to the Cavalry School at Netheravon where the animals were in stables, a vast improvement on the exposed West Down. Some men there had been officially detached from the Fort Garry Horse and the next day its adjutant appealed to them to return to the unit as, having been dismounted during its time on the Plain, it was to revert to being cavalry and sent to France. But Captain Robert Smith, the Remount Depot's adjutant, was anxious to retain the men and invited them to decide how much of what they had just been told was 'bull'. But as Smith could not actually promise anything, the general feeling among the men was to return to the Fort Garrys.

Next day their unit sent a wagon team for the kits of those who wanted to return. When Smith saw the team's horses being put into a stable he ordered that they should not be let out, but this was soon countermanded by the Depot's commanding officer. But both he and Smith seemed to have agreed that the Fort Garrys' driver could not take out the kits and he had to return without them. Some Fort Garry officers came to Netheravon to remonstrate, but still the Depot would not release the men, several of whom of decided to march away of their own accord, only to find Smith had placed a guard on the road. Eventually everything seems to have been sorted out, and on 3 March the men were fallen in to march to Tidworth, though not before they had been offered clean uniforms and five days' leave in London. Three days later, they entrained for Canterbury to report to the Canadian Cavalry Depot recently established there.

Canadian troops in any great number were not seen on Salisbury Plain for the remainder of the war. There had been fears that the Second Division might find itself there, but on 2 February the Duke of Connaught had expressed anxiety about where it would be accommodated. Then on the 12th Carson had reminded Hughes of the terrible conditions on the Plain and suggested that the Second's departure be held back. Ten days later he was advised by the War Office that the Canadian Training Depot would be transferred from Tidworth to Shorncliffe, 135 miles away, around the 22nd or 23rd. On 17 March he reported that all artillery and infantry except the 11th and 12th battalions had been moved to the Shorncliffe area, where they were joined by the 23rd, 30th and

32nd Battalions of the Second Division fresh from home. Having heard much of the First Contingent's deprivations, the new arrivals were delighted with being accommodated in brick buildings in a seaside resort.

A few soldiers continued to be based on the Plain manning the Canadian Surplus Baggage Depot, which housed personal effects that members of the First Division had been unable to take with them. It is probable that these were men not fit enough for fighting and they had the sad duty of returning dead comrades' personal effects to next-of-kin. On at least four occasions they provided detachments for funerals in Salisbury, including a firing-party in October 1916 for that of the 4th Battalion's Private Arthur Chambers, who came from Salisbury and who had died in Chatham from pneumonia after being wounded. In June that year a detachment attended the funeral of Captain James McClure of the 16th Battalion, who had joined the Depot after being wounded in France. He had died of pneumonia in Salisbury Infirmary. It is a little curious that the Depot remained in Wiltshire for so long after the First Division had left as it was isolated from other Canadian units in England.

Formerly a member of the 11th Battalion, Garnett Durham found himself back at Lark Hill in July 1915 after being wounded in France. The camp now had roads and dry streets and very expensive cooking ranges which he thought would have worked well with 60-foot chimneys but not with the short ones that had been fitted. Durham and cyclists from the Fourth Division arrived there in late 1915. Of its 199 cycles on roster, 190 became useless because of abuse and the bad roads. In January 1916 Durham was detailed to make a list of all the Canadian war graves in local churchyards. The following month he moved to Chiseldon Camp, near Swindon in north Wiltshire, where the Canadian Cyclist Corps was based, before returning to France in April.

With there being few suitable alternative large open spaces in Southern England, many artillery units of various nations spent a week or two firing on the Salisbury Plain ranges. A member of Canada's 50th Battery was Robert Gordon Brown, who on 14 January 1917 wrote:

> We had a walk in evening of about 4 mls. from Amesbury station to Lark Hill camp. The week before, the 14th & 16th Bdes. had been here firing. They left their horses & guns here which we use – the 13th & 15th Bdes. On Thurs. the 15th Brigade went firing about 4 mls. from our camp and on Fri. we went. Our battery fired about 92 rounds altogether and didn't do too bad. I was No. 4 on the gun crew that day, my duty being to see that fuses were properly set and to load the gun with

A morass in 1914, the main road through Lark Hill Camp had become a well-surfaced highway later in the war, abutted by pavements, shops, YMCA huts and cinemas.

the 18 pounder shells. Yesterday, the 15th went again and this forenoon, we fired. I was No. 2 this time having to put on the range and open & close the breech. I stuffed my ears but really did not need it. It makes quite a loud report but gun works beautifully. We will have to go twice more, I believe – on Tues. and on Thurs.

Brown remarked that the Australians, now the majority nationality on the Plain, were finding the conditions of a typical British winter hard, even with excellent huts and accommodation. He also recalled the mud and cold Canadians had endured in the first winter of war, and for him this had not changed on the artillery ranges. Nor had the need for waterproof footwear diminished:

The first day we went firing, I got plastered with mud and my feet were pretty wet, so that evening I bought a pair of long rubber boots. We are allowed to wear them on parade if we have them and most of the fellows now have them. They are just the thing for this kind of country and we will likely be able to take them to France with us. I feel pretty well but must try to keep my feet as warm and dry as possible. I can wear two pairs of sox with these rubber boots so that my feet are nice and warm in them.

In 1917 Lieutenant Ogden Dunlap Cochrane, a former *aide de camp* to the General Officer Commanding Toronto Military District, was training as a cadet in the Royal Horse Artillery on Salisbury Plain when he received severe injuries in an accident which led to his death some months later. He was buried in Toronto.

Detachments of the Canadian 224th and 238th Forestry Battalions worked at Stanton Fiztwarren near Swindon. There was one 'Canadian lumber group' at Longleat, one of England's finest stately homes near Warminster, in 1918 and another in Abbey Woods, Hindon, in south-west Wiltshire. Comprising skilled Canadian lumberjacks, the battalions had been formed after shipping shortages had forced Britain to restrict timber imports and rely more on home-grown wood.

In 1917 two field companies of Canadian Engineers, the 14th and 15th, constructed roads, tramways and other works on the Chapperton Down artillery ranges west of Tilshead. Driver William Kellett of the 14th was killed by a train on a level crossing at nearby Codford Camp in July. He was buried in Leeds.

No. 92 Canadian Reserve Squadron of the Royal Flying Corps was formed at Netheravon Airfield on 15 March 1917 and departed for Canada a few weeks later. The airfield had been built in 1912-13 to the east of Netheravon village and a mile from the Cavalry School used as a temporary hospital by the First Contingent. Aviators from many nations were based at the Central Flying School at Upavon and at training depot airfields that were built in Wiltshire in 1917 and 1918, with pupils and tutors suffering frequent crashes, injuries and fatalities, these last leading to a number of victims, including Canadians, being buried locally.

Roderick Ward Maclennan, the son of a Canadian lawyer and a student at Toronto University, enlisted in January 1916, and after serving with the Canadian Army Medical Corps in England was commissioned in to the Royal Flying Corps. His training started in Oxford and continued at Netheravon and Upavon. His published account of this period, in the form of letters home, is a fine description of flying training. When he arrived at No. 8 Training Squadron at Netheravon in July 1917, he found three other Canadians there and, as with so many servicemen, was eager to see Stonehenge, but had the advantage of doing so from 400 feet.

Having gained a little flying experience, Maclennan moved to the Central Flying School at Upavon, which he judged to be 'probably the best of its kind in England' and equipped with a fine supply of modern machines. He noted that 'there are far more colonial chaps than Englishmen and the Canadians easily lead the lot in point of numbers'. The trainee pilots enjoyed 'splendid meals ... such variety and such tasty cooking', this despite much of Britain suffering from food shortages, with civilians finding sugar, bacon, butter and chocolate difficult to come by. Maclennan felt that flying accidents and fatalities were more frequent at Canadian aviation schools than at Upavon, and he described his time at the School as the happiest of his life. Sadly he was killed in action on 23 December 1917, five days after his first patrol over enemy lines.

Lieutenant Harold Leander Hanna of the Canadian Field Artillery and Royal Air Force had completed his training and was due to leave for France when he was killed on Salisbury Plain on 23 April 1918. He had been diving from 2,500 feet when apparently one of the controls gave way and his machine crashed, killing him instantly.

Gavin Baird joined up in Toronto in 1917 and was commissioned as a second lieutenant in the Royal Flying Corps. He sailed to Liverpool and, after a fortnight's leave, was sent to Salisbury Plain to learn to fly large De Havilland bombers which represented a huge advance on the small aeroplanes seen on the Plain in 1914. After Baird and his colleagues got to Salisbury by train they telephoned Lake Down Airfield, three miles south west of Stonehenge, for a car to be sent. On arrival at the airfield they were told they would be billeted in an unoccupied country home at the picturesque village of Berwick St James, about a mile and a half away. Though it was autumn and getting cold, the pilots were fairly comfortable there. In the mornings they would go to the airfield and practice flying and machine-gun firing, dine in the mess at night and then return to the old house.

Pilots such as Baird, Hannah and Maclennan would have flown over much of the ground over which their compatriots had struggled in 1914-15. Since then, there had been many changes in that part of Wiltshire, with two dozen hutted camps and half-a-dozen airfields having been built and the roads much improved. Many bases were served by railway lines, and indeed Lake Down Airfield was now the furthest point of the military track that had been built through Lark Hill Camp in 1914-15 and had been subsequently extended.

Since that time, the Canadian Expeditionary Force had also grown to numbers that not even Sam Hughes might have envisaged when he raised the First Contingent. Eventually there were 260 infantry battalions and 13 regiments of mounted rifles, together with many supporting units. The Force suffered 60,661 dead, or 9.28 per cent of the 619,636 who enlisted. Few of the men who were not members of the First Contingent would have endured so much in training as those who were based on Salisbury Plain in the winter of 1914-15. Many would have been inspired by the accomplishments in battle of the First Canadian Division.

Appendix One

Composition of the First Canadian Contingent

Many recruits to infantry battalions came from Militia units, of which Duguid's *Official History* has two relevant listings, Appendix 83 dated 22 August 1914 and Appendix 85 dated 3 September. These show considerable re-organization between the two dates to accommodate the continuing inflow of volunteers. The latter lists the 9th to 12th battalions in the 3rd Brigade and the 13th to 16th in the 4th Brigade, but on 25 September it was decided to switch the brigades' numbers.

The following roll of units is based on the *List of Officers and Men Serving in the First Canadian Contingent*, compiled by the Pay and Record Office in early November 1914 and reflecting the force's composition shortly after its arrival on Salisbury Plain. Details of the component Militia units, including the numbers of officers and men provided by each, come from Duguid's Appendix 85 of 3 September. Between the 3rd and the Contingent's departure for England a month later, further men enlisted and some of the original recruits were discharged. In addition to the officers and men who left Canada in October 1914, several thousand more sailed to join the First Contingent before it departed from England.

1ST CANADIAN BRIGADE
1st (Western Ontario) Battalion, Canadian Infantry, including detachments from 1st Hussars (66), 7th Fusiliers (146), 21st Essex Fusiliers (229), 22nd Oxford Rifles (69), 23rd Northern Pioneers (152), 24th Grey's Horse (39), 24th Kent Regiment (98), 25th Regiment (97), 26th Middlesex Light Infantry (26), 27th Lambton Regiment (136), 28th Perth Regiment (146), 29th Waterloo Regiment (118), 30th Wellington Rifles (61), 32nd Bruce Regiment (72), 33rd Huron Regiment

(68) and 77th Wentworth Regiment (78). Sailed for England: 1,166.

2nd (Eastern Ontario) Battalion, Canadian Infantry, including detachments from Governor General's Footguards of Ottawa (131), 3rd Prince of Wales' Canadian Dragoons (25), 9th Mississauga Horse (161), 14th Princess of Wales' Own Rifles (76), 15th Argyll Light Infantry (54), 16th Prince Edward Regiment (41), 34th Ontario Regiment (133), 40th Northumberland Regiment (81), 41st Brockville Rifles (83), 42nd Lanark & Renfrew Regiment (128), 43rd Duke of Cornwall's Own Rifles (114), 45th Victoria Regiment (68), 46th Durham Regiment (50), 47th Frontenac Regiment (49), 49th Hastings Regiment (51), 51st Sault St Marie Regiment (Soo Rifles) (126), 56th Grenville Regiment (Lisgar Rifles) (39), 57th Peterborough Rangers (67) and 59th Stormont & Glengarry Regiment (15). Sailed for England: 1,141.

3rd Battalion (Toronto Regiment), Canadian Infantry, including detachments from Governor General's Body Guard (42), 2nd Queen's Own Rifles of Canada (975) and 10th Royal Grenadiers (401). Sailed for England: 1,162.

4th (Central Ontario) Battalion, Canadian Infantry, including detachments from 12th York Rangers (273), 13th Royal Regiment (181), 19th Lincoln Regiment (74), 20th Halton Rifles (171), 25th Brant Dragoons (60), 35th Simcoe Foresters (124), 36th Peel Regiment (230), 37th Haldimand Rifles (76), 38th Dufferin Rifles of Canada (194), 39th Norfolk Rifles (30) and 44th Lincoln and Welland Regiment (202). Sailed for England: 1,165.

2ND CANADIAN BRIGADE

5th (Western Canada Cavalry) Battalion (trained as infantry), including detachments from the 12th Manitoba Dragoons (201), 16th Light Horse, (290), 27th Light Horse (243), 29th Light Horse (200), 30th British Columbia Horse (26), 31st British Columbia Horse (487) and 35th Central Alberta Horse (116). Sailed for England: 1,164.

6th Battalion (Fort Garry Horse), Canadian Infantry, including dismounted detachments from 18th Mounted Rifles (160), 20th Border Horse (123), 22nd Saskatchewan Light Horse (175), 23rd Alberta Rangers (including 21st Alberta Hussars and 15th Calgary Light Horse) (78), 32nd Manitoba Horse (44) and 34th Fort Garry Horse (234). Sailed for England: 1,164.

7th Battalion (1st British Columbia Regiment), Canadian Infantry, including detachments from 6th Duke of Connaught's Own Rifles (353), 11th Irish Fusiliers of Canada (355), 88th Victoria Fusiliers (247), 102nd Rocky Mountain Rangers (123), 104th Westminster Fusiliers of Canada (153) and from East Kootenay (156), West Kootenay (151), Grand Forks (17) and the Nanaimo Independent Infantry Company. Sailed for England: 1,143.

8th Battalion (The Black Devils/90th Winnipeg Rifles), Canadian Infantry, including detachments from 90th Winnipeg Rifles (776), 96th Lake Superior Regiment (316), 98th Regiment (80) and 99th Manitoba Rangers (186). Sailed for England: 1,178.

3RD CANADIAN BRIGADE

13th Battalion (Royal Highlanders of Canada), Canadian Infantry, including detachments from 5th Royal Highlanders of Canada (996), 78th Pictou Regiment (127) and 93rd Cumberland Regiment (133). Sailed for England: 1,167.

14th Battalion (Royal Montreal Regiment), Canadian Infantry, including detachments from 1st Grenadier Guards of Canada (350), 3rd Victoria Rifles of Canada (351), 14th King's Canadian Hussars (7), 63rd Halifax Rifles (26), 65th Carbiniers Mont Royal (337), 66th Princess Louise Fusiliers (32), 69th Annapolis Regiment (35), 75th Lunenburg Regiment (28), 76th Colchester & Hants Rifles (20) and 81st Hants Regiment (20). Sailed for England: 1,165.

15th Battalion (48th Highlanders), Canadian Infantry, including detachments from 2nd Dragoons (32), 13th Scottish Light Dragoons (43), 26th Stanstead Light

Dragoons (25), 31st Grey Regiment (83), 48th Highlanders (836), 97th Algonquin Rifles (266). Sailed for England: 1,160.

16th (Canadian Scottish) Battalion, Canadian Infantry, including detachments from 50th Gordon Highlanders of Canada (262), 72nd Seaforth Highlanders of Canada (542), 79th Cameron Highlanders (263) and 91st Canadian Highlanders (154). Sailed for England: 1,158.

4TH CANADIAN BRIGADE

9th Battalion, Canadian Infantry, assembled from 101st Edmonton Fusiliers (1,247) and Ottawa detachment (77). Sailed for England: 1,207.

10th Battalion, Canadian Infantry, including detachments from 103rd Calgary Rifles (846) and 106th Winnipeg Light Infantry (665). Sailed for England: 1,122.

11th Battalion, Canadian Infantry, including detachments from 52nd Prince Albert Volunteers (150), 60th Rifles of Canada (294), 95th Saskatchewan Rifles (171), 100th Winnipeg Grenadiers (471). 105th Saskatoon Fusiliers (255) and Humboldt (21). Sailed for England: 1,179.

12th Battalion, Canadian Infantry, including detachments from 4th Chasseurs Canadiens (41), 8th Royal Rifles (368), 9th Voltigeurs de Quebec (29), 17th Regiment (7), 18th Franc-Tireurs du Saguenay (3), 28th New Brunswick Dragoons (17), 36th Prince Edward Island Light Horse (11), 53rd Sherbooke Regiment (107), 54th Carabiniers de Sherbrooke & Beauharnois Regiment (113), 61st Regiment de Montmagny (6), 62nd St John Fusiliers (140), 64th Chateauguay & Beauharnois Regiment (30), 71st York Regiment (160), 73rd Northumberland Regiment (76), 74th Brunswick Rangers (73), 80th Nicolet Regiment (1), 82nd Abegweit Light Infantry (31), 83rd Joliette Regiment (26), 84th St Hyacinthe Regiment (12), 85th Regiment (143), 89th Temiscouata and Rimouski Regiment (15) and 92nd Dorchester Regiment (9). Sailed for England: 1,170.

The 4th Brigade was disbanded in January 1915, three of its battalions and the 17th Battalion becoming reinforcing units at Tidworth. Its 11th Battalion replaced the 6th, which was to be re-organized as cavalry, in the 2nd Brigade. A new 4th Brigade was formed in Ottawa. A short-lived 18th Battalion was disbanded on 27 September 1914 and its 366 officers and men absorbed by other units.

The figures below in brackets denote, where known, the numbers of officers and men who sailed for England in early October.

17th Battalion (Nova Scotia Highlanders), Canadian Infantry, including detachments from 78th Pictou Regiment and 93rd Cumberland Regiment (668) (The 17th's small size meant that, unlike the other battalions, it was not one of the four brigades.)

Newfoundland companies (Sailed from Newfoundland: 537)

Princess Patricia's Canadian Light Infantry (1,104)

Royal Canadian Dragoons (575)

Lord Strathcona's Horse (603)

Divisional Artillery Headquarters (28)

1st Field Artillery Brigade (930)

2nd Field Artillery Brigade (803)

3rd Field Artillery Brigade (860)

Royal Canadian Horse Artillery (508)

Divisional Ammunition Column (601)

Divisional Ammunition Park (480)

No. 1 Heavy Battery

Divisional Engineers (759)

Divisional Supply Train (478)

Divisional Supply Column (265)

No. 1 Reserve Park

Depot Units of Supply (103)

Railway Supply Detachment (85)

Divisional Signal Company (203)

Divisional Cavalry (19th Alberta Dragoons) (181)

Divisional Cyclist Company (93)

No. 1 Field Ambulance (266)

No. 2 Field Ambulance (263)

No. 3 Field Ambulance (269)

Clearing Hospital (88)

No. 1 General Hospital (180)

No. 2 General Hospital (157)

No. 1 Stationary Hospital (94)

No. 2 Stationary Hospital (101)

Advanced Depot Medical Stores

Canadian Army Veterinary Corps (27)

Canadian Mobile Veterinary Section

Canadian Veterinary Base Supply Depot

Remount Depot

Automobile Machine Gun Brigade No. 1 (123)

Base Pay Depot Unit

Pay and Record Office, London

Canadian Ordnance Corps

Postal Detachment (13)

Nursing matrons and sisters (99)

Headquarters staff (113)

On the outbreak of war, at least 235 of the 499 members of the Corps of Guides volunteered for the Contingent and were distributed throughout it in various staff and specialist functions, some as intelligence officers.

Appendix Two

Canadian War Graves in Wiltshire

The War Graves of the British Empire register for Wiltshire, published in 1930, lists the graves of service men and women who had died during the Great War period and were buried in the county, including 74 members of the overseas military forces of Canada. It confirms that there had been much exaggeration of the number of deaths (actually of five officers and 63 men) suffered by the First Contingent in England. Private Ernest Robins of Lord Strathcona's Horse thought that the Contingent had lost 600 men from meningitis. The actual toll was 28. On 21 January 1917 Bertie Cox of the 59th Battery wrote home that 1,800 Canadians had died on Salisbury Plain 'from the 1st contingent of 20,000 men'.

There are Canadian graves some way from camps or airfields, and reasons for this may include the churchyard being near where the person died or near the home of a relative. A few members of the First Contingent who perished in England are buried outside Wiltshire. For example Private E. C. Ford of the 10th Battalion expired on 8 November 1914 and was buried in Plymouth (Efford) Cemetery, where other Canadians were interred later in the war, perhaps after dying on or shortly after the voyage from their homeland. It may be that Ford had remained behind in a Plymouth hospital, when his comrades moved to Salisbury Plain. On 28 November Lance Corporal J. C. Morgan of the 2nd Battalion fell off a moving train on the London-Salisbury railway near Fleet in Hampshire, where he was buried. Captain Henry Cook (sometimes spelt as Cooke) of the Canadian Pay Corps shot himself in Kew, south-west London, and was buried in nearby Richmond. Private William Saint of the 5th Battalion died on 2 January and was buried in Cambridge, where he would have been on leave with his family over the Christmas period.

Discrepancies between the dates of deaths given below and elsewhere may be attributed to clerical errors, delays in reporting the death and mistakes in newspaper reports. Unit names are as recorded by the Commission and may differ slightly from those in the main text.

After the First Contingent had left Salisbury Plain, other Canadians were buried in Wiltshire. The number of junior officers interred in certain churchyards later in the war reflects the latter's proximity to airfields, where there were many flying accidents. There are other entries in the register where the deceased had served with a non-Canadian unit and had next-of-kin living in Canada or had been born there. Service numbers are given after each man's name. (Officers did not have numbers.)

Graves of Canadian soldiers in Bulford Cemetery, including that of Lieutenant Ross Briscoe, on the right and marked with a large white cross.

FIRST CANADIAN CONTINGENT

Amesbury Cemetery
Pte Samuel H. Smith 24768, 19 October 1914, 13th Battalion; husband of Naomi Catherine Smith of Newport, Wales.

The War Graves of the British Empire register states that another Canadian grave had been removed, perhaps at the request of relatives for reburial at home.

Bulford Church Cemetery
Pte A. Anthony 46120, 17th Battalion, 25 December 1914.

Pte J. J. Barrett 7020, 1st Battalion, 1 January 1915.

Pte George Thomas Bell 960, Royal Canadian Dragoons, 21 February 1915; husband of Emma Bell of Acton Green, Middlesex, England.

Lt R. D. Briscoe, 9th Battalion, 6 January 1915; son of R. A. Briscoe of Galt, Ontario.

Pte John Kellman Chandler 25935, 14th Battalion, 23 January 1915; son of John K. and Mary Ida Leslie Chandler of Barbados.

Pte Silas Hartley Chase 22559, 12th Battalion, 16 January 1915; son of Melissa Chase of Fredericton, New Brunswick.

Dvr Charles William Crisp 41389, 2nd Canadian Field Artillery, 2 February 1915; son of Mrs E. Crisp of Cambridge.

Pte James William Davidson 46026, 17th Battalion, 17 December 1914; son of Mrs R. G. Hingley of Truro, Nova Scotia.

Pte George Basil Ewens 13492, 5th Battalion, 27 December 1914; son of James Matthewson and Evelyn Bessie Ewens of Bethany, Manitoba.

Pte Herbert French 7145, 1st Battalion, 24 December 1914; husband of Jane French of Lemberg, Saskatchewan.

Pte C. D. W. Gale 18907, 9th Battalion, 15 December 1914; husband of E. A. Gale of Midnapore, Alberta.

Lce Cpl T. Gerrand 12710, 5th Battalion, 11 February 1915; son of David and Alice Gerrand of Winnipeg.

Pte William Goodyear 24133, 13th Battalion, 17 January 1915; son of Thomas and Annie Goodyear of Knaresborough, England.

Pte F. G. Heal 28746, 16th Battalion, 24 January 1915; son of Frederick George and Annie Margaret Heal of Telkwa, British Columbia.

Rev. George Leycester Ingles, Chaplain to the Forces 4th class, attached 3rd Battalion, 1 January 1915; son of Charles Leycester and Frances Helen Ingles of Toronto.

Pte J. J. Laroe 37123, Divisional Ammunition Park, Canadian Army Service Corps, 18 November 1914.

Pte J. G. MacDonald 46971, 17th Battalion, 2 January 1915.

Farrier Sgt J. Mackney 42172, 10th Battery, 3rd Brigade, Canadian Field Artillery, 3 January 1915.

Pte George Meads 33126, 2nd Field Ambulance, Canadian Army Medical Corps, 27 December 1914; son of Richard and Fanny H. Meads of Bicester, England.

Pte H. Morris 16213, 7th Battalion, 20 January 1915.

Pte Percy George Palmer 17044, 7th Battalion, 9 January 1915; son of Emily Morris (formerly Palmer) of Vancouver and the late George Palmer.

Pte H. A. Peden 29008, 16th Battalion, 7 December 1914.

Pte E. H. M. Penn C/37408, 1st Divisional Ammunition Park, Canadian Field Artillery, 3 December 1914; son of John William Penn and Nina N. Hankey (formerly Penn) of Victoria, British Columbia.

Pte F. B. Puddington 46877, 17th Battalion, 31 December 1914; son of the Rev. J. H. and Mrs Eunice C. Puddington of Melvern Square, Nova Scotia.

Cpl Arthur Sydney Randall 25793, 14th Battalion, 29 January 1915; son of William Sydney and Sarah Rebecca Randall of Wilton, Salisbury.

Gnr George Read 40248, 1st Brigade, Canadian Field Artillery, 24 October 1914.

Pte T. E. Trull 9285, 3rd Battalion, 15 February 1915.

Gnr G. A. Wilson 41612, 2nd Brigade, Canadian Field Artillery, 22 December 1914.

Armourer Sgt G. S. Wunsch 21105, 11th Battalion, 19 January 1915.

Pte J. Wylie 46206, 17th Battalion, 5 January 1915.

Nineteen Canadian soldiers were buried in Netheravon Churchyard, many having been patients at a temporary hospital in the adjoining cavalry school.

Durrington Cemetery
Spr George Burnett 45059, 3rd Field Company, Canadian Engineers, 6 December 1914; son of Samuel and Eliza Burnett of Manchester, England; husband of Ellen Burnett of Manchester.

East Harnham (All Saints) Churchyard
Dvr W. C. Campbell 37048, 1st Divisional Ammunition Park, Canadian Army Service Corps, 26 March 1915; son of Mr and Mrs Campbell of Toronto.

Gnr H. E. R. Jackson 44001, 1st Divisional Ammunition Column, Canadian Field Artillery, 8 March 1915.

Maddington Churchyard
Pte William Herbert Vaughan Hartley 25844, 14th Battalion, 19 October 1914; husband of Ellen Hartley of Montreal.

Netheravon (All Saints) Churchyard
Pte George Chittleburgh 26534, 14th Battalion, 4 February 1915.

Pte Henry Holmes 7038, 1st Battalion, 15 January 1915.

Gnr G. R. Hunter 40190, 12th Battery, 3rd Brigade, Canadian Field Artillery, 10 February 1915; son of Mrs R. H. Hunter of Ottawa.

Pte Robert Small Lamont Sidey Lamb 11145, 4th Battalion, 16 January 1915; son of William and Isabella Lamb of Edinburgh.

Pte Bernard Henry McCreedy 6244, 9th Battalion, 20 February 1915; husband of Minnie Rosetta McCreedy of Calgary.

Pte Frederick Williamson McGuinness 24618, 13th Battalion, 9 January 1915; son of William Anthony and Frances McGuinness of Montreal.

Pte Charles Roy MacKenzie 27519, 15th Battalion, 26 January 1915; son of John R. and Elizabeth Smith MacKenzie of Beaverton, Ontario.

Pte Roscoe L. Phillips 27570, 17th Battalion, 16 February 1915.

Pte William H. Phillips 912, Royal Canadian Dragoons, 20 January 1915.

Pte Thomas D. Rose 11397, 4th Battalion, 12 January 1915.

Pte Maxwell Kenneth Smith 13041, 5th Battalion, 6 January 1915; son of William and Annie Smith of Peterborough, Ontario.

Orcheston St Mary
Pte Douglas Kirkpatrick Benham 28958, 16th Battalion, 16 November 1914.

Cpl William Ogden 21506, 7th Battalion, 25 October 1914; husband of Edith Ogden of Manchester, England.

Salisbury (Devizes Road) Cemetery, Bemerton
Pte Edward Daniel Curtin 34593, 2nd General Hospital, Canadian Army Medical Corps, 11 April 1915; son of Daniel and Violetta Curtin of London, Ontario.

Cpl J. A. Mates, 2nd Battalion, 15 April 1915; husband of Sarah Mates of Brockville, Ontario.

Salisbury (London Road) Cemetery
Dvr William Constantine Campbell 37048, 1st Divisional Ammunition Park, Canadian Army Service Corps, 26 March 1915; son of Mr and Mrs R. A. Campbell of Toronto.

Gnr Henry Edgar Randolph Jackson 44001, 1st Divisional Ammunition Column, 8 March 1915; son of Annie M. Jackson of Leicester, England.

Stratford-sub-Castle (St Lawrence) Churchyard
Pte R. G. Carter 16637, 11th Battalion, 26 March 1915.

Tidworth Military Cemetery
Pte George Dean 46285, 17th Battalion, 26 January 1915.

Pte G. Golding 23659, 12th Battalion, 21 February 1915.

Pte W. J. Smith, 28545, 16th Battalion, 8 March 1915; husband of Margaret Smith of West Vancouver.

Pte C. Smollett 30922, No. 1 Reserve Park, Canadian Army Service Corps, 25 March 1915; son of John and Catharine Smollett of Toronto.

Sgt A. T. Underhill 22960, 12th Battalion, 2 March 1915.

Tilshead Churchyard
Pte C. Matthews 33217, 2nd Field Ambulance, Canadian Army Medical Corps, 11 December 1914.

Gnr Walter Pendleton 43171, 1st Heavy Battery, Canadian Field Artillery, 9 November 1914.

Gnr Percy Sawyer 40016, Divisional HQ, Canadian Field Artillery, 21 October 1914.

OTHER SOLDIERS WITH LINKS TO CANADA BURIED IN WILTSHIRE

Bradford-on-Avon (Christ Church) Churchyard
Lt H. C. Jones, 3rd Battalion, 31 December 1915.

Chippenham Cemetery
Pte R. Stubbert M2/268200, Royal Army Service Corps, 14 February 1917; son of W. P. and Caroline Stubbert of Cape Breton, Nova Scotia.

Codford St Mary Churchyard
Pte Oscar Cameron 3367, 59th Battalion, Australian Infantry, 24 January 1918; son of Christopher and Agnes Cameron of Shelburne, Nova Scotia.

Durrington Cemetery
Sec. Lt Joseph Claude Barker, 109th Squadron, Royal Air Force, 19 May 1918; son of John J. and Evaline Barker of North Bay, Ontario.

Lt O. J. Marchbank, Canadian Engineers, attached Royal Air Force, 2 June 1918.

Figheldean (St Michael) Churchyard
Sec. Lt Herbert Henry Ezard, 24th Squadron, Royal Flying Corps, originally a member of the Canadian Army Service Corps, killed whilst flying, 30 May 1917; son of Dr E. H. and Mrs Mary Ezard of Cambridge, England.

Sec. Lt I. W. Hathaway, 12th Training Depot Station, Royal Air Force, 11 August 1918; son of William A. and May Elizabeth Hathaway of Toronto.

Sec. Lt Howard Stanley Nolan, General List and Royal Flying Corps, 27 July 1917; son of W. H. and Lydia P. Iris Nolan of Montreal.

Mere Cemetery
Pte James Edward Chalk 516301, Canadian Army Veterinary Corps, 26 June 1920. Born at Mere.

North Wraxall (St James) Churchyard
Pte C. E. Coles 2140532, 1st Reserve Battalion, 21 October 1918; son of Mrs Julia Coles of Yatton Keynell, Wiltshire.

Purton (St Mary) Churchyard
Pte R. S. Grimes 447150, 29th Battalion, 13 October 1916.

Salisbury (London Road) Cemetery
Pte Arthur Edward Chambers 22004, 4th Battalion, originally of the 11th Battalion with the Contingent on the Plain, 28 October 1916; son of John and Sarah Chambers of Salisbury.

Sec. Lt Charles Hedley Edgecombe, 11th Squadron, Royal Air Force, 6 October 1918; son of Mr and Mrs Fred B. Edgecombe of Frederictown, New Brunswick.

Capt. James McClure, 16th Battalion, 17 June 1916.

Sec. Lt William Everett Sinclair, General List and Royal Flying Corps, 15 March 1918; son of Laura Belle Paterson of Winnipeg.

South Newton (St Andrew) Churchyard
Sgt G. M. Tyrell 246073, 58th Broad Gauge Railway Operating Company, Canadian Railway Troops, 7 May 1918; son of Henry and Harriett Tyrell of Ottawa.

Sutton Veny (St John) Churchyard
Sec. Lt Harry Bronard Ward, No. 12 Training Depot Station, Royal Air Force, 23 October 1918; son of W. D. F. and Mary Ward of Nova Scotia.

Swindon (Radnor Street) Cemetery
Spr W. Bramble 193713, Royal Engineers, 3 January 1917; husband of R. Bramble of Toronto.

Tidworth Military Cemetery
Pte D. Berard 23628, Canadian Divisional Cyclist Company, 2 December 1915.

Sec. Lt Fleetwood Earnscliffe Daniel, Royal Flying Corps, formerly 9th Battery, Canadian Field Artillery, 20 December 1915; son of Joseph William and Sarah Lydia Daniel of Toronto.

Pte Walter Theodore Dickson 487532, 89th Battalion, 23 July 1916; son of Peter and Dora Dickson of Vernon, British Columbia.

Lt George Jamieson Downey, 3rd Battalion, King's Own Royal Lancaster Regiment, 25 April 1918; son of John Downey of Ottawa.

Lt Harold Leander Hanna, No. 3 Training Depot, Royal Air Force, 23 April 1916; born at Kaslo, British Columbia.

Pte Robert Frank Kneller 3310136, 58th Battalion, 17 February 1919; son of Edward and Mary Kneller of Ayr, Ontario.

Trowbridge Cemetery
L Cpl Edward Joseph Hollis P/8999, Military Police Corps, 6 November 1918; husband of Rose Annie Morgan of Galt, Ontario.

Upavon
Sec. Lt Russell Roberts Caldwell, Central Flying School, Royal Air Force, 15 September 1918; son of David and Bella Caldwell of Loverna, Saskatchewan.

Lt Frederick Henry Choate, Lord Strathcona's Horse and Royal Air Force, 4 June 1918; son of Charles A. and Nannie Choate of Ingersoll, Ontario.

Sec. Lt Harold Augustus Freeman, Central Flying School, Royal Air Force, 9 September 1918; son of Binney Smith and Edith L Freeman of Victoria, British Columbia.

Sec. Lt Lawrence McClean Lord, Central Flying School, Royal Air Force, 15 September 1918; son of the Rev. C. S. and Mrs Mary Lord of Fenelon Falls, Ontario.

Sec. Lt William Kay Misenhimer, Central Flying School, Royal Air Force, 6 September 1918; son of H. Kay and Mary A. Misenhimer of Strongfield, Saskatchewan.

Sec. Lt Oscar Lancelot Nicholls, Central Flying School, Royal Air Force, 24 December 1918; son of Robert Andrew Nicholls of Cannington, Ontario.

Sec. Lt Donald Springer Osborne, Central Flying School, Royal Air Force, 5 October 1918; son of Robert Bryson and Charlotte Mary Osborne of Preston, Ontario.

Sec. Lt Stanley Cecil Paice, Royal Air Force, 6 April 1918; enlisted in Royal Canadian Horse Artillery at Kingston, Ontario.

Sec. Lt Allan Gibbs Ridout, Central Flying School, Royal Air Force, 28 July 1918; son of Andrew William and Isla Ridout of Montreal.

Lt L. R. E. van Buskirk, Fort Garry Horse and Royal Flying Corps, 9 December 1917.

Probationary Flight Officer Clarence Earl Young, Central Flying School, Royal Air Force, 10 November 1918; son of David John and Catherine Young of Kingston, Ontario.

Yatesbury (All Saints) Churchyard
Lt W. E. Carter, Lord Strathcona's Horse and Royal Flying Corps, 22 March 1918.

Lt J. T. Gibson, Royal Flying Corps, 10 February 1918; son of Alexander and Charlotte J. Gibson of Fredericton, New Brunswick.

Sec. Lt Marcus E Rowe, 62nd Training Depot Station, killed whilst flying 19 August 1918; born at Springhill, Nova Scotia.

Lt C. G. V. Smith, 66th Training Squadron, Royal Air Force, 21 May 1918; son of Henry Valentine and Kathleen Smith of Vancouver.

In Durrington Cemetery, a mile north east of Lark Hill, a plaque has this message written in English and French:

FIRST CANADIAN CONTINGENT
ON 14TH OCTOBER 1914 THE FIRST CONTINGENT OF 33,000 CANADIAN TROOPS
ARRIVED AT PLYMOUTH FROM GASPÉ, QUEBEC AND ENCAMPED IN THE
AREA IMMEDIATELY WEST OF THIS CEMETERY

THEY SUFFERED EXTREME HARDSHIPS DURING THE EXCEPTIONALLY
SEVERE WINTER OF 1914-1915 AND MANY THOUSANDS WERE TAKEN ILL
WITH INFLUENZA AND RELATED DISEASES

MANY DIED AND WERE BURIED IN LOCAL CEMETERIES

FROM THIS CONTINGENT WERE DRAWN THE 1ST CANADIAN DIVISION WHOSE
FIRST MAJOR ENGAGEMENT WAS AT THE SECOND BATTLE OF YPRES
IN APRIL 1915

ON THE ANNIVERSARY OF THAT BATTLE, THIS PLAQUE WAS DEDICATED ON
22ND OF APRIL, 1979 BY THE HONOURABLE PAUL MARTIN P.C. C.C. Q.C. HIGH
COMMISSIONER FOR CANADA

A plaque was unveiled in the Guildhall, Salisbury in September 1915, with this inscription bearing the names of James Macklin and Francis Hodding, respectively Mayor and Town Clerk of Salisbury:

Dulce et decorum est pro patria mori
To the honour of
those brave men of the
Canadian Expeditionary Force
who on their arrival in England
to fight for their Empire in the
Great European War
were stationed and trained on
Salisbury Plain
many being the guests of the Citizens
and by their gallantry at the Front
have since shown themselves to be
worthy Sons of their Mother Country.

This plaque in Durrington Cemetery commemorates the Contingent.

Bibliography

Colonel J. G. Adami, *The War Story of the Canadian Army Medical Corps 1914-1918* (c1920)

Alfred Herbert John Andrews, diary, Canadian Letters and Images Project

Anon, *A Brief Outline of the Canadian Grenadier Guards and the First Months of the Royal Montreal Regiment in the Great War* (Montreal, 1926)

W. J. Bailey & E. R. Toop, *The Canadian Military Posts* (c1984)

Gavin Baird letters, Canadian Letters and Images Project

Harold Baldwin, *Holding the Line* (Chicago, 1918)

A. M. de Beck, editor, *Canadian News Souvenir Edition in Honour of the Canadian Contingent* (1915)

Frederick McKelvey Bell, *The First Canadians in France* (Toronto, 1917)

Charles Wallace Bishop, *The Canadian Y.M.C.A. in the Great War* (Toronto, 1924)

S V Brittan diaries, Imperial War Museum, London

Richard Broadhead, *Salisbury Soldiers* (Stroud, 2007)

Bruce Brommell letter, 18 November 1914, Nova Scotia Genweb website

Frank S. Brown, *Contingent Ditties: Other Soldier Songs of the Great War* (1915)

Robert Gordon Brown letters, Canadian Letters and Images Project

Walter Bruce *et al, Historical Records of the Argyll & Sutherland Highlanders of Canada* (Ontario, 1928)

Raymond Brutinel tapes, transcribed by Dwight G. Mercer, George Metcalf Archival Collection, Military History Research Centre, Ottawa.

J. F. Cadenhead, *The Canadian Scottish: Papers by a Private* (Aberdeen, 1916)

James M. Cameron, *Pictonians in Arms* (New Brunswick, 1968)

Kenneth Cameron, *History of No. 1 General Hospital, Canadian Expeditionary Force* (New Brunswick, 1938)

Len Campbell, *The First Canadian Contingent* (Durrington, 1994)

Canadian Field Comforts Commission, *With the First Canadian Contingent* (Toronto, 1915)

Charmion Chaplin-Thomas, 'Canadian Aviation Corps', *Maple Leaf* No. 5, 1 February 2006

N. M. Christie, editor, *Letters of Agar Adamson* (Nepean, 1997)

Bertram Howard Cox letters, Canadian Letters and Images Project

Richard Cramm, *The First Five Hundred* (Albany, 1921)

T. S. Crawford, *Wiltshire and the Great War* (Ramsbury, 2012))

A. C. Critchley, *Critch! The Memoirs of Brigadier General A. C. Critchley* (1961)

Colonel J. A. Currie, *The Red Watch* (1916)

Frederic C. Curry, *From the St. Lawrence to the Yser: With the 1st Canadian Brigade* (1916)

Howard Curtis letters, Canadian Letters and Images Project

D. G. Dancocks, *Gallant Canadians* (Calgary, 1990)

Colonel A. F. Duguid, *The Official History of the Canadian Forces in the Great War: August 1914 to September 1915* (Ottawa, 1938)

G. W. Durham papers, Imperial War Museum , London

Ron Edwards, 'The Houghton Machine Gun Detachment', *Journal of the Military History Society of Manitoba*, 1998

David R. Facey-Crowther, *Lieutenant Owen William Steele of the Newfoundland Regiment* (Montreal, 2003)

R. C. Fetherstonhaugh, *The 13th Battalion Royal Highlanders of Canada 1914-1919* (Toronto, 1925)

R. C. Fetherstonhaugh, *The Royal Montreal Regiment, 14th Battalion* (Montreal, 1927)

R. C. Fetherstonhaugh, *No. 3 Canadian General Hospital* (Montreal, 1928)

R. C. Fetherstonhaugh, *A Short History of the Royal Canadian Dragoons* (Toronto, 1932)

J. F. C. Fuller, *Memoirs of an Unconventional Soldier* (1936)

George Gibson, *Maple Leaves in Flanders Fields* (Toronto, c1916)

Richard Grant, *S.O.S. Stand To* (1918)

D. Graves, *A Crown of Life: The World of John McCrae* (Staplehurst, 1997)

Basil Green typescript memoir, *The Autobiography of an Almost Nonagenarian*, Imperial War Museum, London

Sandra Gwyn, *Tapestry of War: A Private View of Canadians in the Great War* (Toronto, 1992)

Ronald G. Haycock, *Sam Hughes: The Public Career of a Controversial Canadian, 1885-1916* (Waterloo, 1986)

Eric Hearle letters, Canadian Letters and Images Project

Ian Hicks, editor, *Early Motor Vehicle Registration in Wiltshire 1903-1914* (Trowbridge, 2006)

Ralph Hodder-Williams, *Princess Patricia's Canadian Light Infantry* (Toronto, 1923)

M. S. Hunt, *Nova Scotia's Part in the Great War* (Halifax, 1920)

A. M. J. Hyatt, *General Sir Arthur Currie* (Toronto, 1987)

Andrew Iarocci, *Shoestring Soldiers: The First Canadian Division at War, 1914-1915* (Toronto, 2008)

Imperial War Graves Commission, *The War Graves of the British Empire: Wiltshire* (1930)

Glenn R. Iriam, editor, *In The Trenches, 1914-1918* (Kenora, 2008)

N. D. G. James, *Gunners at Larkhill* (Henley-on-Thames, 1983)

N. D. G. James, *Plain Soldiering* (Salisbury, 1987)

Louis Keene, *Crumps* (Boston, 1917)

W. S. Lighthall memoirs, Imperial War Museum, London

'M.B.', 'Queen's Canadian Military Hospital', *British Journal of Nursing*, 24 October 1914, 326-7

Brian McGill, *Village under the Plain: The Story of Market Lavington* (Warminster, 1995)

J. Kennedy Maclean and T. Wilkinson Riddle, *The Y.M.C.A. with the Colours* (c1915)

Roderick Ward Maclennan, *The Ideals and Training of a Flying Officer* (Manchester, 2009)

Sir Andrew MacPhail, *Official History of the Canadian Forces in the Great War 1914-19: The Medical Services* (Ottawa, 1925)

W. W. Murray, *The History of the 2nd Canadian Battalion* (Ottawa, 1947)

Colonel George Nasmith, *On the Fringe of the Great Fight* (Toronto, 1917).

G. W. L. Nicholson, *Canadian Expeditionary Force 1914–1919* (Ottawa, 1962)

Harold R. Peat *Private Peat* (1918)

Kenneth Radley, *We Lead, Others Follow: First Canadian Division, C.E.F. 1914-1918* (Ottawa, 2003)

Gordon Reid, *Poor Bloody Murder: Personal Memoirs of the First World War* (Oakville, c1980)

Captain James Ross letters, Canadian Letters and Images Project

Reginald H. Roy, editor, *The Journal of Private Fraser: Canadian Expeditionary Force 1914-1918* (Nepean, 1998)

Brough Scott, *Galloper Jack* (2003)

Frederick George Scott, *The Great War As I Saw It* (Toronto, 1922)

J. E. B. Seely, *Adventure* (1930)

Val Shushkewich, *The Real Winnie* (Toronto, 2003)

John Siggers, *Wiltshire and its Postmarks* (Devizes 1982)

A. J. Stacey, *Memoirs of a Blue Puttee* (St John's, 2002)

A. G. Street, *The Gentlemen of the Party* (1936)

J. E. Sutton typescript of taped reminiscences, Imperial War Museum, London

Christopher Sykes, *Nancy: The Life of Lady Astor* (1972)

Major R. H. Tait, *The Trail of the Caribou* (Boston, c1933)

Arnold Warren, *Wait for the Waggon* (Toronto, 1961)

Jeffery Williams, *First in the Field: Gault of the Patricias* (1995)

S. H. Williams, *Stand to Your Horses* (Manitoba, 1961)

S. F. Wise, *Canadian Airmen and the First World War* (Toronto, 1980)

Larry Worthington, *Amid the Guns Below* (Toronto, 1965)

Urchfont Parish Millennium Group, *Urchfont by Any Other Name* (Urchfont, 2001)

H. M. Urquhart, *The History of the 16th Battalion (The Canadian Scottish)* (Toronto, 1932)

Various, *Canada in the Great World War*, vol II (Toronto, c1918)

List of Officers and Men Serving in the First Canadian Contingent of the British Expeditionary Force, 1914 (1914)

Maidenhead Advertiser, Manchester Guardian, New York Times, Portage Le Prairie Weekly Review, Red Deer News, St Lawrence Republican, Salisbury Times, Salisbury Journal, Scotsman, The Times, Toronto Globe, Toronto Star, Western Evening Herald, Wilts, Berks & Hants County Paper, Wiltshire Advertiser, Wiltshire Gazette, Wiltshire Telegraph, Wiltshire Times

Canadian Expeditionary Force mail arrangements, POST 29/1272B, Royal Mail Archives, London
Kitchener papers, PRO 30/57/56, National Archives, Kew
Soldiers' attestation papers and unit war diaries, Library and Archives Canada

Canadian Expeditionary Force Study Group: www.cefresearch.com
Canadian Great War Project: www.canadiangreatwarproject.com
Canadian Letters and Images Project: www.canadianletters.ca
Great War Forum: http://1914-1918.invisionzone.com

Index

Page numbers in bold denote illustrations.